You Can't Come In

A Memoir of Vietnam and Its Aftermath

By

Martin D. Alexander

Edited by

Dan Crissman

You Can't Come In: A memoir of Vietnam and its aftermath (2nd Edition)

Anh Yêu Em Nhiều Lắm

Kiém Liên, 1969

Acknowledgements

First and foremost, I want to thank my lovely and beautiful wife of twenty years. Karen has been extremely supportive of this written project, her input, feedback, patience, and encouragement have allowed me the time, energy and resources to make this happen. I love you, Karen. You mean the world to me.

Mr. Hal Kaller, a very thoughtful man with whom I've had the pleasure of many weekly conversations, story-telling and constructive analysis over a period of many years. I am forever grateful for your insight, compassion and ability to help me overcome anger at myself, and the world in general. Thank you, Hal, for your understanding and allowing me to vent.

And thank you to Dan Crissman, a most professional editor to whom I will be forever grateful. Your thoughtful critique, recommendations to purge superfluous episodes, and keeping me on track to tell my story have been helpful to the highest degree.

Much has been written about the pros and cons of the military action in Vietnam between 1960 and 1975. That era was a time when our nation called, and many fled to avoid military service. Those that did answer our nation's call generally came home to an ungrateful nation. To the men and women who were there, I thank you.

As each generation pass onto the next, the story of our nation's involvement in Vietnam will be reduced to ever smaller sections in academic text books, if at all. Its history will be defined by socio-political reflections and opinions. I want to contribute to the national story of what it was like, for me in the United States Army, during that most spectacular, and controversial period of our nation's past.

A family tradition of military service had been one of the building blocks of my youth. My dad was in the Army during World War II. My two grandfathers were in the Army during World War I. One of my brothers was in the Army during the Vietnam War; and, the other, an Air Force pilot and the first commissioned officer in our family, had gut-wrenching military missions elsewhere. Two of my sons, following in the footsteps of their maternal grandfather and with my full support, are careerists in the United States Air Force.

Contents

Preface

It's been tough adjusting to civilian life, even decades after leaving Vietnam. Admittedly, it could be my problem—viewing myself as a marked man, wearing a badge of honor that few recognize and a majority of others couldn't possibly understand. It's frustrating. It's very difficult to connect with civilians. Even among veterans we have a separation of comradery, a disconnect, that some just don't understand. Some call it a caste system.

In the military, a caste system that was, in many respects, unofficially defined yet encouraged. Generally, it separated commissioned and warrant officers from enlisted men, non-commissioned officers from lower-ranking pay grades, skilled trades from non-skilled, and combat soldiers from support personnel. Notwithstanding our own biases, as veterans we collectively separated ourselves from our civilian families, neighbors, friends, and acquaintances. The thinking could be summed up as "if you weren't there, you wouldn't understand." That may be true.

Keeping notes, writing a journal, or even writing a book was not something I seriously considered when I joined the United States Army during 1966. They frowned on us keeping record of military events, especially within combat zones, for fear that the information in diaries and journals may find its way into enemy hands and compromise current or future operations. In the stories that follow, which are presented as accurately as possible, I would like to share some of my Army experiences from 1966 through 1970 to include two years in a combat zone. There are quotations throughout attributed to certain people, myself included. I did not record those statements or otherwise document in any way what was said at the time. But, to the best of my recollection, the quoted words are what I remember being said. For the last fifty or so years, I have heard them over and over again. In each case, I believe it unnecessary to explain each quote with the disclaimer, "to the best of my recollection, this is what was said." So, let it be known, here and now, the quotes may not be entirely accurate. They are only what I recall being said.

Vietnam felt like a war to a select few who were there. The Vietnamese believed it was. Her people suffered the consequences of one ideology fighting another, defending against invading Japanese, occupying

French forces, insurgent communists from the north, and a host of allies coming to their defense since the 1950s as they struggled to form a representative government. From the mid-1960s to the early 1970s, American troops dealt with violence and death on a daily basis, always aware that the next moment could be their last. I thought it was a war.

But, was our involvement in Vietnam actually a *war*? I suppose the answer to that depends on whom you ask. To the men and women engaged in combat action and hostile fire, being killed or wounded, searching for the oftentimes-elusive enemy, it was, indeed, a war. To the newspaper men, "war" was easier to say and print than "police action," and it fit on newspaper headlines better. But, what exactly is a *police action*? That name is defined as military combat action by our regular military forces against another without a formal declaration of war. The Gulf of Tonkin Resolution was passed by Congress, giving President Lyndon B. Johnson the legal foundation to wage an undeclared war, or "police action," in Vietnam, just as President Truman had done a decade earlier in Korea.

Vietnam meant many things to me. As a destination, it was a place we went to, and deep down not knowing if we'd ever return. Yet, we pushed forward anyway. Youthful bravado and a naïve reliance on stateside military training made us believe we were invincible. But once we were actually there, we became aware of a new reality, and for me it was kill or be killed, shoot first and ask questions later. It was a place to disassociate the enemy, whoever they might be, by believing they were inferior. Using terms that were neutral (*target*) or derogatory (*dink, gook*) became common, and it weighed on my mind to begin speaking of people in such a manner. It made us veterans, some with combat experience and many others without. Every soldier, sailor and airman there became brothers (and sisters) to each other, notwithstanding the natural rivalry between the different branches of service. We came home, alone and detached from what I suppose was the most intense year-long experience imaginable, the ultimate us-against-them in warfare. As part of our life-long resume, it was either a plus or minus. It all depended upon whom was making the evaluation.

The title, *You Can't Come In*, is a reference to one very early morning in Bien Hoa, Republic of Vietnam on January 31, 1968. Attempting to enter a bunker during a rocket attack was denied because of what three inside perceived as it being overcrowded. It wasn't. Later, when I came home, I was kept at arms-length by a society that didn't understand what I'd been through. I soon learned I was like most Vietnam veterans. We left one battle overseas. Coming home we had to fight another for personal survival and self-respect. My story reveals how it felt for me, and, I think, other Vietnam veterans coming home to American soil, to become the pariahs of civilian society. Our own nation closed us out and never really let us back in. *No, you can't come in* is the message we heard loud and clear.

Combat veterans, in particular, seem overwhelmingly to have undergone a personality change to those who knew them before they went to war. On the battlefield, they have crossed the line that some may call *innocence* by either killing someone and/or almost being killed. That experience can never be undone. It changes a person in ways that are personal and difficult to explain. To the uninitiated, it is almost impossible to understand. That became a wedge to reintegrating back into society.

Likewise, having circled the wagons for decades against overly generalized vitriolic accusations, it had become very difficult to allow those having never set foot in Vietnam into our world. So, we kept you out. We felt no one else could understand what it was like going there, being there, and coming home to a nation that couldn't care less. The emotional pain and suffering had been stifled for too long. For many years, I thought tears were for crybabies, not combat veterans. I was wrong.

A word of caution. I most certainly would not recommend this to be read by children. Salacious details have been omitted, just in case. Some of the words and phrases used, well-known by adults and, I think, necessary to be included, would not be appropriate for them. In the pages that follow I have described events that have had the most effect on me that some readers may find offensive. Sorry 'bout that. After all, *it don't mean nuthin'*.

There is so much to understand about who we were and the skills involved to do our job that I've devoted a few pages to explain that what we needed to know to survive. No room for mistakes.

Without further delay, I offer… my story.

Chapter 1

RA

I considered myself a typical middle-class kid in a quiet, developing suburb west of Chicago. I wasn't rich, nor was I poor. My early thoughts about the military were the summer games we played in the neighborhood; choosing sides, building forts, and assembling weaponry such as make-believe wooden rifles, rocks and dirt-balls, and prairie-stalk spears. When we finished our war-for-the-day, we'd go home for dinner. In high school, I continued the combatant role as a high school junior varsity wrestler for two years. Our coach worked our butts off in practice, and only in hindsight was I grateful for that. Busting ass or not, it was tough competing for a spot on the varsity team. I managed one, just one, meet; and, I won in 21 seconds with a pin.

I've always told people I'm from Chicago, even though I only lived within the city limits for three years as a child. If I told them I was from a small suburban village twenty minutes west of the city, as I occasionally did, further explanation was required. But I was born in Chicago. So were my parents. My grandparents emigrated from Germany, France, Belgium, and Greece to Chicago during the late 1800s and early 1900s. My maternal great grandfather, who was from Prussia but lived in Ohio for most of his life, was working there during the Great Chicago Fire of October 10, 1871 and sustained serious burns and survived. My older sister, Sharon, who I never knew, was born there. My oldest kid brother, Steve, was born there.

We moved to the suburbs when I was three. Villa Park, to be exact. The home of Ovaltine, that favorite chocolate-powder additive to milk enjoyed by so many children. Our two younger siblings, Scott and Suzanne, came into this world soon after, calling Villa Park their hometown. Twenty minutes due west of downtown Chicago on I-290, we had the best of all worlds: the peaceful, tree-lined streets of a small village; yet, close to the hustle and bustle, the history, reputation and sophistication of downtown Chicago.

We had all of the modern conveniences of suburbia at that time: a color TV; a stereo radio/record player console; a wall phone with push button dialing (as opposed to the rotary dial) and a new system called "call waiting"; a natural gas stove, furnace and clothes dryer; and a recent model Oldsmobile with automatic transmission.

It was a time when blue jeans were beginning to be accepted as approved attire for school, as long as they were clean and not worn out. Boys still wore a shirt, tie, and jacket for school events such as dances or concerts. Girls wore skirts and dresses no shorter than at or below the knee. Tobacco products were forbidden, as were fighting, cussing and drinking alcoholic beverages (though a few did). The use of marijuana and/or other illegal narcotic and chemical substances were so far removed from our concept of prohibited activities that they weren't even considered.

In our home, obedience was expected. Our parents divorced when I was sixteen years old. During the next eighteen months, both remarried. Mom and her new husband, Bill, moved to Michigan about a year later with two of my siblings, Steve and Sue. Dad, our step-mom Cathy, Scott, and I stayed at home with our new sister, Janie. I graduated from high school during June 1965. I was kidding myself by thinking I'd be going to college in the fall. That summer I continued working at a discount retail store, where I worked while a senior. In September, I started working in the mail room at Kiwanis International in downtown Chicago, at the corner of Erie and Rush.

My decision to leave home came about slowly. My usefulness as the oldest son was being exploited. I became a convenient babysitter for my infant sister. Most of my friends were gone. Approaching the age of eighteen, I realized my opportunity to leave was at hand. I was excited to begin the next phase of my life. It was easier than expected when I left home two and a half months after my birthday, celebrated most unceremoniously. I couldn't get out of the house fast enough. I had enough of *growing up*, it was time to sprout my wings and fly.

The winter of 1965-1966 in Chicago was very windy and cold. But then again, weren't they all? When I think about the winter seasons in the greater Chicagoland area, they all seemed to be the same. The occasional sunny sky, the faintest shade of light blue and gray punctuated by a few small white clouds here and there. Steam and hot air rising as white vaporous plumes from chimneys and furnace exhaust pipes on roofs of buildings, too numerous to count. Cars and trucks, partially camouflaged in varying shades of gray up to three feet off the street from road salt, moving about in straight lines and some vanishing around curves. Thin layers of road salt, waves of swirling snow blanketing most roads, naked and cold, sometimes lifted up and set free by street-hugging and fast wind currents. Glistening icy spots, hidden at night and known as *black ice*, revealed by the new day until they evaporated into nothingness, sometimes. I wanted to leave.

I had no car of my own. I'd use Dad's for dates. He strongly encouraged me to get a car when I was a senior, but instead I chose a Honda 90; a motor scooter, really. Ninety cubic centimeters of pure, unadulterated power. I preferred calling it a small motorcycle to avoid embarrassing myself for making such a stupid choice. Riding it on the Eisenhower Expressway back and forth to work during the winter was brutal. Winter rush hour going home, riding into the prevailing western winds and hugging the white fog line to avoid being side-swiped by cars or trucks, being alone, freezing, and going no faster than 45 mph on the freeway (if I crouched down far enough) for the thirty-minute drive gave me plenty of time to think. How could I leave home with the least amount of disruption?

It was time for me to go. I felt it in my bones, literally. It was an urge that became uncontrollable, running away from home in an honorable way. Dad was so unpredictable it was often impossible to know what set him off. His mood would change as quickly as flipping a light-switch. I paid more attention to the fifteen-minute evening news. The fighting in Vietnam was still going on, heavier than just a year before. I didn't want to miss it, but didn't know why.

Propaganda was not a word or concept I was familiar with during the months before and after I graduated from high school. During 1965, there was nothing officially negative about our involvement in Vietnam. Some young men were protesting, but I didn't so much as see them protesting our involvement there but rather the Selective Service draft. Quite a few young men my age were getting drafted. Many were college students and preferred to keep it that way. The nightly news began airing stories about a few of them burning their draft card in public; a criminal offense, I heard. The Selective Service developed official deferments, such as a college deferment if the person was a full-time college student in good standing; medical deferments, such as 4-F; and hardship deferments, such as being the sole remaining son in the immediate family whose brothers may have been killed in Vietnam; and later, marriage deferments. When I registered, none of these applied; I was 1-A.

Our government, I believe, was in cahoots with Hollywood to promote the idea of war. There were quite a few military-themed programs shown during prime time TV: *Combat*, a drama about World War II starring Vic Morrow; *McHale's Navy*, a comedy starring Ernest Borgnine in the starring role and Tim Conway as Ensign Parker, his bumbling sidekick; *Hogan's Heroes*, a comedy starring Bob Crane as the titular hero and Werner Klemperer as Colonel Klink; and *Twelve O'clock High*, a drama starring Robert Lansing. The wholesome town of Mayberry on *The Andy Griffith Show* gave way to *Gomer Pyle, U.S.M.C.*, with Jim Nabors in the title role giving a lighthearted face to military life. Even the dramas contained a hint of comedy and sharing of experience with the viewers that made military life livable (no pun intended). The good guys (us) may have got wounded, some shipped home (and out of the series), but no one was killed to the best of my recollection. The bad guys (them) always suffered the worst.

Music was another form of pseudo-government propaganda. During high school, a very popular country march song, and movie of the same title, was *Sink the Bismarck*, sung by Johnny Horton. The one that had the most impact on me, as a high school graduate, was *The Ballad of the Green Berets* by Barry Sadler. Under President Kennedy's Administration, the Army Special Forces gained a certain mystique as the best kind of soldiers we had. They had the reputation of being the toughest and most talented in warfare. The green beret, their headgear, became emblematic of their status as the epitome of the American soldier. So, in part, the lyrics to the song told of soldiers fighting fearlessly, men of their word, bravery; silver wings on their chest, coveted by many but earned by only 3%.

I didn't want to be a Green Beret. I wanted to join the Air Force, as did many others, apparently. The recruiter told me there would be a two-month wait to get in, but I was impatient. If I waited, the war might be over before I got there. So, I thought it would be a good idea to check in with the Army recruiter. There was no waiting to get in there. None at all. Just pass the tests. So, I started the ball rolling. Any patriotic motives for enlisting were actually secondary to my primary goal of leaving home at 18 years of age.

Monday, March 7, 1966 was the day I enlisted into the United States Army for a term of three years. After being tested academically to insure I qualified for the school I wanted, my mechanical aptitude score was among the highest of my panel; not great, but high enough. Though it was not my original intention, one of the guys from the discount store where I used to work also wanted to sign up, too. We had worked together quite often. After I left, he stayed. So, with my casual friend named Chuck Bailey, we enlisted on the "buddy program." Chuck and I would remain together during basic training. Chuck lived about a mile from me. He was from a broken home, as was I. After high school, he hadn't yet found his calling. Neither did I. To both of us, military service was a good way to get out of town and away from our families, and start living our adventures.

I had the Army's guarantee of going to helicopter maintenance school. It was up to me to pass the course.

As we were leaving the house to pick up Chuck, Dad, being a Tech 4 Sergeant (three-stripes and a "T") during the "Big One" (European Theater, World War II) gave me a bit of advice in private, "Keep your mouth shut, do what you're told, do your best and you'll do fine."

We picked up Chuck from his house, and then to the Armed Forces Induction Center in Chicago. Dad drove us in his polished yellow Oldsmobile. Chuck was always quiet, an introvert, maybe. Dad, being in sales, was charming and tried to engage him in conversation. True to form on the way to Chicago, Chuck probably didn't say twenty words. I didn't find that unusual, actually. It had been my idea to join the Army. He didn't have anything else going on, except working at the discount store in hardware one day, or housewares the next. He thought it seemed like a good idea to enlist together. Was he having second thoughts? Dad dropped us off, leaving without any fanfare. Chuck and I were off on our great adventure.

At the induction center, we lined up for in-processing. Physical exams, hearing tests, prodding, probing, going from one station to another, following directions, never leaving the building. Each of us was assigned a service number. Ours started with an RA[1]. The service number for draftees began with "US", rather than "RA." Little did I realize that day how important the "RA" would become during the next three years. It set us apart from the draftees.

Those who enlisted were processed first. We were separated into the branch of the military each of us chose and herded into a room where the oath of enlistment was read by a captain. Raising my right hand just above my shoulder, palm facing forward toward the American flag, I repeated the oath of enlistment, phrase by phrase, along with the others:

> *I // ("state your name") Martin D. Alexander // do solemnly swear // that I will support and defend // the Constitution of the United States // against all enemies // foreign and domestic // that I will bear // true faith and allegiance // to the same // and that I will obey // the orders of the President of the United States // and the orders of the officers appointed over me // so help me God.*

And then we were done. Waiting for bus transportation to take us to basic training, we sat around with no TV, no radio, and no snack bar. Some read a book. Others were in small groups talking amongst themselves. Chuck and I walked around a bit, not wanting to lose sight of our stuff. None of us were permitted to leave the building. So, in one of the lines of chairs, set up like inside a bus terminal, we sat down, waited and watched the draftees process in. A few other guys joined us. This was not the place to heckle. In a manner of speaking we were all in the same boat.

Every one of us was committed to six years of military service. Draftees would serve two years on active duty; RAs three, four or six. Draftees then would have four years of reserve duty, two active and two inactive. Three-year RAs have one and two, four-year RAs have just the two years of inactive reserves. The period of active reserves, meaning once-a-month weekend duty and one two-week field exercise per year,

---

[1] Regular Army. The "US" stood for United States, a generic label for those drafted.

would be waived if that person spent a year in a combat zone like Vietnam. None of the draftees had a choice of school, military occupational specialty (MOS), or branch of service. But it didn't have to be like that. In that building, a draftee's destiny could be changed immediately by accepting the cadre's offer to enlist for a minimum of three years—just one extra year. If that was done, the "new" enlistee could attend a school of choice, if qualified, and join the ranks of the RAs. This offer was made repeatedly, but only a few took advantage.

Those that chose to remain a draftee were instructed to line up and count off by fours. One by one, the draftees counted off in sequence: *one, two, three, four, one, two...* and so on. The *ones* were told to go into one room. On the way, they were informed they would be in the Army. Then, the *twos* did the same thing, and were promptly informed they'd be in the Air Force. The *threes* were next, informed they would be entering the Navy, and finally the *fours* were told they were going into the Marines.

Throughout the day, there must have been at least five hundred guys processing in. It was organized, thorough, and efficient. Towards the late afternoon, groups were beginning to leave for basic training or boot camp. When I watched those going into the Air Force line up at the door, I thought about my first choice and the two-month wait. Was it worth it to get in? Did those guys also have a two-month delay? If only I had waited, I'd be in that line or one very similar to it. But, the Air Force was not going to happen for me.

Chuck and I boarded the bus with all the others destined for Fort Polk, Louisiana. As we left the building, evening rush hour was just beginning. I looked out the window at the traffic, the cars, trucks, busses and motorcycles. I did not regret leaving. I was actually excited. As we travelled southward, small talk among us revealed we were not all from the Chicago area. Some came from lower Illinois, Indiana, and Wisconsin. Soon, the chatter died out as each of us either fell asleep or had nobody left awake to talk to.

Eventually, we arrived to our destination. Our bus entered the Army base, and stopped at the gate. The driver spoke to the guard through his opened window. Inside the bus, guys were waking up to the sound of the air brake, hissing, and the change of forward momentum coming to a standstill. The night air during March in Louisiana was quite unlike that of

Chicago. It's warm and muggy. You could feel the humidity. No snow, no ice, no blowing wind. I was really gone.

Except for a fire light on nearly every building illuminating the doors of white, old, World War II–era wood-frame structures, and the occasional street light, it was very dark on base. The temperature, at 2:30 in the morning, was maybe sixty-five or seventy degrees.

Entering the post, and driving a few more blocks, we arrived to our destination. The pneumatic door at the front of the bus opened with a hiss. We were in the midst of darkened two-story wooden barracks. A single-level structure stood apart, alive with lights and activity. We would soon learn this small building contained the orderly room and supply room.

As we filed out of the bus, a buck sergeant wearing a well-tailored and heavily starched khaki uniform and Smoky-the-Bear hat yelled at the top of his voice. Looking at one of our guys with eyes of certain hatred and contempt, and a face that could win the war by itself.

"YOU PEOPLE ARE LATE," he hollered, "WHY ARE YOU LATE? GET IN LINE OVER THERE." The guys who had gotten off the bus first were lined up, shoulder to shoulder, facing away from the orderly room.

Someone behind me made a crude comment, barely audible. A few guys snickered. I might have, too. Focusing his contempt at that guy and using his words as a spear the buck sergeant said, "YOU." His eyes narrowed as he took a few steps toward him, "WHAT DID YOU SAY?" He didn't give him two seconds to answer. Then, he continued, "DROP AND GIVE ME TWENTY PUSH-UPS."

As the rest of the guys spilled out of the bus, each man followed the one in front of him to get in line quickly, as instructed. One by one, they stepped around the man on the ground doing his twenty.

Because of my being on the wrestling team in high school, and having survived the torturous physical training under the watchful eye of our coach, I was still in very good physical condition. Push-ups were a breeze, but there was no way I was going to tell *him* that. So far, knocking out twenty didn't seem to be much of a corrective measure.

Basic training began. Our unit was "B-3-5": B Company, 3rd Training Battalion, 5th Training Brigade at Fort Polk, Louisiana. We were a bunch of civilian kids, ranging in age from eighteen to twenty-four but most at the younger end. Most of us were white. We were separated into equal number groups, later identified as platoons, and led first to the supply room to get our bedding, then to our barracks, one platoon each. As Chuck and I and the others marched to our building, as only a bunch of civilian kids could do, our sergeant told us to halt. Standing at attention, with the necessary encouragement to help some of us along, he called for the draftees to step forward and form a group in front. About a third of the group formed a line, and the sergeant instructed the rest of us, the RAs in our platoon, to enter the barracks and select a bunk. Top or bottom, it didn't matter.

As we entered the building, I noticed some guys already there, inside and sacked out. We weren't the first to arrive. Chuck grabbed the top of one bunk and I took the top of the bunk next to his. We each had a gray, metal wall locker about twenty-four inches wide and six feet tall, and a wooden footlocker about three-feet wide, twenty-inches tall, and twenty-four-inches deep. This would be our home for the next eight weeks. As we were getting settled, the draftees had entered and picked their bunks.

The second order of business was to get instructed about our fire watch. We had two pot-bellied stoves for heat, one upstairs and one down. SFC[2] Vega-Barrera, our drill sergeant, told us about how fast these old wooden buildings could catch on fire. "Just the other week, one barracks burnt to the ground. I could have been prevented if the fire guard didn't fall asleep," he said convincingly. We believed him. As a preventative measure, each of us would have a fire watch detail. One man from each floor would stay awake for an hour, keeping alert to any sign of fire and/or smoke so as to wake everyone up to get out, and then wake up the next guy as the relief guard. We'd start at the bunk closest to the door and work our way around. This would be our nightly routine until we completed basic training.

"It's late, men, get some shut eye," the drill sergeant said as he and his sidekick buck sergeant left the building. So, with that, they left and we went to sleep. I looked at my watch. It was ten-to-five. As I drifted

---

[2] Sergeant First Class, E-7.

away, I was excited to be where I was. SFC Vega-Barrera, probably in his late thirties, seemed nicer than I expected a drill sergeant to be. I expected him to fit the only example I knew of—Sergeant Carter on *Gomer Pyle, U.S.M.C.*— but he didn't. His assistant, the buck sergeant, was another story.

"EVERYBODY UP! OUTTA BED, LET'S GO, YOU'RE WASTIN' DAYLIGHT!" Some of the guys around me started to grumble as this buck sergeant went bunk to bunk, banging on the metal frameworks with something hard, a piece of metal, maybe. Noise, commotion, chaos. "OUTSIDE IN THIRTY MINUTES. MAKE YOUR BEDS, GET DRESSED, LET'S GO, YER LATE," he bellowed as he walked from the far end of our barracks, down the aisle, and out the side door. It was still dark outside. I stole as glance at him as he walked past me. I couldn't help but wonder how in the world his khaki uniform looked so perfect. His black boots shined like glass. The creases in his heavily starched pants and long-sleeved shirt were impeccable, both tailored to perfection. The upper point of his three-stripe rank patch was perfectly centered on the crease. His brown felt Smokey-the Bear hat, with a strap behind his head, tilted forward, just above his eyebrows. The brim of his hat, strangely enough, perfectly flat all around. He wore an olive-drab web belt, three inches wide, snuggly around his waist. Every minute detail, perfect. No loose threads, no wrinkles, no area worn or thinned out.

The first day in B-3-5 was busy. After breakfast, we marched to a building for our haircuts. Forming a very long line outside, we took our turns to enter. Inside, six barbers and six chairs. We had no choice of style, they were all going to be the same, hair cut close to the skin about a quarter of an inch long. Then, each of us had to pay a dollar for our five-minute haircut. Chuck confided in me that joining the Army might not have been a good idea as we stood in line waiting our turn. It was like an assembly line; guys going in one door with various lengths and styles of haircuts, and coming out the other end as "skinheads," though that moniker was not yet in circulation.

Then, we marched over to another long building to be issued our uniforms: three sets of fatigues, three hats (a very ugly fatigue hat, a Garrison hat, and a Service hat), Class A uniforms (one green and two khaki), a black tie, white boxer shorts and T-shirts, two sets of black boots with green boot socks and a pair of low quarters with black dress socks, two white towels and washcloths, a green canvas duffle bag printed with our name and service number (complete with either RA or US), and field gear such as a poncho, pack, web belt, a couple of ammo pouches, etc.

Back in the barracks, we learned how to make our beds with "hospital corners," tight enough to bounce a quarter off the top blanket. Our gear went into the wall locker just so, and, using a folded white towel for the upper tray of the foot locker, other items were placed inside. Socks were rolled in a certain way, as were the skivvies and towels. No allowance was made for individual preferences. Everybody followed the same instructions to make each display of gear identical to another. Going from one person's area to another, one would not be expected to tell the difference except for the name tags. Details was the name of the game. Nothing short of perfection was expected.

One of the guys had his radio with him. He had found a station that played music most of us enjoyed. "Monday, Monday," by the Mammas and Pappas, came on, and to me it seemed to embody the folksy way-of-life of the times. I liked that perceived life-style, but knew it was unattainable given my present situation. Folk music, back to basic living, hootenannies—it all meant something to me, though I found it almost impossible to articulate why. But, that song would always remind me of my first day in the Army.

Guys from California were a little different from Midwesterners like me. We had two or three in our platoon. They were draftees, and a little older than the rest of us. Because of that they seemed more mature, not succumbing to resistance of authority, emotional outbursts, or just being stupid. It was as if they were "college guys," and the rest of us were a bunch of "high school guys."

Over the next few days, every one of us did something wrong to merit the "drop, and give me twenty" routine. There were a few who were selected by the drill sergeants a little too often, maybe. Me? At least once every couple of days, at first. But I think I was adjusting to the Army pretty well. My measurement of success was how often, or not, I got into trouble. In front of the cadre, I kept my mouth shut, did my best, and didn't complain. This seemed to be a very wise bit of advice from Dad.

The Army's *Daily Dozen*[3] physical training was not difficult, nor were the foot marches we had. SFC Vega-Barrera was tough but also a good leader.

For the first few weeks, we called home (collect, usually) on Saturday afternoons to check in with our parents, girlfriends, or anyone else important enough to call. There were two pay-booths, adjacent to each other, located nearby. Because we were restricted to the company area during the first month, permission from the drill sergeant was required to leave the area and use the phone. Most of the time no less than three or four guys waited his turn at each phone, standing away to provide some degree of privacy. We didn't have all the time in the world, so each of us tried to limit our calls to twenty minutes.

About three weeks into basic training, I called home as usual. The routine was Dad would talk first, pass the phone to my stepmom Cathy, and if my brother Scott was home, then to him. On this call, Dad told me that the Air Force recruiter from Elmhurst called "just the other day" asking for me. Apparently, there was an opening for a couple recruits sooner than expected, and I was invited to sign up immediately. Dad let him know I had enlisted in the Army two weeks before.

I couldn't believe what I heard. I much preferred the Air Force, but it was too late for me. There was no such thing as quitting the Army once you're in. Transferring from one branch to another simply didn't happen. I was in the Army now, like it or not.

Nearly every guy in our platoon smoked cigarettes. We were taught how to field strip them when the smoking was over. Filter cigarettes were not too common, so field stripping was easy; just twist the cigarette butt between your fingers, allowing the remaining tobacco to fall to the ground (always outside the buildings), and roll the remaining paper into small balls and cast them aside, allowing the weather elements to finish the work.

I didn't smoke, but I thought it might be time to start. I wanted to be an adult, being eighteen and all. Wanting to live up to the *sophistication* (at least in my eyes) of being from Chicago and knowing that ciga-

---

[3] Bend and reach, rear lunge, forward lunge, high jumping, squats, deep knee bends, bent-leg body twist, full-body twist, pushups and single-leg push-ups, sit ups, face up and face down prone leg lifts, and mountain climber.

rettes were not good for you, I began smoking a pipe, a la Hugh Hefner. Bad idea. Too much work, and not enough time.

When we were in the field, we could only smoke when the drill sergeant allowed us to take a smoke-break. "Smoke 'em if you got 'em, bum 'em if you don't." The others were already taking their first drag of a cigarette by the time I removed my pipe and bag of tobacco. The others were nearing the halfway point of their cigarettes by the time I had the bowl packed, just right and not too tight, and lit the pipe with my Zippo lighter. A couple puffs and maybe the tobacco caught. Maybe it didn't. Then, just as my pipe began to fire up and I took a few drags, the drill sergeant bellows out, "OK, put 'em out." Eight to ten minutes was never enough time.

Basic training taught us first aid, breaking down the M-14 (7.62x51mm) rifle for cleaning, fire watch and guard duty, drill and marching, the Military Code of Justice, and learning how to rely on each other. We eventually qualified with the M-14 rifle at 400 meters without a scope. I qualified as a Sharpshooter. The lowest qualification was Marksman and the highest was Expert. We trained with the bayonet and pugil stick, and hand-to-hand and judo techniques. We cleaned the latrine spic-and-span every day, washed and waxed the barracks floor by hand, and learned how to use the electric buffer. I quickly found that operating the buffer was *the* best job to get, and I jumped at the chance as often as possible.

There was a technique to be mastered with the electric buffer. The controls were similar to a motorcycle handle bar, but smaller, with the on/off lever on the right side. Depressing the lever starts the rotating buffer-head. Tilt the handles to the left moves it left, tilting to the right moves to the right. It didn't take much effort to move the buffer one way or the other. Straw bristles were standard on the buffer-head to clean the floor. Polishing would require a felt pad that kept its place by the weight of the motor area.

Working together taught us teamwork. Getting into trouble, as a group, because of one person's screw-up also taught us teamwork. What we learned, most of all, was attention to detail. No loose threads, no missing buttons, and no dirt or dust anywhere. These were old, wooden barracks, so you'd expect there to be dust somewhere, no? Not in basic training. If you couldn't clean it up, you painted over it because you would never hide it from inspections. I learned to appreciate detail work.

I continued to call Dad about once a week, but after a few weeks he told me to stop calling collect so often. It was getting expensive. So, unless there was something important going on, write a letter. I knew he was right, but his request hit me like a ton of bricks. All of a sudden, I realized I was on the outside looking in. Letters? That would take days to get delivered. It would be at least a week before I got a response to my letters, *if* one of them wrote back right away. Sure, I received letters at mail call, but it was not the same as a phone call. I missed that connection. I understood Dad had his new family, and so did my mom up in Michigan. I don't want to admit feeling left out, abandoned maybe, but for these reasons the Army was a good place to be.

By May, we were nearly done with basic training. As Private E-1s, we sure weren't in it for the money. Paid once a month in cash, our net pay was about $75. It was close to "another day, another dollar" as they've said since World War I. We mostly remained confined to our company area. The mess hall was located there as well. The only time we were allowed to leave the company area for enjoyment was when we earned the right. We'd be able to go the Post Exchange (PX) or movie theater, a short walk away, if we earned that privilege. Our platoon did qualify towards the end of basic training, week number seven. The one movie playing was the Beatles *Yellow Submarine*. A few of us jumped at the chance to go. Not because we thought it would be a good movie, but the Beatles were popular and it was a chance to get away. Contrary to our expectations, the movie was a waste of our time and our limited financial resources. It was silly and nonsensical. For one, I saw this as nothing more than a showcase for a few songs. Besides, living in a yellow submarine…what the hell does that mean?

The city of Leesville (better known to us as Diseaseville) was off limits for us. Not really sure why. Actually, I think I do. Most of us were eighteen or nineteen-years of age, immature in many aspects though we would argue aggressively that was not the case. Testosterone was running high, notwithstanding the saltpeter rumored to have been added to our meals since we arrived. We were likely kept out of town to protect the citizens of that community. Let's face it: post-adolescent testosterone plus a few too many three-point-two beers (alcohol content of 3.2 percent) equal trouble. And, after being confined to the company area for weeks, except for training, I'm sure at least a few of us would have acted like animals if let loose upon the locals.

We had no say in the matter. We were, after all, basic trainees. We had no rights. But, what we did have was unity, teamwork, and *esprit de corps*. We learned where one was weak, another was strong. Together, we could not fail any challenge, even if it meant bending the rules a bit. Just don't get caught! Like siblings, bickering among us was expected; but, as a family, we could not be defeated. When the chips were down we pulled through, together. Our platoon, our company, our base, our Army was that family—unified and loyal to one another.

By the end of eight weeks, the orderly room didn't seem to be a place *verboten*. The faces inside were familiar; the people, friendly. We'd get our orders for AIT (Advanced Individual Training) there. A handful of guys, mostly the draftees, were going to remain at Fort Polk for their "AIT"— advanced infantry training at Tigerland. The rest of us waited for our orders to send us to our school of choice.

Chuck and I parted ways after basic training. Except for an exchange of one or two letters, we lost touch. All of us had a "delay in travel" of about three weeks to get to our next base. Aside from actual travel, what are you going to do with two and a half weeks of free time, except go home? There was enough money allocated in our travel pay that flying home on military standby and then going to the next base on standby was just enough. For us to qualify for standby status, we'd have to wear our Army uniform while we traveled, which was no problem. We were proud to be in the Army. I think maybe the draftees were, also. Wearing our uniform with pride, we left Fort Polk as active duty soldiers. Our only ribbon, for the National Defense Service Medal, became our first badge of honor.

About eighteen days later, I went to Fort Rucker outside Dothan, Alabama. I expected to be there for four months. With duffel bag in hand, I got onto a shuttle from the airport that went directly to Fort Rucker. This base was essentially an aviation training base for pilots, and fixed and rotary-wing aircraft mechanics.

The first two months were basic fixed-wing aircraft training. This was more or less an introductory course for aircraft maintenance. The basic aero-dynamic principles, electrical systems, and engine operating methods were taught. If we successfully passed this two-month stage, we'd go onto the next. Most of us did fine. The second two months were specifically about the Bell Iroquois "Huey" helicopter's maintenance, up-keep, and rotary wing principles of flight.

There are four forces at work with aircraft: gravity, thrust, lift, and drag. Of course, what goes up must come down. Our job was to make sure the aircraft systems worked properly and that when the pilot wanted to land, he did so under his control, not by chance. Maintaining a helicopter required attention to detail, and lots of it. Fluid levels had to be filled ex-actly to the line. Safety wire had to be twisted perfectly and in the correct direction to prevent the bolt-nut from loosening. Maintenance logs and various forms had to be kept up. Bearings and push-pull rods were al-lowed only so much "give" before it was time to replace. Filters and screens cleaned or replaced on a very strict flight-time schedule. Adjusting the trim on the main and tail rotor blades was required to reduce vibration in flight and we learned how to do that, as well. The instructors taught us everything we needed to know about the mechanics, hydraulics, avionics, electrical systems and an overview of weaponry.

Dad, Cathy, Scott and Janie came down to visit me one weekend. My step-mom was from Alabama, so she probably still had family in the state to visit as well. Her son, who lived with his father in Tennessee, had died a year or two before. Dad, acting out his protective instincts, didn't want her to go out of state to the funeral where she may run into her abu-sive ex-husband. But, now, maybe they also went to Tennessee as well to visit her son's gravesite. But they didn't share any plans with me about going anywhere else, so I never knew. They stayed for the weekend and left.

It was also here where I met many guys who would be with me for the next twenty months. Three guys in particular, Don Garceau, Tom Lovetere, and John 'Babe' Leone, would become my very close friends. There were other guys I met as well, but these three and I formed a bond. They were slightly older than me by months, maybe a year or so. Back home I was the older brother. With these guys, I was like the younger brother. Collectively, they took me under their wing. Surprisingly, I liked that status. We shared the same moral values, a deep sense of patriotism, and we were each single. These guys became my family.

Don was the oldest among us four, from northern Massachusetts. Although we were all single, he was the one who was most settled down, almost as if he was actually married. Responsible, contemplative, and mature are words I would use to describe him. He had a quick wit and dry sense of humor and fit into the group almost as a counter-point to our antics.

Tom, hailing from East Boston, was extremely proud of his Italian heritage. His dad passed away on Tom's sixteenth birthday. He loved his mother, the matriarch of his large family, more than anyone or anything else in the world. He was a smooth operator, serious and a natural born leader, at least among us. As the youngest in his family he had been protected by his brothers (one twenty years his senior) throughout his life. Yet, he was street smart and could hold his own in any situation. He was also the mechanics' mechanic. His skill with car engines was unsurpassed.

Babe was the steam powering our collective engine. Also of Italian heritage but from New Jersey, he had an older car that later was very useful during our excursions. Tom made sure it ran well. Dark sunglasses were as part of Babe's persona as were his always present smile and jovial attitude. He was stocky and somewhat muscular, just enough to impress every girl he met. Or, so he told us. Hence, the nickname Babe (magnet). Hanging around him didn't result in us meeting a lot of girls, but it was fun trying. But, just ask him. He *was* the lady's man.

Being from the Chicago area, I was actually the odd man out (not Italian or from Massachusetts), but we all connected. Tom and I spoke often about the Greco-Roman relationship throughout history, and it helped us bond a solid friendship. Don, Tom, Babe, and I were all "northerners," not from Texas or California, which probably made us that much closer. People from Texas are proud of their large state, as everything in Texas is bigger and better than anywhere else according to them. People from California were more laid back. They seemed to have a unique outlook on things, preferring the surf, sun and women. But, there was something about California guys that seemed peculiar, strange almost. They weren't like the rest of us, somehow. Guys from those two states had unique personality characteristics that were *different*, to put it politely, from anybody else. We were "Yankees" to those who hailed from the Southern States. In a form of soft rivalry, we were frequently reminded the southern Confederacy was alive and well. Most of all we were all friends.

At the end of June, we all got 'promoted' to E-2. Unless you were a screw-up, the promotions were automatic and came with a slight pay increase. But still, our sleeves were empty. No insignia would announce our rank to the observer.

Don, Tom, Babe and I did almost everything together. Babe went back to New Jersey one weekend and came back with a used '58 Ford Fairlane. He, Tom, and one or two others would take it on weekends to visit the beaches at Panama City, Florida, a little over a hundred miles to our south. Not wanting to risk being AWOL[4], I never made it there, however. Strangely enough, I don't regret not going. As a passenger, I wouldn't have had any control about when to leave except for a suggestion, and I was accustomed to playing it safe and being where I was supposed to be on time. I never wanted to be late getting back to base. An Article 15, non-judicial punishment (possibility of reduction in rank, fine, and/or extra duty) meted out by the company commander was something that I could not afford to happen.

That summer in Alabama was unmercifully hot and humid. We were allowed to shorten our fatigue shirt sleeves, uniformly rolling them up to just above the elbows. Our barracks, the same style as at Fort Polk, had no air-conditioning. A few guys bought small electric fans at the PX which helped a bit. Our classrooms were air-conditioned and the cool temperature inside was always a welcome relief. As soon as training was done for the day, all of us made a bee-line to the mess hall for chow, and then the barracks to change into civilian clothes if we planned to go into town; or just lounge around in our fatigue pants and T-shirts, telling stories, goofing around, and so on. None of us had much money, so staying on base was what we did most of the time.

A cafeteria was nearby, and I'd go there alone or with one of the guys for a hamburger and Coke, maybe a three-point-two beer, just to get away from the company area. Inside, it was abusively bright; neon lights in the ceiling, walls at least twelve feet tall and painted white, a light gray

---

[4] Absent With-Out leave, not having permission to be off base.

tile floor, and pale green vinyl covered aluminum chairs and Formica table tops. It was too clean—almost sterile clean—and uncomfortable. It had a jukebox at one corner, filled with all the popular 45 rpm record songs, and a few others I never heard before. But getting near it seemed almost impossible. A group of young Negro[5] men, roughly ten to fifteen, were almost always seated at the tables near the jukebox.

It was from this group that I heard for the first time, "What's the word?" addressed by one guy to a new arrival.

The other guy would respond, "Thunderbird."

"What's the price?" was the second question.

"Thirty-twice."

I thought that was such a weird greeting. When I got back to the barracks, one of the guys explained it to me. Thunderbird is the name of a cheap wine. It used to cost sixty cents a bottle some years before, hence "thirty-twice." It was a favorite, low-cost alcoholic beverage that easily fit the budget of low-paid privates. I heard this same exchange from different demographic groups all the time. It didn't matter who you were.

They liked certain vocalists and certain styles of music, so different from what I was accustomed to. If I heard "I Feel Good" by James Brown & the Famous Flames once in that cafeteria, I heard it a hundred times. He was their favorite singer, as were, to a lesser degree, Smokey Robinson and the Miracles, Wilson Pickett, The Supremes, Lou Rawls, Percy Sledge and Eddie Floyd. For all intents and purposes, that jukebox was theirs.

Around this time, I gave up smoking my pipe, which had gotten to be ridiculous. Too many steps involved and material to carry around made me envious of those who smoked cigarettes. My buddies, and nearly everyone else I knew, smoked cigarettes. Why shouldn't I? I wasn't in sports at high school anymore. Smoking then would get you kicked off the team in a heartbeat. That no longer concerned me.

The worst thing about smoking was the morning after. Heavy smokers sometimes were short of breath. Some coughed up a luggie first

---

[5] The term, African-American, was not used at this time in our history.

thing in the morning. But then, after they'd have their first cigarette of the day and a cup of coffee, everything would be fine. I knew of no one, personally or by hearsay, who died of cancer from smoking cigarettes. So, I started with Lucky Strikes, the brand my dad smoked.

Very near the end of our Alabama training, the cadre gathered the class for a meeting. We were congratulated for completing our training and were reminded how important Hueys were becoming in military plans and operations. They told us that we would go on our next assignment directly to either South Korea or Vietnam, or be assigned stateside to form aviation companies. There were no other options. We were told that both countries were technically in a state of warfare. South Korea had an armistice, rather than a peace accord with the North. As such, they were technically in a state of war since the early 1950s. But, there would be no actual enemy action expected there, only in Vietnam.

During training, there was almost no talk among us about the possibility of any of us going to Vietnam, though we knew in the back of our minds it was a likely destination. None of us had even been to Vietnam. We were brand new helicopter mechanics. As far as I knew, none of us pictured ourselves as crewman. My mental picture assigned that role to other guys, other job skills. For all I knew, that job was a different MOS and didn't apply to us.

An officer asked who among us wanted to be assigned to South Korea. About a third of the guys raised their hand. I did not. Tom, Babe, Don and I sat together, looked at each other for mutual confirmation and kept our arms down. I actually wanted to go to Vietnam, but not right away. If I chose Korea, it would be a thirteen-month tour of duty, a month longer than Vietnam. I suspected there would be a lot of time doing not much at all, just being mission ready. The demilitarized zone separating the two Koreas did not come to my mind at all, nor did being assigned to a unit in or near Seoul, the capital. I envisioned being stationed in an isolated area, maybe in the countryside somewhere, bored to death. Besides, it's really cold in Korea.

Those selecting Korea were dismissed to follow a couple sergeants into another area for additional assignment information. Those remaining in the room had chosen Vietnam by default. The only difference was: now or later. We had no choice in that. Our new assignments would be prepared and given to us before we left Fort Rucker.

Our orders came through quickly. My next assignment was going to the 69th Aviation Company at Fort Bragg in Fayetteville, North Carolina. I quickly learned that a few of us had the same unit assignment, including Don, Tom, Babe, and a few other friends. School was over and we departed to the four winds.

Because Babe had his car, he drove and took Jim "Smitty" Smith with him. They first went to Charleston, South Carolina, then on to Fayetteville and Fort Bragg. Other guys went their different ways. A few of us, including Tom and me, took the train.

Tom and I arrived at the train station in Dothan wearing our khakis[6] and looking sharp. Our train to Fayetteville, North Carolina had arrived at the station. As Tom and I climbed aboard and entered one of the passenger cars, there were only a few people inside. I immediately saw two girls sitting together at the far end, away from anybody else. I nudged Tom. He saw them, too. We sat down in the vacant double seat in front of them. Both girls were very good looking, our age, and not wearing any rings on their left hand. After a brief but productive conversation, Tom and one girl moved to another bench seat on the other side of the isle while I joined the other. Maybe two rows separated Tom and me. It was night. It was semi-dark inside the car. Some lights inside the passenger compartment had been turned off and others dimmed so that passengers could sleep or rest. It was perfect for us.

The sound of iron wheels hitting he joints of the rail was subtle and hypnotic. The back and forth sway of the car was comforting. The girl in my arms snuggled close and warm. The remainder of the train trip was not put to waste, as any red-blooded American GI would know. I knew her name only for those few hours. Her pretty face, soft skin, velvet lips, and Southern drawl during our brief get-acquainted conversation were gifts from God Almighty. Thank you, Father in Heaven.

---

[6] Long sleeve khaki shirts were removed from the uniform of the Army during this summer. With long sleeves one would be able to wear the unit patch on the left sleeve near the shoulder, the cloth rank insignia (we didn't have one yet), and black tie that would be tucked into the shirt just beneath the third button from the top. But, with short sleeve khakis, no cloth insignia was worn except for the rank patches; no tie, just an open collar shirt.

We arrived at Fayetteville around four or five o'clock in the morning. Tom and I said our good-byes to the girls, grabbed our bags and got off the train. They remained on the train. As we stood on the platform, still wet from a recent rain, we looked for them through the coach window. It was still dark inside and out except for the pale lighting from the station's lamp posts. As we stood together and watched, Tom and I were sure we saw a slight movement of a hand-wave as the train moved forward and left the station. Neither one of us had gotten their contact information or even their full names, but it didn't matter. Like two ships passing in the night, we went our separate ways, never to see each other again.

Each with our duffle bag on the right shoulder, we walked along the rain soaked concrete platform to the end where we found the shuttle to take us to the Army base. We were the last two guys who got in the vehicle, and off we went.

Chapter 2

E-3

It was the first week of September 1966. The 69th Aviation Company at Fort Bragg was just our destination, not our unit. We were there to be part of a new aviation company. Except for its name, the 187th Aviation Company (Airmobile Light) did not exist yet, physically. Tom and I were among the first four people to sign into the new company, making us some of the originals in the unit. The day after, another guy with rank signed in. He was a Private First Class, and for that day he was our acting first sergeant. Then, a staff sergeant signed in, and he became our acting first sergeant. Within the next week more arrived—enlisted, NCOs, warrant and commissioned officers. With this bunch, Babe and Don arrived, too.

The four of us were together again. As the numbers grew, we finally moved into a different company area on base. We took over the upper floor of an old wooden barracks. My brothers were back and I felt good about that; complete, almost. Our clan grew to include Cody, Ouellette, Jensen, Peniska, and a few others. The aircraft had not arrived yet, so much of our time was spent at the baseball field we had set up in a nearby empty field across the street. We'd play against others in our company. There was no organized schedule. Just play ball when it was possible. These opportunities became scarce as the days passed.

Babe was the most flamboyant on the team. He'd walk up to the batter's box wearing his sunglasses, strutting about as if he were Babe Ruth. He was our showman. Though he rarely hit a home run, he played the part well. Tom, his sidekick, was more serious at playing ball. I imagined him as the embodiment of the Boston Red Sox; there, on our field, a no-nonsense player with a quick eye for the ball.

Rounding out the four of us was Don. Confident and wise, he didn't strike me as being too serious about the game. Neither was I. Hit the ball, get on base, try to make it in to home plate. For the moment that's what mattered.

We had fun, as much as our meager monthly pay would allow. A base service club was next door.

After work and chow at the mess hall, we sometimes went next door to the service club, a two-story building for recreation, lounging, and to watch TV. A couple of pool tables were upstairs, and these were usually busy with one or two guys methodically pocketing each ball with as few moves as possible. We'd noticed something else in each room: metal pedestal ashtrays. A lot of them. "You know, guys, we could use one of those in our barracks," I said to the others. We all nodded in agreement. I think Babe was on board with this idea first. Having a pedestal ashtray in the barracks would add a touch of class. Tom saw it as more of a challenge than anything else in how to get it out of the building. Don, my anchor to responsible behavior, grudgingly went along with the plan.

We rationalized it in our favor. Everything in the service club belonged to the Army. We were in the Army. Removing property from one Army area and putting it into another Army area didn't seem to be a crime, just a minor relocation. But, at the same time, we knew it belonged in the service club. They had so many, though. They wouldn't miss just one. We knew another thing, too. Don't ask. The problem with asking for permission is that the answer might be "no." And if you got that as your answer, you were stuck. We also knew it would be impossible to just walk out the front door carrying the two-foot tall metal ashtray without being seen and confronted.

We planned our operation. Don and I would go upstairs into the pool room, wait until it was vacant, with Don acting as the lookout. Babe would be on the ground, below the window, with Tom as his lookout, waiting for the signal to catch the parts of the ashtray. I selected the cleanest one, opened the window, and waited a few minutes. The ashtray had a top that could be untwisted from the base, we had made sure of that. It reduced the weight, somewhat. I took the top off and, looking outside first to make sure someone was still there to catch it, dropped it. Then, I took the base, a little heavier, and dropped that, too. Through our coordinated efforts, we had liberated the tray. This became our first successful military operation. I couldn't allow myself to consider that we stole that ashtray. It was a *military mission* of our own creation, and it took some effort to believe that. I didn't feel guilty at all.

In short order, assignments were made within our new company. Some of us were assigned to one of the three flight platoons, and the others to the maintenance platoon. We were 67N20s[7]. But not the gunners. There was one guy on our floor who outranked all of us. Specialist Fourth Class Fred Thompson was a gunner[8] in our unit who had seen action in the Dominican Republic recently and wore an 82nd Airborne patch on his right sleeve. He was very likeable, but was a year or two older than most of us. I guess in many ways we still acted like kids, but he was mature by comparison.

Babe, Don, Tom and I were assigned to the gun platoon as crew chiefs under Staff Sergeant (SSG) George "Sarge" Grabbenstetter. *Crew chiefs*, mind you. Why us? I could only guess it was because of our strong military demeanor and superior knowledge of what makes helicopters tick. We considered the gun platoon to be the elite platoon in the company. But, maybe what we thought of ourselves only had meaning *to* ourselves. From a pragmatic point of view, it made sense. Gunships would have a lot of weight due to fuel, a crew of four, weaponry and ordnance. The less weight of the crewmen, the more weight could be added for the other things. And, in hot humid climates, it takes more power from the engine than in cooler climates to pull pitch and take off. For our eight soon-to-arrive gunship aircraft, the enlisted crews for each were roughly five-foot-eight to five-foot-ten and weighed no more than a hundred and fifty pounds each, on the average.

There was one minor problem. The aircraft hadn't arrived to Fort Bragg yet. We were told they'd be new helicopters, straight from the Bell factory. All we had to do was wait, go on various details, look busy and stay out of trouble.

We soon learned that our Sarge (Grabbenstetter) was not a taskmaster. He was very pragmatic. One time I walked into the latrine at our barracks and found him sitting on one of the toilets[9] reading a tech-manual. Always multitasking.

During one weekend in November, Babe and one or two others got a pass from the orderly room for an overnight stay. They intended to drive

---

[7] A numerical designation for second echelon Huey rotary wing aircraft mechanics. The '67' denoted the aircraft type and the '20' our skill level.

[8] Frederick D. Thompson, from Lynn, Massachusetts, was sent to an infantry unit soon after we arrived in Vietnam. Rumors of his death in Vietnam seem to be incorrect.

[9] There was no modesty in the barracks. Each latrine had a row of toilets, a row of sinks, a row of urinals and open showers. Barriers or privacy walls did not exist.

up to New England. On the way, Babe got pulled over for speeding. He was stopped by the state police, and some altercation between him and the trooper resulted in them being locked up in a small detention cell for the night. The First Sergeant got involved as a result of their call. He gave Babe a lawful order to return to base, immediately if not sooner. They came back the next day. After an animated discussion about the pros and cons of being absent without leave (AWOL), the company commander put Babe on extra duty, namely kitchen police (KP), for two weeks to work sixteen to eighteen hours a day.

While we waited for our aircraft, we would take rides in the deuce-and-a-half to the airfield, probably to get acquainted with the airfield operation (official reason), or to keep us busy to look like we're doing something constructive (unofficial reason). Meanwhile, Babe was busy scrubbing pots and pans, cleaning the kitchen grease trap, washing meal trays and utensils, table tops, the floor washed and waxed, or whatever else the cook-NCO-in-charge thought needed to be done. By the time the workday was over, Babe was too tired to do much of anything but make a few jokes about his predicament.

Then, suddenly, it was official. The 187th Aviation Company was going to South Vietnam. A vast majority of us were neophytes. As far as we knew, there was only one enlisted man in our company who had been to Vietnam, Pearle Ettinger. We were rather 'gung ho' about our perceived destiny of going to war. Most of us had no misgivings about Vietnam. We believed in our mission, that of protecting the elected government of South Vietnam against the communists from the north and their agents in the South. Yet, we didn't dwell on the fact of actual battle, for that was still a concept beyond our naïve understanding. After years of being told about the danger of Communism and its threat to our nation and allies by our politicians, it was our turn to be on deck. Batter up. The Republic of Vietnam (RVN) was a signatory to the SEATO[10] Treaty. The enemy attacking our ally was the North Vietnamese Army (NVA), communists from North Vietnam supported by the Russians, our enemy. In the South, there were the Viet Cong (VC), an insurgent group who were supported by North Vietnam, conducting guerilla warfare against the government of the South.

---

[10] South East Asia Treaty Organization

We knew about communist regimes, the enemy of the free world. China was a closed nation[11] that supported North Korea, also a communist regime. The USSR was our main Cold War enemy, communist as well. Millions of people were murdered or imprisoned just for disagreeing with, or escaping from, their government. The Domino effect of one nation falling to communism after another is what we had to stop.

Vietnam had a long history of war and invading armies. The Chinese dynasties had once governed the country for a thousand years. During the late colonial period, the French took over control for about a hundred years, until the Japanese occupied the country during World War II. When that war ended and with the defeat of Japan, the French came back. Their attempt at colonial rule ended with their butts getting whooped at Dien Bien Phu in 1954, thus ending the French-Indochina War. Afterwards, in compliance with the Geneva Accords, the country was separated into the North and South pending the outcome of elections scheduled for 1956. Suspicious of election fraud, the American and South Vietnamese recommendation to have the voting process supervised was refused by the North and the Soviet Union, and the two halves of the country remained as separate entities.

We understood the legal and moral commitment on our part to support the government of South Vietnam, whether we as individuals liked it or not. You harm one, you harm us all. It was the same thing with NATO[12]. Some would say that the conflict in Vietnam was nothing more than an internal civil war. As such, the U.S. had no business getting involved. But there were two Vietnamese distinct governments: one north and one south, one communist and one not. The Viet Cong was not a political party, vying for control through elections in the south. They were an armed, non-uniformed, communist *militia* hell-bent on toppling the elected government of the Republic of Vietnam in the south in order to unify the Vietnamese people under communist rule. We all saw our mission through those terms, and we accepted it.

After the official announcement of our mission, it wasn't too long before the helicopters arrived. They were all new and right out of the Bell

---

[11] Chinese contact with the 'outside' world was negligible; hence it was a closed society until the aftermath of U.S. President Richard M. Nixon's diplomatic visit during 1972.
[12] North Atlantic Treaty Organization

factory box, just like they told us. Our platoon had eight Bell UH-1C model Iroquois helicopters with a 540 rotor-head system and enhanced hydraulics. The main rotor blades were wider than the B models, providing more lift with a heavy load in hot and humid weather. Seventeen Bell UH-1D models (one for the maintenance platoon and eight each for the two lift platoons) arrived as well. These type of rotary-wing aircraft were known better by the slang-term *Hueys*. The "UH" in UH-1C (or D) represented *utility helicopter* (U-till-i-tee----Hue-ey).

The electrically operated weapons systems for the C models arrived later. Each of our C models had two seven-tube rocket (2.75 inch) pods, one on each side of the ship. The pilot of the ship would be known as the *aircraft commander* (or A/C) and would control the launch of rockets by aligning the ship to the target. Two gunships had a 40mm grenade launcher that was affixed to the nose of the ship. This system used a hundred-round ammo box. The other six gunships had two mini-guns (7.65x51mm six-barrel Gatling-style rotating barrels, the M134 version, with ammo trays that could hold thousands of rounds), one on each side of the ship, each capable of firing thousands of rounds per minute. The co-pilot, to be known as the *pilot* (or *peter-pilot*) would operate the grenade launcher or mini-guns using a flexible targeting device.

The flight crews would each have to pass an annual Class III Flight Physical to qualify for flight status. At the risk of over-simplifying the medical examination (which checked nearly everything), the emphasis was on dental, eyesight, heart rate, blood pressure, color blindness, ears and hearing, and general physical fitness suitable for an occupation involving equilibrium, sustaining variations in altitude and air pressure, potential for motion sickness, and being able to conduct our flight duties while not aggravating a pre-existing medical condition. It was a required annual examination and there was no getting around it by anyone.

Crew chiefs and gunners were assigned together as a team, and each team assigned to a ship. As such, that ship was our responsibility. The aircraft commander and pilot would change from one ship to another, but not the *crew chief* and *gunner*. On gunships, the crew chief's position was on the left side of the ship, seated directly behind the peter-pilot. This way, he would be able to maintain eye contact with the aircraft commander, who was seated on the right side in front. The gunner would sit on the right side of the ship, behind the aircraft commander. On the other Hueys, the crew chief sat on the right side, and the gunner on the left.

I still couldn't believe our luck. Tom, Babe, Don, me and a few others working as crew chiefs? Each with our own helicopter? We didn't ask for that type of job, but I'm glad I was selected. Still, we had no real idea what it would involve once we got to Vietnam. We had no one to ask. I was thinking more of a defensive posture, heavily armed to return fire if we got shot at by the enemy. Being the aggressor was the furthest thing from my mind. It could be I just didn't want to face reality. After all, it had been almost ten months without TV, except for *McHale's Navy* or *The Monkeys* occasionally in the barracks, and almost no exposure to the news. No one actually said, "Look, this is what you'll be doing in Vietnam"— not even PFC Ettinger, our only Vietnam veteran.

Ettinger was in the Special Forces (so we heard) and got busted down to a PFC (E-3) from a buck sergeant (E-5). To get back to Vietnam, he was assigned to our unit as a UH-1D gunner. Along with most of my friends, I stayed clear of him, thinking he was a bit too animated when venting his anger. A few wall lockers in his barracks bore the marks from his karate chops and Tae Kwon Do kicks. Besides, he wasn't in our platoon. He was a nice guy, it turned out, and we were fortunate to have him.

Our time was split between the airfield, the gun range, and going into town. Don and I also had a special assignment. We were to design and paint the company sign that was to be posted in front of the orderly room near the road. The wording was to be "187th Aviation Company (Airmobile Light)". All they wanted was a block-letter sign, nothing fancy. But, I didn't know that. I designed a creative image of a UH-1 helicopter formed by the letters

"A I R M O B I L E – L I G H T."

It was somewhat flamboyant. The first sergeant (who we called "Top") and the company commander were kind enough to allow that sign to be posted, but before long it was replaced by more traditional signage and mine disappeared.

Don and I were assigned the two ships with 40mm grade launchers, ship numbers 66-00672 and 66-00671, respectively. Tom and Babe were assigned ships with mini-guns. We flew a bit during the winter, enough to earn our crewman wings[13] and received our orders to wear them. Wow, were we proud. We'd have to buy them at the PX, they weren't issued, but we were happy to pay. The metal ones were sterling silver, and the cloth ones were white on an olive drab green fabric matching the color of our fatigues. All of our fatigue shirts and fatigue jackets would have to be turned in to get the cloth patch sewn on. In the meantime, we wore the metal pin-on. To me, and I suppose the others, too, these wings were more important than our newly attained rank of Private First Class. The new paygrade, E-3, had a single "mosquito wing" chevron[14] stripe that would be sewn onto our uniform sleeves.

By flying a minimum of four hours per month, we'd qualify for the standard $70 flight pay per month. We were each issued a flight jacket, aviation sunglasses, white flight helmet, and M-60 (7.62x51mm) machine gun. Of course, the M-60 was kept in the arms room when not in use. The new M-16 rifles (M-16A1, firing 5.56mm x 45mm NATO rounds, with a 20-inch barrel) were not available to us at Fort Bragg. We also had no access to the M-14, even though that was the rifle model we all qualified with during basic training. It was being phased out in favor of the M-16.

Out in the gun range, we practiced firing the M-60 a few times. It wasn't exactly a real firing range, per se; just an open field that was quite spacious inside hundreds of acres. I was a light weight (125 pounds, maybe), so when it was my turn, I fired the twenty-three-pound machine gun from my shoulder as instructed. The recoil pushed me back a couple feet. After a few minutes of laughter from everyone at my expense, one of the officers propped me up from the back with his extended arm so I wouldn't fall backwards when I continued to fire. We did not fire it from either a bungee cord or metal post such as would be installed on each ship, or from a seated or prone position. Just freehand standing up. As our company was gaining proficiency at Fort Bragg, only the pilots worked on the mini-guns and 40mm grenade launchers. The enlisted men could watch and learn, but no hands-on. They cleaned them, loaded the ammo, and made ready for flight as we looked on at arms-length. But, we were all new.

---

[13] Award of Aircraft Crewman Badge (Permanent). January 21, 1967, 187th Aviation Company (Airmobile Light), Fort Bragg, NC; Unit Order number 4.
[14] Years later, this rank insignia would represent the E-2 pay grade. The PFC insignia became the mosquito wing with a rocker beneath.

Throughout my training, I had been getting letters from Barb, my girlfriend from high school who had moved with her family to North Carolina at the end of our junior year. We wrote back and forth about once a week ever since. I had a huge crush on Barb. Losing her to another state about the same time that I lost half of my family to another state was tough. At eighteen years old, she was still living at home in Charlotte. Now, I was in Fayetteville, just a short drive away. We decided to have a double date.

She arranged a blind date for Don with one of her girlfriends. He and I borrowed Babe's car and went. Once there, we met them and changed cars because Barb was much more familiar with the area and driving around was easier than giving one of us directions. The four of us went to a nightclub. In that the club was located in a dry county[15] we stopped at a liquor store on the way to pick up a small bottle of rum first. There wasn't enough rum in that small bottle for the four of us to get anything more than a slight buzz. With each round of Coca-Cola at our table, Barb's friend poured a little rum from the bottle that she kept hidden in her purse.

The evening was enjoyable and I was very happy to see Barb again. Before we knew it, it got late and we had to return to base. When Don and I got out of their car, I stayed back a bit as Don went to Babe's car. When I kissed Barb goodbye, her hand cradled my face, and I cradled hers. It was a long kiss, but there was no real spark that made it special. Don and I left after the girls drove away.

Part of the drive back to base was filled with laughter and jokes back and forth as we compared notes. The other part was in silence. The hum of the car's motor and tires rolling over the pavement was mesmerizing. My thoughts about Barb consumed my mind. She and I shared something very personal during the couple years we wrote back and forth every other week. Our kiss was… well, it was disappointing. I wanted the sparks to fly, but it simply didn't happen.

I fought the realization that Barb and I had, as she once wrote, a platonic relationship. I didn't want to accept the impact of her message at the time, even though I had to look up the word in the dictionary to under-

---

[15] A dry county is one where alcoholic beverages are not sold. Most of the time only spirit alcohol (whiskey, rum, vodka, etc.) is prohibited, allowing for beer and wine only.

stand what she was implying. It was the first time that word was introduced to me. Now, the full impact of our relationship was just then beginning to sink in. Don and I didn't talk about this on our way back to base, but I gave it a lot of thought.

Weeks later Tom, Babe, Don and I got a three-day pass. Babe drove us to East Boston where Tom and I were dropped off first. Then, Babe and Don continued on towards northern Massachusetts and over to New Jersey.

I stayed with Tom at his home on East Saratoga Street in East Boston. It was in a nice, traditional neighborhood of older brownstone-type homes. I met his very Italian family and found them to be absolutely wonderful people. His mom cooked a feast of a meal for dinner on Saturday night. A huge bowl of spaghetti and homemade meatballs was passed around the table. Moving my glass of wine aside, I filled my plate, being careful not to outdo the others at the table.

Picking up my knife and fork and selecting a section on the plate, I began cutting the long noodles to a size that would fit onto my fork without any long ones dangling. I didn't want to splash any sauce on my shirt.

"Maaty [my name spoken with a Boston accent], what're you doing?!" Tom asked in a very loud voice. "Are you cutting the pasta?"

His mom looked at me with a polite, but disapproving glance. I could read her thoughts. *Where did you say your friend is from?*

The silence was deafening. Before long, everyone at the table leaned forward, just a bit, looked at me with the fork in my left hand, knife in the other.

As far as I knew, you cut the noodles to fit on your fork, lift and eat, and don't slop the sauce. What's to know? That's how we ate it at home, at church potluck dinners, and anywhere else where spaghetti was served. Back home, the idea was to eat and finish your supper, sponge-up the sauce with bread, and continue until the plate was clean. Even in the Army's mess hall, we ate spaghetti the same way.

But here, you would have thought I committed a Holy sin by the way Tom and his family reacted. They made it abundantly clear in a very nice way that I should properly twirl the noodles and sauce onto my fork by using a spoon as the base.

Spoon in left hand, fork in right. Scoop up a bunch of noodles, stick fork into it, and twirl it around until the noodles are nicely wrapped around the fork. Lift and eat. Repeat as required.

"I have it now," I said as I looked up to see approving smiles all around.

"We'll make an Italian out of you, yet," someone said.

On Sunday, Babe and Don picked us up. It was time to get back to base. Traffic wasn't bad at all. Babe drove for a while but didn't want to drive the entire way back, so Tom took over. It was a long drive. Just as we entered North Carolina, we realized we were almost out of gas. We were running on fumes by the time we saw a gas station off the exit that was still open that late. Unfortunately, the ramp was an incline, forcing us to go upwards to the overpass. We could see the station right at the top. Our speed had been about 80 miles per hour on the highway. We slowed down as we made the exit, but worried the car might cut out midway up the ramp.

Tom made a suggestion. When the car slowed down enough, Babe and I would bail out from the back seat and push it, while still rolling, to gain a few extra yards so we could reach the overpass. The trick was doing so when the car was coasting fast enough to make it up the hill. When we seemed to be going slow enough, Tom would give us a signal to execute our plan.

Moments later, about halfway up the ramp, Tom yelled, "Go." Or, at least that's what I heard. Babe and I bailed out from the rear passenger doors, he on the left, me on the right, at the same time. I hit the ground and rolled a few times, then got up and ran to catch up to the still moving car. Babe rolled out, too, and did the same thing. When we got to the car and began to push, we could hear Tom yelling at us. He was in a panic.

"Why'd you guys jump out when we were still going 30 miles per hour? Are you crazy?"

Don got out and began pushing from the passenger door. We barely made it, with a few scrapes and bruises but otherwise no worse for wear.

Some weeks later, Tom took one of his trips back home to see his mom. We were getting close to the end of our time at Fort Bragg, and weren't sure if any of us were going to get a chance to go home beforehand. Babe drove him the airport and expected him to call later on when he was ready to be picked up in a couple days, maybe Sunday night. From Saturday afternoon on, we usually had the rest of the weekend for ourselves. We covered for Tom at the Saturday morning formation, though he left the night before. His plan was to make the visit and get back to the company area by Monday morning before formation. Nobody would be the wiser.

Monday morning arrived. Tom was missing and we had no word from him. The company formed up and a call went out to the platoons to make a verbal report of the men being present or accounted for, a standard procedure. He wasn't present and no one knew where he was. Babe never got a call from him to be picked up or explain why he was late. I didn't know, nor did Don. There was always the option to cover for your absent buddy, as long as you knew what was going on. But, we didn't. Anticipating the first sergeant's command for the platoon sergeants to *report*, our platoon sergeant, Grabbenstetter, asked Babe about Tom's whereabouts. He struggled with what to say. There was a risk of making a false report if he indicated Tom was accounted for, and he wasn't. Babe would be considered disloyal by his buddies if he reported Tom missing and unaccounted for, something nobody wanted him to do. But he had no choice. Babe felt bad, as if he would betray Tom. So, he told Sarge, "I don't know where he's at right now."

And, Grabbenstetter reported to the first sergeant, "All, but one man, present and accounted for." Sarge had to cover his ass, too.

"You have one man missing? Who?" the first sergeant asked.

"Yes, that's correct. Leone."

Later on, Babe told us his report about Tom being unaccounted for made him a pariah to a few guys. Some of them, who usually joked with him in the mess hall, turned against him. Even Top later asked Babe why he couldn't have covered for him. It wasn't much longer, maybe an hour later, when Babe was summoned back to the orderly room. Tom's mom had called. She said Tom had been in a serious automobile accident on Sunday night. His injuries required hospitalization and, as a result, he wouldn't be back to duty for some time.

If Babe had reported Tom as either present or accounted for during the formation, the call from Tom's mom would have blown the lid off that short-lived attempt to cover for him, and Babe's report would have been false. He could have faced charges and maybe the stockade.

When Tom got out of the hospital, he returned to base. Because he was absent without leave, an Article 15 proceeding was conducted by the company commander. Tom, a private first class, E-3, was busted down to a private, E-1. He remained a private until we left for Vietnam.

The temperature in North Carolina was getting chillier, and the sky grayer, by the day. Guys were going home for Thanksgiving, mostly the married ones, those above PFC, and others who got their request in first to take leave. There had to remain at least a skeleton crew in the company area. I stayed. I really didn't want to go home.

As I sat in the barracks and thought about the Thanksgiving dinner they would have at the mess hall later that day, Sarge came by the company area. Moments before he walked into the barracks and saw me, the other guys had left the building. He invited me to his living quarters to have dinner with him and his wife. Having dinner with the platoon sergeant and his wife, off base in their apartment, I felt privileged and honored. Mrs. Grabbenstetter was from Germany. She spoke with a heavy German accent, but was fluent in English. A very nice woman, and a very good cook. It was the first and would be the last time I saw her until many years later at one of our company reunions.

Christmas came and went without much fanfare. Then New Year's Eve. The letters back and forth with Barb continued weekly. A few letters back and forth from home, but no more phone calls.

Our time at Fort Bragg was coming to an end. Before we were to leave, a few men in the company had been selected to accompany our aircraft being transported to Vietnam on an aircraft carrier. Among those selected were Tom, Babe, Don, and me. Our written orders from the 187th Aviation Company (Airmobile Light) at Fort Bragg, Unit Move Order Number 1, dated 6 February 1967, had us report to the 56th QM Depot, Lathrop, California on 22 February 1967. There were twenty-seven of us going by boat: pilots and crew chiefs. We had a travel delay that enabled me to go home for a few weeks before leaving the United States. So back home I went.

Winter in Chicago was still cold and windy. Nothing had changed. Dad still had the only car in the family and went to work every day. Travel for me was, therefore, limited to thumbing a ride, walking, or walking the two miles to the train station at the north end of town and taking the train to go downtown. My finances were still limited, even as a private first class. While I was back in Villa Park, I took a girl named Deb from Bellwood out a few times. I had met her when I was in high school, though she went to a different school. Most of my friends from high school were not around, having gone to college or military service. My best friend Dick Johnson was at college in Virginia. My wrestling buddies Ken Dempsey and Deak Cunningham were nowhere to be found. People thought Ken might have joined the Air Force.

I did not go to Michigan to visit Mom, Steve, and Sue. I was still struggling with my emotions about them. I missed my brother and sister and it hurt. It would not have been that difficult for me to get to Detroit by train or plane. I thought about the cost and logistics of going, but decided against it. At home, Dad didn't take any time off from work except for Saturday and Sunday. Scott was busy with school and being on the basketball team where practice kept him late. Cathy stayed home all day, being the dutiful housewife and taking care of our sister, Janie, then about twenty-months-old.

It was maybe a couple weeks into my leave when Dad received a phone call from a man identifying himself as my first sergeant. I was not home at the time. He told Dad that there was a problem with loading the helicopters onto the boat. I was to delay my reporting-in until a week later. Well, Dad was a war veteran himself and not stupid. He knew the consequences of missing a military departure time, especially when en route to a combat zone. Prison, at the very least. We waited for confirmation to arrive in the mail. I didn't. Just the phone call.

Dad was suspicious. He reasoned that the caller could have been anyone, maybe someone with a nefarious reason to have me report late and miss the boat's departure.

He asked, "Do you know of anybody who wants you to miss the boat?"

"No," I replied.

We didn't know for sure. So, Dad encouraged (read *insisted*) me to obey written orders, unchanged, and I left as scheduled.

I could have checked with telephone information to get the number of our company orderly room at Fort Bragg, but didn't. I really didn't want to confirm I could stay home for another week. I wanted to go. Imagine being all set, emotionally, to leave on a certain date. My excitement, anticipation, and sense of adventure of beginning the long journey to Vietnam, halfway around the world, was at an all-time high. To confirm I'd have to stay home one more week was akin to having detention after school was let out. No, I did not want to confirm the message Dad received.

Deb accompanied us to O'Hare International Airport. She was a good casual girlfriend, though our relationship was mostly adolescent and physical. We shared a good hug and kiss goodbye. I did not want to let go, but not because I didn't want to leave. Confusing. As I got onto the plane, my window seat provided a good view of the people inside the gate area of the building. I noticed Dad, Cathy, Scott, Janie, and Deb all standing at the window. We waved to each other as the plane rolled away from the gate. I had no foreboding of anything going wrong, and was excited to be on my way.

I arrived to the place where I was supposed to be at Sharpe Army Depot in California on February 22, 1967. I was the only guy from the 187th there. No one said anything to me about being the only one to sign in. They provided me with a place to bunk down. They had nothing for me to do, and, like a typical private, I didn't really ask for any work to keep me busy. I figured one of the NCOs would let me know. No one did. It would be a week before anybody else showed up. I don't remember what I did during that week other than waste time, walk around, eat and sleep. Eventually, our first sergeant arrived. It wasn't long (an hour or two) after his signing in before he found me. He asked if I had gotten his message to delay my arrival.

"Well, yes, I did, Top," I replied. I told him the reason why I arrived early, following written orders and such. He seemed to understand.

The rest of the guys finally showed up: Tom, Babe, Don, and the others. We had a little time to waste waiting for the ships to be completely loaded on the boat[16]. In the absence of anyone telling us to stay, we went sightseeing. Renting a car, the first place was Sacramento, the capital city of California. What struck us odd was the style of the town: quiet, small, and not as busy as one might expect for a capital city of a huge state. Unlike Chicago or Boston, this place was almost a ghost town. Then again, maybe it was a Sunday.

The second place we went was to check out the Haight-Ashbury district in San Francisco. All of us had heard of that district as being ground zero of the counter-culture movement, where hippies, half-naked women, and 'flower children' were in abundance. We arrived during the late morning. Standing at the famous intersection of Haight and Ashbury Streets, I looked up at the street signs to make sure we were *there*. Where were the half-naked women? The hippies? We didn't see anyone who fit our stereotype of what a hippie might actually look like—no rose-colored glasses, no cloth headbands, no bra-less attire or exposed boobs. To be honest, we were quite disappointed.

Then we checked out China Town, walking around the shops and restaurants. We stuck out like sore thumbs, clearly not fitting in with the surroundings. Not at Haight-Ashbury, not at China Town. Our haircuts were short, military-style. Our civilian clothes were so bland, so Sears-like, compared to the casual groovy-style of young Californians. We ate an early dinner and left to go back to base.

We had one guy in our company who was trying desperately to stay behind and not go to Vietnam. He was a Spec Four, I believe, though I can't recall his name. The day we were leaving he was at a phone booth, screaming at somebody through the handset. I stood a few feet away, wait-

---

[16] Navy people tell me that "boat" is the wrong term for an aircraft carrier.

ing my turn. I heard him say he had been accepted to go to OCS (Officer Candidate School) at Fort Benning, Georgia. Because of that, he wasn't supposed to be going to Vietnam with the 187th. I had never witnessed such desperation in a young man as I did with that guy. When he was off the phone, he told me he called the OCS school commandant, his state representative's office, his dad, and one or two other people of importance. He thought nobody was listening. But, it worked. He did not leave with us.

Some of the guys were a little opinionated about his efforts to avoid going with us. Why would he wait until the last day before leaving for Vietnam to make his calls? Why hadn't he done that in the weeks before? Did reality hit him like a ton of bricks? Did he realize that once on that boat, he was stuck for three weeks until we arrived in Vietnam?

At one of our reunions years later, I asked about him. He did go to OCS as planned but broke his leg during training, causing him to end his candidacy. When he healed months later, he was sent directly to Vietnam.

From the Alameda Naval Air Station near San Francisco, we arrived at the USS Kula Gulf. From the dock, it looked large. Built during 1943, the Kula Gulf was a leftover from World War II. It was reclassified as a cargo ship and aircraft ferry during 1959. It was about the length of two football fields. During 1967, the permanent crew consisted of Merchant Marines.

At least twenty-five helicopters were cocooned in dark weatherproof wrapping and were positioned and secured for travelling on the high seas, strapped down on the top wooden deck as well as the steel deck below. I noticed a fixed-wing plane secured below deck, too. There was a huge elevator platform that could be raised from the lower deck to the top in order to move aircraft. There were no naval weapons aboard that we knew of, somewhat of an odd detail for a boat going to war-torn Vietnam.

Except for food and bunks, there was nothing soft on that ship. Everything was made out of iron and steel: stairs, floors, walls, ceilings, rivets, cabinets, you name it. And, everything was painted gray except for a few signs and lettering.

Leaving California on March 4, 1967, we passed the notoriously impregnable Alcatraz prison and went under the Golden Gate Bridge, which actually looked red to me. We found our berths. We would sleep on canvas cots hung in stacks from the ceiling. One side along the length was connected to the wall and the other side strapped, the outside edge of each to the one above and below. Each bunk was about 18 inches from each other, ceiling to near the floor. There was just enough room to crawl into and turn over if needed. Near the sleeping quarters was the galley (mess hall) where we would eat. Just off that was the radio room with a shortwave radio that I would soon become familiar for my needs.

I'm not sure how many men were assigned certain jobs on this boat, if any. But, I was put in charge of the daily newsletter to be distributed to the guys. Don was assigned as well. Together, we would make this detail work. A small broom closet was where we set up the office. The table inside had a manual typewriter, a mimeograph machine, paper, wall lamp, etc. I learned how to type, make copies, collect news, operate the shortwave radio, and find our position in the ocean. Any news I learned from the radio, as well as pin-pointing our position in a graphic sketch of the Pacific that I prepared, was included in the newsletter.

Days later, we bypassed Hawaii. We were so far away that the islands never came within eyesight. I had no misgivings about it; after all, what would we have done there had we been closer? The weather, near Hawaii, was beautiful, sunny, warm winds, blue sky, smooth water. But we had our share of rough seas, huge waves, and dark skies, too.

We were approaching a significant event: passing through the Equator. The ship's crew had informed us about its importance. Preparations were to be made. A detail was selected among our men, working closely with some of the ship's crew, to gather all necessary materials. Certificates would be prepared, costumes made ready. Men were selected to perform specific roles during the ceremony. To me, it seemed silly, so I kept busy with the daily paper.

We passed the Equator on March 12th. There was something called the Dominion of the Golden Dragon, a rite of passage that required initiation. When I saw the craziness of what these guys were doing, I avoided them like the plague. One guy was dressed as King Neptune, another as Davey Jones, and yet another as Queen Amphitrite, the sea-goddess and wife of Poseidon. These men were wearing costumes made up from supplies from the galley. When I saw one guy wearing a mop-head as hair and another with make-up and red lipstick, guys getting splashed by buckets of seawater (which I had to assume was fresh from the ocean and extremely cold), I knew it was time for me to get lost. I went back to my office and stayed out of sight. Some might say I hid, but I prefer to think I was busy doing something really important like dusting my typewriter or cleaning the desk.

A few more days later we passed through a few islands of the Philippines. These were close enough that the inhabitants were able to travel out to our ship and offer us their greetings. I watched in anticipation as a group of eight traditional outrigger canoes made their way towards us as we passed slowly. It was if the Captain of the ship knew they were on their way and slowed down just enough to make this encounter happen. Recalling the movie *Mutiny on the Bounty* with Marlon Brando, we half expected the women to be topless and the men, doing the rowing, wearing warrior gear.

Tom, Don, Babe and others were with me on deck. We chatted among ourselves while each of us had our eyes glued to the approaching entourage. Each canoe held about four men and three women. Their bronze skin tone, at a distance, contrasted nicely to the muted, sun-faded pastel colors of the tropical South Seas traditional skirt worn by each. We were getting riled up in anticipation of the topless women. We were sure they were topless. For a bunch of 19 and 20-year-olds, we still managed to behave ourselves.

All of the men in the canoe out-riggers were rowing in unison, one woman between each man. I saw what appeared to be a lot of skin as they got closer and made sure the other guys saw the same thing. Slightly over a hundred yards off, the men were, indeed, topless and wore flower leis. Each woman, standing tall between each rower, also wore the same type of skirt and leis. We watched them arrive closer, but noted they also wore tan and beige tropical blouses. We visually inspected each female occupant out there, just to make sure none were topless, but all were fully clothed. I thought immediately of the paintings by artist Paul Gauguin from the late 1800s, depicting Tahitian women in all their glory. It was disappointing to know that modesty now prevailed. So much for stereo-types.

So far in our voyage, we had all types of weather suitable for the South Seas. There were storms, rain, thunder and lightning. We had days full of sunshine, no shade and no wind to keep us cool. The seas ranged from choppy and rough to smooth as glass.

The ocean has many moods, from rough waves breaking at six feet or more with high winds during a storm to being so calm and smooth as glass with nary a ripple or wave. Albatross and porpoise accompanied us most of the way from California. Some fish were florescent and you could see them at night. The sky at night was literally glowing with the bright-ness of stars, far away galaxies, reflective planets, and the moon. So many points of light. To really describe it accurately in words, without seeing it firsthand, would be an injustice. The sight was overwhelming.

A few guys stayed on deck as much as possible, even sleeping there during the night. Tom and Babe spent as much time there, too, to keep cool with the ocean breeze. I was not one of those guys. Below deck, Tom's bunk was just above mine. When he reclined in his, when I was in mine, there would be a measurable distance of no more than six inches between my chest or shoulder and the bottom of his canvas bunk. So, it pleased me that he spent a lot of time on top deck. It gave me all the room I needed.

Each day brought us closer to the realm of combat, that ancient struggle of good versus evil, yet so new to us. The thought of the next twelve months was in the back of our minds every day, though we seldom wanted to talk about our fears and apprehensions. None of us wanted to admit it to anyone. Day by day, we were building our bravado, our cour-age, and exploiting our youthful zest.

Then, Vietnam was finally at our doorstep. It took us twenty-two days to cross the Pacific Ocean. At night, we anchored about a mile or two off shore. Except for the faded gray mountain range in the distance and the darken thin line at the horizon that was *terra firma*, there were billowing clouds in the far distance and flashes of light behind that. We asked each other if it was lightning or bombs bursting. None of us knew for sure, but we discussed and analyzed each possibility. There were no sounds except for muffled ocean waves beating against the stationary ship's hull and quiet talk among the men.

Our discussions turned to protecting ourselves in the event we were to storm the beaches the next day. I think many of us had watched one too many war movies. Our personal weapons were locked away in a Conex[17]. A couple guys found where it was placed, but no one knew if, or where, we had any ammo. We were a little apprehensive about that fine detail, but what could we do? Some of us found sleep to be most welcome at this point of our journey. A few of the more nervous types stayed awake and kept watch for enemy action against our anchored ship.

I awoke the next day and went top-side to sunny skies. The ship's loudspeaker informed us we were at Vung Tau, an in-country R&R[18] city. Also, so we were told, it was used by the Viet Cong for the same purpose.

"Well, who's who?" we asked one another. "Do they wear uniforms?" For the most part, no. We were cautioned to be careful.

As of 1000 hours we would be allowed a twenty-four-hour shore leave. We were excited to be walking on firm dirt once again. In groups of ten or so, they ferried us to shore in a small, motorized boat.

I was delayed in leaving. Tom, Babe, and Don had apparently gone ahead on their own, as I couldn't find them when I was ready to go ashore. It didn't really matter. I was thinking they were probably on shore by then. I did find my buddy Jack, another PFC who'd been with us at Fort Bragg. Still on the boat, he and I were among the last small group to leave. The boat ride took about fifteen minutes. As we got closer, I could see the buildings, the dock area, and people standing about. This part of Vung Tau was definitely not a military base. It looked more like a large ocean-side fishing village, which it was, I suppose. The civilian men wore faded, loose clothing and a few wore wide, conical, straw hats. As a group, they were a short people, thin, and very tanned. The young Navy skipper reminded us that the last boat to return to ship the next day was at 1000 hours.

"Don't be late," he said, "or you'll be stuck on shore."

---

[17] A steel container about 10' x 10' x 10'. One end had double doors which could be locked. These were common containers used by the military for storage.
[18] Rest and Relaxation. A three or five-day vacation of sorts used to take a break from normal duties in a combat zone.

As instructed, we took no weapons and wore civvies for our first entry onto war-torn Vietnam. We perceived no danger in Vung Tau, though we remained alert for anything out of the ordinary. In the business area of town many women were dressed in white long silk dresses over black silk pants (Áo Dài) and wore the same wide conical straw sun-hats (Nón Lá) as the men. In town, men were dressed either in the well-tailored, faded green fatigue uniform of the South Vietnamese Army, or the front-buttoned shirt (usually white) and trousers (usually black) that were familiar to us. Footwear, except for those soldiers wearing boots, for both genders were mostly sandals or, as we called them in the States, flip-flops.

Jack and I went on our own. We noticed a few hotels and bars, homes, merchant areas, and so on. The streets were dusty concrete or hard-packed dirt, and wider that what you'd imagine for a non-industrialized country. Tall leafy trees on either side gave ample shade from the sun. The vehicles were smaller than what we were accustomed to back home. There were many motorbikes and three-wheeled taxi Lambret-tas[19] moving about. Thirsty, we were in search of a local bar, tavern, any-place to get a beer and relax on solid ground.

Not finding a traditional watering hole, we picked a hotel. It looked clean enough, actually better than we expected. Jack and I each got our own room. Mine had a bed and sink with running water. The bed cover was reasonably clean, so I lied down for a few minutes. On the ceiling were three small lizards—geckos, maybe. I watched as they scurried this way and that, staying still, and moving about. It was my entertainment for about a half hour. Soon, Jack was knocking at the door.

"Let's go downstairs for a beer," he said. I agreed, and we found the lounge.

The local beer was called 33 La Rue, or *Ba Muoi Ba* (pronounced bah-mee-bah; or, Bamiba)[20] beer, brewed in Saigon. It wasn't like the three-point-two beer we drank in the states. With this beer, a buzz developed after drinking just two. As we sat at a table in the lounge, talking and

---

[19] In the front of the three-wheeled Lambretta was what appeared to be a small motorcycle with a seat for the driver. The back half had a roof, open sides, and seating for two on each side on benches.
[20] In some parts of Vietnam, some GIs would pronounce it as *bom-de-bom*. This is also the Vietnamese pronunciation of the number "thirty-three". Other names used by GIs were 'Panther Piss', 'Thirty-three', and 'Poison.' It was rumored to have been made out of formaldehyde, but that was never proven.

looking around, we saw a couple of girls at the end of the room, and they saw us. The taller of two young Vietnamese women came over to our table, the other one tagged along at a respectable distance behind her, and asked to sit with us. They were good looking. They appeared to be our approximate age, but it was difficult to judge. They had all their teeth, unlike some very old women here and there, and their long, black hair was neatly brushed. All in all, quite attractive.

We took them up on their offer. Once seated the waitress came to our table. They each ordered a *Saigon tea*. Their drinks arrived costing us two bucks each. It was a very small "V" shaped cocktail glass, similar to a small Martini glass, holding about an ounce and a half of colored liquid. As the four of us sat there getting acquainted, our curiosity about their drinks got the best of us. We asked and were allowed a taste. There was no kick. It tasted like sweet, colored water. Jack and I joked with them about the drink being nothing more than Kool-Aid. They didn't know what that was, unsurprisingly. So, two bucks for a shot-glass worth of Kool-Aid, just to keep them at the table talking to us. Maybe we'd get lucky after a few.

One of the young ladies spoke broken English so we were able to communicate a little bit. She seemed intelligent, but not arrogant. The talk began by covering general questions: our first names, what state were we from, what was it like in America, are either of us married, do we have girlfriends, and so on. Nothing was asked or said about our job in the Army, where we were going (we didn't even know yet), or the cost of dillying our dallies. By mid-evening, "fearful" of their safety in getting home due to a local gang, we were asked to escort them home. Apparently, this gang did not take too kindly of Vietnamese women talking with Americans and would rough them up or extort money, if given the chance. So, we took them home. On the way, no incidents at all.

By the time we got there, it was too late for us to go back to our rooms. Anyway, I wasn't sure if we could find our way back. So, Jack and I stayed with them that night, he and the older one in one bed and me with the other girl nearby. We knew these young women were not going to be our girlfriends. We had no misgivings about developing a long-term relationship as we most likely would never see them again. We were gentlemen as much as circumstances would allow, but we all knew why we were there.

Needless to say, I had a *very* good night's sleep. Welcome to Vietnam.

Chapter 3

Stop Him

Waking up that first day was very quiet. A peek out from the window found the warm morning sunlight had worked its way down through a labyrinth of leafy tree branches. From a short distance, the occasional muffled sounds of mopeds and Lambrettas interrupted the tranquil setting. Old women, maybe neighbors, talked to each other quietly in their native tongue. Their language sounded musical and pleasant. Of course, I couldn't understand a single word of what was being said, but it was spoken with an almost sing-song cadence. A few birds chirped, almost as a response to the muted chatter of these neighbors. I couldn't help but wonder if animals all communicated in the same language world-wide, or if these birds had their own regional dialect. How many beers did I have last night?

The charm was interrupted by the unmistakable and distinct WOMP, WOMP, WOMP of a Huey flying by overhead. Stepping outside, I looked up and noticed the thin barrel of mounted M-60s pointing out at ninety-degrees on each side of the ship. Jack was still sacked out. I was wondering where to get a cup of coffee and maybe something to eat. I wondered if there was someplace nearby. I doubted we'd find any restaurants, and wasn't too confident that the hotel where we had a room had any food to offer.

"Aw, shit," I exclaimed as I checked the time. "We've got to get going. Jack, get up. We're gonna be late."

There wasn't much time to spare to get to the boat, our only way back to the Kula Gulf. Our 24-hour leave was up at ten o'clock. Up and dressed, we bolted out of the small two-room house. Nestled among similar houses, the winding pathway to the main road was easy to find and we walked very quickly, deciding not to run. Somebody might think we committed a crime and, thinking we were making our escape, shoot us. No thanks. We'll walk.

The dock wasn't too far away. As we approached, neither Jack nor I recognized the few guys already on the waiting Navy boat. We jumped on board and I caught my breath. From a short distance, three other guys were running towards us. They were in our company from Bragg. When they got on, we shoved off.

It was just past 1000 hours when we made it back to the Kula Gulf. The upper deck was full of guys working to remove the dark fabric cocoons from the helicopters. Babe and Tom were on that detail and busy at work. I didn't see Don, though he may have been elsewhere on the upper or lower deck. Not knowing if this was a detail still looking for people to work, or not, Jack and I immediately went below deck and busied ourselves with packing our gear and otherwise looking busy. I didn't volunteer to work. Months before, we learned the way to avoid work details was to look busy doing something else, like spit-shinning your boots in the barracks. Whatever we did, look busy doing Army stuff. Most of the time it worked. At nineteen years and two months old, my willingness to look for work was not quite well developed and still needed improvement.

We spent a few days in Vung Tau. I found the barber shop—or rather, three chairs placed in an open-air section of our area, no walls or roof, just the chairs and a counter set against a tent used by someone else. The barber was an old Vietnamese man who worked with a hand-squeeze type (non-electric) hair-clippers. A one-minute massage followed the cut, smoothing out the knots in my shoulder muscles with quick and measured karate chops. Then, he rolled my head from the left to the right, and back again. Soothing, in a way. Before I realized what was about to happen, he cradled my head from behind and gave it a quick jerk to set my vertebrae back into alignment. I heard a loud crunch from my neck. That had never been done to me before, and I wasn't too keen on having it done again.

One staff sergeant from the area gathered a few of us together to explain the dangers of the forty-millimeter grenade. He held one in his hand as he explained how it was armed internally by spinning the grenade laterally.

"Don't toss it up, don't spin it, and don't throw it back and forth with anyone. Doing so will prove disastrous and you'll blow yerself up."

He told us that a month before, two guys were playing catch with a forty-millimeter and it went off, killing both. That made quite an impression on me, and probably on the other guys, too. Just like the barracks that burnt at Ft. Polk.

Somehow, we kept busy for the next week. We did not return to the civilian part of Vung Tau but stayed on base. It might have been more of a matter of limited finances instead of getting approval to go off base. As E-3s, we were paid $128.70 base pay at the end of each month, in cash. It was up to each of us to manage our finances. I was fortunate. I had no bills to pay each month except for haircuts, and maybe laundry services if I chose to use that instead of the Army's laundry. After taxes, and any other deductions were taken, my net 'take-home' pay was more like $78.00 or so, excluding flight pay. Now, being in Vietnam, I would also get combat pay (about $65) in addition to increase my monthly income. And it was all tax-free.

We were told to exchange our American money for Military Payment Certificates (MPC), a form of paper currency in various denominations ranging from five cents to ten dollars.[21] The reasoning was that the US dollar had a value worldwide, whereas the MPC had no value except in our theater of operations among our American personnel supply lines. If the North Vietnamese Army captured a bagful of MPC, taking it back to Hanoi would be worthless; just paper. Some guys never saw the wisdom of this and continued to use the greenback for various transactions. For every US dollar going into the hands of the Vietnamese, it was certain that some of it was being funneled to Hanoi to purchase military equipment in the world market, and equipment to be used against us and our allies.

After roughly three weeks since we arrived in Vietnam, it was time to go. The advance party had been working on our new company area in Tay Ninh, setting up tents, work areas, etc. while we stayed in Vung Tau getting the Hueys ready to go. Our manpower numbers shrank in tandem with the number of ships remaining in Vung Tau. Finally, after twenty-two days at sea and another three weeks in Vung Tau, we were on our way to join the war. Travelling by helicopter, as we approached our new base at Tay Ninh, one huge mountain caught our attention. It stood alone, like an overgrown cyst on the earth's surface. Northwest of Saigon, Tay Ninh Province juts into the adjacent Cambodian border almost like a short peninsula. The capital city of the province, by the same name, is where our company was based. Upon arrival, we had a new name: the 187th Assault

---

[21] The twenty-dollar MPC wasn't available until 1968.

Helicopter Company, 269th Combat Aviation Battalion, First Aviation Brigade. Tents had been constructed over concrete floorings. Inside each tent were metal cots, wall lockers, and foot lockers. Tents were assigned for the enlisted men of each platoon, the officers, clerks, and so on. The mess hall was a large and long tent. The orderly room was operating in a tent. Maintenance had a large rounded-ceiling hangar tent for aircraft inspections and repair.

The food and drink in the mess hall was a little different from what we were used to. Milk, in a can, was reconstituted, meaning the concentrate was mixed with water at the factory. The white milk was horrible. The chocolate canned milk tasted better. They kept the cans of milk in a large container filled with ice and water to keep it as cool as possible, but often it was lukewarm. When available, they also provided milk that was cooled and dispensed in a stainless-steel machine, the type you might find in any mess hall stateside. Mashed potatoes were dehydrated and mixed with potable water. The meat (pork chops, hamburger, etc.) tasted odd. Somebody told us they were dehydrated, too.

Maybe a mile from our base was that single cyst mountain, about 3,200 feet high. Called the Black Virgin Mountain (a/k/a Black Lady Mountain or Mountain of the Black Virgin) or to the Vietnamese, *Núi Bà Đen* (pronounced: Nuey-bah-din), it could be seen for miles away and often became a visual landmark back to Tay Ninh. What concerned us about this mountain was its close proximity to the end of the Ho Chi Minh Trail, about 30 kilometers to the west on the other side of the border with Cambodia. Also, it was rumored that the sides of the mountain were crawling with enemy forces, notwithstanding an American Army signal unit[22] stationed at the summit.[23]

The helicopters had all arrived from Vung Tau. The gunships were ready to go. One day, Major Joe Burns, our platoon commander, called the platoon enlisted men together. Sitting in a tent near the flight line, he explained we needed to have a call sign for radio communication. The com-

---

[22] The 372th Radio Relay Unit out of Sobe, Okinawa, a secretive section of the American Security Agency. The cover unit was the 25th Infantry Division, 125th Signal Battalion. Among other unit representations, the Army 5th Special Forces Group personnel were also here, providing security.

[23] There are many stories about this mountain that occurred during the Vietnam War. I encourage further research for the reader, especially regarding the Viet Cong 82mm mortar and rocket propelled grenade assault and penetration of the base perimeter on May 13, 1968. The American casualties were 24 killed, 35 wounded, 2 missing; and, of the bad guys, 25 VC confirmed killed.

pany call sign was *Blackhawks*, but each platoon needed its' own. After a few suggestions were made and discussed, we finally approved the name of *Rat Pack* for us. The officers would each use this as their call sign. Maj. Burns would be "Rat Pack Six", or "Rat-6" for short (the "6" representing the commander). Only our platoon pilots had numbers assigned to each of them. Always use their call signs on the radio.

And, there were a few phrases we needed to learn:

Transmission	Meaning
Copy or **copy that**	I understand your message.
Roger or **roger that**	Your information is received, loud and clear.
Over	I'm done transmitting, waiting for your response.
Out	I'm done talking. No need to reply.
E.T.A.	Estimated Time of Arrival
At (or watch) your six	Directly behind you
Whiskey, Tango, Foxtrot	What The Fuck?
LZ	Landing Zone
Victor Charlie	Viet Cong
Klicks	A distance of one thousand meters, one kilometer
Alpha Oscar	Area of Operation, AO
Say again	Repeat your last transmission, or clarify

We were never to use anyone's name, unit name or location, cussing or vulgar words, or the term "repeat" on the radio. "Repeat" was reserved for the artillery, also known as *Red Leg*, when another salvo was being requested.

The pilots used the avionics to communicate with the others crew members and anyone outside the aircraft. The crew chief and gunner usually were limited to using it for crewman-to-crewman communication and ADF (Aircraft Direction Finder, a/k/a armed forces radio) for entertainment. During missions, we were able to monitor the other frequencies. Strict radio communication discipline was expected.

Sgt. Grabenstetter asked me to design the Rat Pack logo. It would be used as a platoon pocket-patch (including the unit and platoon names) and painted onto the nose of our gunships. Two ships would just have just the words "Rat Pack" because of limited space due to the 40mm turret on each. He wanted the rat to look mean, and I obliged. He had the design put on pocket patches embroidered by a Vietnamese woman who worked on base. Each patch was encased inside a plastic sheath with a leather strip at the top. Everyone in our platoon, including the pilots, began wearing this patch buttoned or sewn to his right shirt pocket. The first patches were not as good as my drawing, but passable.

American forces were located on our side of the airfield runway. On the other side were the Philippinoes. They were in Vietnam, not to engage in battle, but as a civic action force. Their uniforms were tailored, pressed and starched. Their sandbagged bunkers, as far as I could tell from our flight line, were perfect: straight edges, uniformed height and width, even the sandbags were groomed to have smooth sides, straight edges and corners. It wasn't long before I learned other countries were represented in Vietnam, including Republic of South Korea (ROK), New Zealand, Australia, and Thailand, where many of the U.S. Air Force aircraft were based. Many people at home were not aware of this then, and still not today. We were not alone in our fight against the communist aggression in Vietnam.

Many times, we helped the 9th Royal Australian Air Force near Vung Tau. They used the UH-1D Huey as well to insert their troops in the field, extract them at the completion of the mission, and for Medivac. They did not have gunships, so we flew cover for them. As far as missions go, theirs was no different from our methods and tactics.

Most of the time I had very little contact with my Australian counterparts. But one time we were grounded at the Aussie base because of weather. The rain, a heavy downpour, wasn't expected to end until an hour later, so we were released to get some lunch. The Aussies had a tent near the flight line, and within eyesight of our ships. That was where we'd get our food. We greeted the enlisted crews of their ships and exchanged a couple stories over lunch. One thing that stood out to me was their canned beverage: gin and tonic. Hard alcohol in a can? Wow! I'd never seen that before.

Soon enough we began to lose some of our guys to other more experienced assault helicopter companies. They, in turn, reassigned some of their experienced guys to our unit. This was called an infusion. Very soon after arriving in Tay Ninh, Babe was transferred to the 71st Assault Helicopter Company at Chu Lai. He had only two weeks at Tay Ninh to get used to things before he left. All of a sudden, he was gone. I didn't have a chance to bid farewell to a good friend. I wouldn't see or hear from him for the next 45 years or so. Tom also left the unit within a week or two later, transferred to the 118th Assault Helicopter Company in Bien Hoa. I didn't have a chance to say goodbye to him, either. But, I would see him in a few months. Both were just gone. No party, no handshake, no nothing. Again, I forced myself to suppress the emotional pain of losing those close to me, just as I did when I was sixteen as two of my siblings moved to Michigan with our newly remarried mom.

Don was still around. As we both crewed 40mm gunships, our missions varied. Only one of our type of ship would be on a fireteam. They would avoid assigning our two ships together to form a fireteam.

We learned a lot of combat mission techniques from the new guys coming into our unit. Not having shot our M-60s from a moving helicopter back in the States, we honed our skills by learning how to lead the target depending on the direction of flight versus the movement of the target, and taking in consideration the altitude of the ship (aircraft) through trial and error. There must have been some mental geometric mathematical equation at work. We dispensed with the Army issued ammo box that was originally attached to the M-60 that held one hundred rounds. It wasn't nearly enough. The replacements we used were empty smoke grenade boxes because they held just over two thousand rounds. We needed every bullet. That box would be on the ship's floor and the belt of ammo being fed into the M-60 would be loosely draped over the upper leg or knee as we sat hunched over the box.

Inside the gunships, our M-60s were supported by a single bungee cord attached to the top of the cargo door, enabling the door gunner to move it around easier. We always flew fully armed, ready to go, no matter what type of mission it was. Our job as a crew chief was also as a door gunner in flight, essentially an aerial machine gun nest.

The D models were referred to as *slicks*, because, as carriers of troops and/or cargo, they had only two mounted M-60 machine guns; one on each side. Both were attached to an upright metal brace affixed to the ship. These machine guns used butterfly triggers (usually two hands were used to aim and fire). Their crew chiefs and gunners sat in a four-foot by three-foot cubby-hole, one on each side, behind the cargo area. Due to this confined space, and seated behind the gun mount, movement was limited. Some called it a *suicide seat*.

All flight crews were issued flack-jackets, a chicken plate[24], and later, Nomax (fire resistant) gloves. Our stateside fatigues had been exchanged here for jungle fatigues and leather boots for jungle boots. The pants had cargo pockets, one on each leg. The shirt, not to be tucked in, had diagonal pockets. The rank insignia remained the same as stateside and were sewed onto the shirtsleeve. The flight helmets remained white. Our unit patch (1st Aviation Brigade) was a gold bird-of-prey with wings straight up on a blue background. The bird was in the forefront of a red-handled sword, also pointed upward. It was only an in-country unit patch, as the brigade was not represented at any other posts outside of Vietnam. The M-14 rifles were replaced by the M-16. Full automatic was standard. The magazines held twenty 5.56mm rounds each.

We had never shot the M-16 before. We didn't even qualify with them. They were issued to us as a back-up weapon. The primary weapon for crew chiefs and gunners was the M-60. We didn't qualify with these, either. Pilots were issued a .38 caliber revolver as their back-up weapon, usually secured on their person with a government issued shoulder holster.

There was trouble with the M-16. The bolt malfunctioned too many times, not due to the weapon not being cleaned and lubed with LSA, but due to mechanical and metallurgical problems. Eventually, they were replaced and the rifle worked fine.

At the end of March, our slick platoons were deemed mission ready. The pilots had been working with various assault helicopter companies in the 145th Combat Aviation Battalion (CAB), and the 11th CAB. The difficult and exact training in tactical helicopter approaches and

---

[24] A bullet-resistant ceramic chest-plate, fitted inside a harness, designed to be worn over the chest.

emergency procedures were compounded by the unfamiliar verbiage of the "red-leg" artillery:

"Arty" for artillery;

"FO" for forward observer;

"Contact Fire Mission" for the highest mission priority, that of supporting the infantry actively engaged with the Viet Cong;

"Danger Close" for firing artillery rounds to within a hundred meters of friendlies;

"GT" for gun target;

"Fire for Effect" meaning arty firing continuously, at maximum capacity until the cease-fire order is made by the FO.

If our gunships weren't available to prep the landing zone (LZ), arty would do the same, calling it "time on target" (TOT), and using various impact patterns. The "Daisy-Cutter" was an artillery round designed to explode between one and six feet off the ground, maximizing enemy casualties. "Beehive" rounds used six thousand steel darts, detonating about 50 meters from the cannon, sending the darts in a 60-degree pattern at a velocity of two thousand feet per second towards the enemy. On occasion, an artillery round didn't have enough power to arrive at its target and was called a "short round." A "tree-burst" occurred when the round hit a tree or one of its branches and exploded prematurely. Easy stuff.

The assistance of experienced men being brought into the 187th taught us techniques and methodologies, tactics, and so on. We received some information about the enemy. One of the hints about identifying the enemy was: you would know them when they were shooting at you. Our exposure to Vietnamese people was limited. A few worked on the base for laundry, sewing, etc., but not in our company area. The village of Tay Ninh, just outside our base perimeter, was off limits; too dangerous. Unless authorized to leave we were restricted to the base. There were other American units here, among them being a hospital and dispensary.

Crewing a gunship meant you were always looking for the enemy, always. That was our mission every time we flew. How to find them? Experience would help. The VC could be, and most of the time were, anywhere. We learned to search through treetops to see the ground underneath by focusing our eyes to do so. We searched the branches of trees, the ground underneath, rice paddies, fields; any place where Charlie could hide. Identifying the enemy, wearing clothing no different from the villagers, often depended on location and the intelligence briefings from various sources. There were no loose cannons among us. We all followed orders, or faced some form of disciplinary repercussion if we didn't.

While the pilots, seated not four feet in front of us, flew the ship, maintained radio communication, checked the maps and coordinates, monitored ground action, and made large orbits around the LZ, my gunner and I monitored the sky and ground. Always watching. Because we commanded the skies, there were no enemy aircraft in South Vietnam that we needed to worry about, especially there in III Corps. But, we were always on the lookout for friendly aircraft to prevent mid-air collisions.

Using the horizon as a reference point, aircraft above the horizon were above us. Any below were at an altitude lower than us. Determining the speed, altitude, and direction of other aircraft was essential. If another aircraft was spotted at a distance we'd notify the aircraft commander using a clock method to report its position relative to us. Imagine looking down on the ship, with the nose to the front, that would be 12 o'clock. Ninety degrees to the right would be 3 o'clock, the rear of the ship would be 6 o'clock, and the left side 9 o'clock. Each hour hand of the clock would be a position. We might say: *Sir, we have a fixed wing aircraft at our two o'clock, high*; or, *Sir, I spotted people and equipment moving along the trail at our eight o'clock.*

Monitoring the ground for well-beaten trails, military equipment, people in civilian clothes (or khaki uniforms) carrying weapons, manmade structures where they don't seem to belong, bunkers and tunnel entrances, and anything else that seemed out-of-place was reported to our pilots. Selecting various landmarks, it was easier to get a fix on the location of friendlies, the target area, and enemy activity.

Being on the lookout also meant searching for weapons on the ground. Some, too large to hide underground, would often be camouflaged with leafy twigs and branches or other forms of cover. While booby traps and punji stake pits primarily affected the infantry, automatic weapons like the AK-47 automatic rifle, .51 caliber machine gun, and the rocket propelled grenade (RPG) affected aviators. We all knew it could take only one, well-placed round to destroy a helicopter in flight.

We learned why the enemy used the .51 caliber for a bullet size. If they captured the ammunition from one of our .50 caliber weapons, the round casings would fit into the chamber of their .51 caliber guns, but their ammo would not fit inside ours. However, there were few occasions when we found the VC in possession of a .51 caliber gun. Their weapons of choice were usually the AK-47 and the RPG.

Let's face it, flying in circles for hours at a time, seeing the same real estate time after time can become dangerously boring. Our flight missions were usually categorized as a combat assault (CA)[25]. Orbiting the landing zone (LZ) and surrounding area of operation (AO) searching for the enemy and providing air cover for the grunts (infantry, no disrespect intended) was extremely monotonous. Many veterans have described war as hours of boredom interrupted by moments of terror, and I found that adage quite true.

For each crew member of the ship, we had an array of radio communications available. One of the toggle switches connected us to the ADF (essentially the Armed Forces Radio Network in Saigon for music and news). Another toggle switch was for a hot mike[26], and the others were for the various tactical radio frequencies (FM, UHF[27], VHF[28]). The crew members could pick and choose which channel and when they wanted to listen. Almost always we listened to the ADF.

Our company's first crash, on April 3, occurred on top of Song Be Mountain, about 3,500 feet in elevation. One of our slicks was sent there to deliver radio equipment. Air turbulence, down draft, and other aerodynamical problems caused the ship to crash, injuring all crewmen aboard. The injuries to both pilots were serious enough to send them to Japan for recovery. The enlisted men's injuries were such that they were able to return to work within days, minus one aircraft. I wasn't that acquainted with them, in part because the slick platoons were different than us in terms of

---

[25] A flight mission that exposed the crew to anticipated (potential) enemy action was called a Combat Assault. Missions that were milk-runs, such as picking up the payroll, test flights for maintenance, and administrative purposes were not.
[26] A hot microphone enabled you to communicate with everyone without pressing the transmit button.
[27] Ultra-High Frequency
[28] Very High Frequency

missions, methodologies, and general mental attitude meaning we were aggressors; they were defenders. But, at the same time, they had nerves of steel.

Each evening one team of two gunships was scheduled to be on standby. This meant that if anyone needed the help of close air support, day or night, the *standby team* would respond. Because Don and I were assigned the "hogs"[29], we never flew in the same fire team, either at night or during the day. The hogs were usually the second ship of a two-ship fire team. The reason we were in back was if the lead ship, with mini-guns, received fire from the ground while flying over the VC, the hog could provide cover and hopefully eliminate the threat by firing a volley of grenades at suspected enemy locations. But still, the ship with mini-guns could do the same thing.

A typical mission consisted of one gunship fire team and two or more slicks. The passengers in the slicks were usually the infantry and loaded up either at our base or near Cu Chi. We would all become airborne as a *flight*, one ship after another, and head to the LZ, usually an open field or series of rice paddies. Depending on the intel received, the slicks may hold back their landing while the gunships prepped the LZ by strafing the adjacent tree lines and obvious hiding places. Otherwise, we'd all go in together, with the flight leader choosing exactly where to land. Of course, common sense prevailed. Infantrymen (the grunts) would be inserted into the LZ where they would best be able to accomplish their mission in the shortest amount of time.

Pilots had a lot on their mind, too. Ideally, they would want to descend and lift-off into the wind, if at all possible. They needed to be aware of lift, downdraft, cross-winds, payload and weight, air temperature, flight controls and instrument readings, the safety of crew and passengers, proximity to other aircraft, and the distance between the rotor blades and potential obstructions. As the slicks landed, consideration was given to the option of landing on one or both skids, or hovering off the ground close enough for grunts to jump out without breaking a leg. Pilots had to make sure not to crash, beware of enemy activity and be brave enough to stay

---

[29] Variations existed among different units. Some *hogs* had no 40mm grenade launcher in front, but instead a much larger load of 2.75-inch rockets, e.g. 20 rockets per pod for a total of 40 per ship.

there if being targeted. And when the troops were out, you had to get the hell out of there, fast—all without breaking formation if at all possible.

Depending on the type and duration of the mission, grunts would carry the gear needed. That could range from as little as their weapon, canteen(s) of water, ammunition, helmet, food, and anything else deemed necessary for a day's outing. Or, the carry-load could be much greater and include a rubberized mat and sleeping bag, change of boots and socks, and excess food, water and ammo. It was not unusual for the grunt, with full load, to jump out of a hovering slick, land into a watery rice paddy, and sink up to his upper torso.

The gunship fire team never split up, such as one taking the left flank while the other took the right. It was a team, pure and simple, and we stayed together. More often than not, we flew at treetop level within the area of the LZ. Up close and personal with the enemy. It was easier to see the whites of their eyes that way. At treetop level, the enemy would have had a difficult time seeing us if we were overhead, zooming along at a hundred miles an hour.

But there were problems. In my ship, on many occasions, mud and vegetation debris from the 40mm impact sites would spray up and we'd fly right into it, striking the ship's chin bubble. Sometimes that debris cracked or broke the Plexiglas, requiring me to make the repair or initiate replacement.

On occasion, a replacement part was not available. To remain mission-ready, it would be up to the crew chief or maintenance personnel to repair the damage to the Plexiglas. With a crack, a small hole would be drilled at each end to prevent it from becoming longer. If the crack was already long, a series of small holes would be drilled on each lateral side. Safety wire would then be laced through these holes and twisted closed to secure each side of the crack together. Sort of a Frankenstein-ish scar across the window.

The M5 aircraft grenade-launcher system had a maximum rate of fire of 220 rounds of 40mm grenades per minute. The maximum effective range was 1,500 meters. Our sheet metal guys quickly replaced the original 150-round ammo box in the cargo area with a 500-round box that worked very well. Aiming it, the peter-pilot used a drop-down targeting device and trigger.

One of our biggest early missions came on April 10. As usual, the Rat Pack crew chiefs and gunners weren't privy to the main mission objectives except for the obvious: follow orders. At the A/C's discretion we would get briefed about the mission at hand. Our company was supporting the 2nd Brigade, 25th Infantry Division based out of Cu Chi, and the 36th Vietnamese Ranger Battalion. The number of Hueys waiting for the grunts to load up was more than I had ever seen. There must have been over forty slicks. Gunships were everywhere. Everybody waiting. Nerves settled by idle chit-chat, checking maps for the umpteenth time, smoking one cigarette after another, or day-dreaming while listening to the ADF. Excitement was in the air. You could feel it, mentally and physically. I was pumped and ready to go.

We finally got the order to go, and over the course of the next couple hours, six hundred grunts were inserted into various LZs in the AO. We kept busy doing the same thing, over and over again prepping LZs, responding to the numerous contacts with Charlie, re-arming, re-fueling as necessary and returning, orbiting the AO waiting to be called to a certain location. During one of the insertions, my ship took a hit in the tail boom. Except for the tail rotor drive shaft and control linkages, most of the tail boom is hollow. The bullet caused no damage except for the two holes, one on each side. This was the first of many times my ship caught a round from the enemy.

Three days later, one of our gunship teams encountered heavy, automatic fire from numerous Charlie locations. During a gun run, just as one of the rockets was fired from the right pod, a round struck it as it left the tube, causing it to explode. The gunner on the right side, PFC Howell, was severely wounded. His right arm nearly severed.

By the end of the day, everybody heard the story. The crew chief, Spec Four Hester, responded immediately. Seeing the gaping wound, blood everywhere, he reached into Howell's opened chest cavity and pinched an artery. The bleeding stopped. Because of air turbulence inside the ship, blood had sprayed everywhere. Meanwhile, the explosion caused significant damage to the ship. The hydraulics and control linkages were severely damaged. The A/C had a choice to make, and it had to be made immediately: Land the ship in the closest area that seemed safe to avoid going down and crashing, maybe killing all aboard; or, fly to the nearest base to get Howell the medical attention he needed to live. He chose the latter. The doctor at the base credited the crew, especially Hester, for saving Howell's life. He was recommended for the Distinguished Flying Cross (DFC) for his actions under enemy fire.

The DFC is a coveted award for heroism or extraordinary action in flight. It is ranked just below the Silver Star, and above the Bronze Star for valor, Air Medal for valor, and the Purple Heart. It is rarely awarded, and when it is, usually pilots are the recipient. So, for Hester to be recommended for this award reveals much about his heroic action under enemy fire. A very significant award.

Days faded into one another. More missions, more strafing gun runs, more hours spent in the sky, orbiting a piece of real estate that somebody, somewhere else, thought to be important. More sweeps by the grunts, more injuries and fatalities. On the go, everyday. It was a blessing when the flight hours reached the point when a special 25-hour aircraft inspection was required. But once grounded we were anxious to get back in the mix. We missed it. I missed it.

My first confirmed kill came not long after. Later in life, certain geo-physical aspects would open my mind's eye to that uninvited memory. The season would have to be just right. Hot, but not so much to cause sweating. The radiance of the sun perfectly positioned in a pale blue clear sky; no clouds, just the bright mid-morning sun. The momentary sighting of a stand-alone hundred-yard line of not-so-tall green, leafy trees. Observing a well-used footpath along one side of the tree line where the beige trampled earth had become hard as rock. The feel of a strong, steady breeze on my skin, so similar to the wind rushing into the helicopter from the open cargo doors. Sensing my eyes, shaded by a hat or overhang like a flight helmet, but only if the shade was at just the right angle.

Here's what happened: An ARVN[30] force tasked with capturing a Vietnamese man needed assistance from our unit. It would require two of our slicks to transport the ARVNs and one fire team of gunships for cover. The mission would take place at mid-morning with minimal cloud cover, so it was expected to be a cold LZ—meaning no hostile ground fire. Just drop the ARVNs off, give them time to apprehend the man, and provide

---

[30] Army of the Republic of Viet Nam.

close air support if required. Once he was secured, we'd leave. No problem. We'd be back to Tay Ninh by lunch.

Our team was flying on one side of a tree line. The slicks were on the other. We were all heading in the same direction. As the ARVNs were dropped off just in front of an isolated thatched building, a man, about twenty years old or so, bolted out the back door to escape. Carrying no weapon and wearing only red shorts, he did not hesitate as he ran in the opposite direction from the ARVNs, following a well-worn path along the tree line. He was on my side, about a hundred and fifty yards off, as we made our second orbit approaching the area about two hundred feet in the air.

Through my headset, I heard one of my pilots telling me, "Stop him. Try shooting a few rounds in front of him." I did so, but the guy kept running. The dirt in front of him kicked up dust plumes.

"Stop him. Stop him," came the command again. The man kept running. I kept firing and, using the tracers as my guide, purposely missed him, hoping the guy would get the message. I did not have orders to kill him, just to stop him. He had run a distance of at least halfway along the trail, dodging my hail of bullets.

Stop him. Stop him. But he wasn't stopping.

Major Joe Burns, my A/C, slowed the ship down and swung the tail boom to the right, giving me a better angle and more time to shoot. It seemed as though everything was in slow motion. The guy just would not stop.

Then, he stumbled. Did I hit him? Didn't see any blood. The man jumped into a bush at the far end of the tree line.

Stop him.

I didn't know if the guy had weapons in the bush, maybe an AK-47 or RPG. There could have been a tunnel there for him to escape. Or maybe he was trying to save his own life by finding cover. It could have been all three or any variation. Stupidly, I kept firing into the bush until the order to cease fire order was given. It was, and I did.

The ARVNs came around and found him dead in that bush. No weapon. No tunnel. Just him with a bunch of bullet holes in his body.

Going back to base, I didn't know what to think. I tried to collect my thoughts and feelings. Honestly, at first, I couldn't explain what I was thinking or feeling. How was I *supposed* to feel about this? I didn't know. Sadness, more than anything else, overcame any other fleeting emotion in the aftermath of that killing. There was no moment of joy, nor did I feel proud. The fact was an unarmed man, running away from his pursuers, had been killed. The lives of his family changed at that moment, and I was responsible. They, too, became casualties of this aggressive act that most certainly could have been avoided. I expected to feel some remorse. But this particular emotion (intense sadness) was new to me, and there was no name by which it could be identified. To my knowledge, I had never killed anybody before. Yes, I had been on combat assaults before, strafing treelines and such, getting shot at by the rarely-seen enemy, but never actually seeing the men or weapons I was shooting at.

Inside the open cargo doorway, buffeted by the wind, I sat on my small nylon and aluminum seat not really knowing what to think. I lit a cigarette. There were no tears. Not a word was spoken about this by anyone connected to me by intercom. But I knew I had screwed up the mission big time.

When we landed, I unbuckled my seatbelt and hesitated a bit, not wanting to appear anxious to cry on somebody's shoulder over this, but I did want to talk to Major Burns before he left the ship. As soon as he stepped out of the ship, I was there at his door. For the first time, he and I spoke as human beings, not as officer to enlisted man. I wanted to express my confused feelings to him, the way I thought I felt.

The words formed in my mind, but couldn't come out: *Did I understand his orders correctly? By directing me to stop him, did he, or the other pilot, mean for me to kill him? Why didn't that guy stop when he surely must have known he was being chased and then shot at by me, missing him? I wasn't out to kill him. Didn't he know that? Why was he being apprehended? Was he Viet Cong? A deserter?*

But the big question on my mind: *Was this shooting justified?*

"I'm sorry about killing him, Sir," were my only words to Major Burns. "He just wouldn't stop."

Quite tall and lean, Major Burns was older than most of us, probably in his late thirties. He was cool under fire and a born leader. He had been our platoon commander since Fort Bragg. He was very kind, almost fatherly, as he consoled me.

He explained, "Look, these things happen in war. We have a duty and sometimes people get killed."

After he and the other pilot left I tried to focus on my job at hand. Keep busy, walk around the ship to check for damage. Wait for the fuel truck to arrive. Clean up my brass casings, scoop them into an empty ammo box to be disposed. Detaching it from the bungee cord, I broke down my M-60 to clean it thoroughly. Maybe just a little extra cleaning was necessary this time. My gunner cleaned the forty-mike-mike and reloaded the rocket pods. Updating the logbook, and seeing my gunner leave with a hand-wave, I was alone. My eyes began to well up with tears, making it difficult to see as I stared at the page. But not one fell.

Who was that man? Why was he running? What must have gone through his mind as I was trying to stop him? When I hit him? Was he out of breath? Did he think of his family? Did he know he was going to die? Was he a deserter? An escaped prisoner? A Viet Cong? A spy? Was he a draftee who didn't report in? He ran away not to be captured by the descending ARVN squad sent to apprehend him, so clearly, he had a reason. But what was it? I would never know.

Chapter 4

The DFC

I woke up in the middle of the night burning up by fever. It had been a few weeks since my first kill. I couldn't get that guy outta my mind. Remorse, regret, guilt; I didn't know how to handle it. Maybe this was punishment of sorts. I could tell my temperature was very high, though we didn't have access to a thermometer in the company, nor a medic. In the morning when everyone was getting ready for the mission, one of the guys summoned our platoon sergeant. Grabenstetter arrived at our tent and checked my forehead for a fever with his calibrated back-of-the-hand. He confined me to bed rest. I don't remember much of that day.

With no improvement, later that day Sarge took me to the nearby hospital.[31] I had a fever of 104 degrees and was admitted. The cause of the fever was unknown. It was not malaria, but officially diagnosed as an Unknown Fever Origin, referred to as UFO. While there, I slept. I do not know if other people were in the ward with me. Sarge visited me once (that I know of) to check on my condition and if I needed anything. He told me I had missed out on a major operation.

Our ships had been authorized to evacuate a large contingent of grunts just near the Cambodian border. On April 18, five slicks and two gunship teams were sent to assist a Vietnamese or Montagnard Civilian Irregular Defense Group (CIDG) outpost near the Cambodian border. The VC and North Vietnamese Army were attacking, and the CIDG were at a risk of being overrun. The weather was terrible. Visibility was not quite a thousand feet. Heavy rain, strong winds, turbulent air currents would have caused the faint-of-heart to turn back. But, not our guys. We had received word the CIDG had sustained twenty-three men wounded and one killed. They needed to be evacuated. When our ships arrived, the base was still under fire. Undaunted, our gunships did their thing while the slicks did theirs. Under heavy ground fire, all were evacuated safely.

Our missions kept coming at us. We were establishing routines, and our reputation grew. I didn't go on all the missions even when I

---

[31] 45th Surgical Hospital (MUST), Tay Ninh, Vietnam. This was a forward-based surgical hospital.

wasn't sick. We had eight gunships in our platoon. Most missions only required two, sometimes four. The initial tactic of remaining at the AO for hours at a time during the entire mission softened up a bit. Once the grunts were inserted into the LZ, sometimes we were released to depart the AO. We would either go back to base, set down in a field somewhere waiting to be called back, or go onto another mission. Otherwise, we stayed at the AO to provide close air support until they were done. That meant long hours, many times six to eight, before being released. The only break during that time was to refuel and rearm as necessary. With a full tank of JP-4 fuel, we could remain in the air for up to two hours at a time.

If we stayed near the AO and shut down in an open field waiting to be called back, we'd open the C-rations to grab a bite to eat. Some of the food tasted much better when heated. That was no problem. Opening a can of cookies or crackers using a supplied P-38 can opener, we'd empty it out, squeeze the upper edges together a bit to form a platform, scoop dirt or sand into it, then add *belly fuel[32]* to ignite. Of the twelve different meals, the beans and franks were the worst cold, but heated they tasted pretty good. Not liking the taste of lima beans, it was traded or given away every chance possible.

Another thing we learned about food in the field: there is a correlation between how hungry you are to the tastiness of the food. Sometimes it was not possible to heat the food, but if you're hungry enough it didn't matter. A case of C-rations contained twelve individual boxed meals. Secured by 20-gauge wire wrapped around, the case required a wire cutter to open. If that wasn't available, and it sometimes wasn't, we used the three-pronged flash suppressor of the M-16 to twist the wire until it broke. It pretty much always worked, and there was no damage to the rifle end[33]. A different entrée was in each box. A sealed brown packet inside each meal box contained gum, toilet paper, salt and pepper, a small box of four individual cigarettes (Lucky Strikes, Pall Mall, Winston, etc.), and so on.

The slicks had their own way of flying in formation. Each aircraft would be assigned a number, one through however many ships there were

---

[32] Beneath the ship was a release valve to access and drain JP-4 fuel. It was designed to allow any water that condensed inside the fuel bladder to be removed. Doing this was one of the daily routines for our inspection of the ship.

[33] The rifle manufacturer, Colt, redesigned the flash suppressor a year or two later to eliminate the three-prong design. By connecting the three ends, it was no longer usable to break wire.

in the flight. Apparently in reference to each position as noted in chalk on the blackboard in operations, the lead ship would be *Chalk One*, the second was *Chalk Two*, and so on. That position was to remain intact as much as possible during the mission. If it was necessary to communicate by radio, the chalk number would be used to communicate to the flight commander or the command & control ship[34], thereby identifying the crew without broadcasting crew names, ship number, etc.

As our mission count rose, we honed our skills to perfection on how to strafe tree lines and other suspected hiding places. Flying at ninety knots or so—about a hundred miles per hour—while shooting laterally an M-60 at a stationary target on the ground can be tricky. Factors to consider include the speed and altitude of the aircraft, bullet drop due to gravity, leading the target (in reverse, because we're moving, not the target), the tilting of the ship in relation to the target, location of friendlies and noncombatants, etc. And when the target is moving, the dynamics of shooting changes slightly. The easiest way to shoot was to follow the tracers[35] and adjust the aim as required. Every fifth bullet was a tracer-round. It was easy to visually follow a series of red-dots, as they appear to be, to the target area and to adjust targeting without using aiming sights.

Enemy casualties were not always obvious. After strafing, especially in a hot LZ, the dead often remain where they were killed. If they were shooting from a hidden place in a tree, when killed they might drop to the ground. Or not. When the grunts come through to make their sweep of the AO, they'd find the dead VC most of the time and would credit us with the body count, unless they knew the kill was theirs. If it was ours, the crew usually took the credit as a team effort. Sometimes, the crew knew which one had made the kill.

Enemy body count, reported to higher command, was important for the mission planners and S-2[36]. We didn't keep track of that number and it really wasn't that important to us, except as a personal "accomplishment" for some guys. We weren't rewarded for having an enemy

---

[34] The C & C ship would fly at a higher altitude and monitor the overall mission, sort of having a 'big picture' look at the operation while in progress.
[35] Bullets having a small pyrotechnic charge ignited by the burning gun powder. These bullets usually have a colored tip to identify the color of the burning chemical composition.
[36] Military intelligence officer at the battalion level.

body count in any sense of the word. But, my ship had many confirmed kills during many missions.

Mission after mission helped force the experience of my first confirmed kill to the back of my mind. Dwelling on it did not help. Keeping busy was the best remedy. Killing the enemy became our true mission. We weren't called out just to escort the slicks in and out of LZs, but to hunt down and kill the enemy where and whenever possible. Our enemy body counts grew larger, a little at a time; not that we were keeping track of that sort of thing.

Direct firefights were funny things. Sometimes I'd see Charlie shooting at us or one of the slicks, but most of the time I never did. A few shot at us from where they hid in tree branches, and a few out in the open. But, most of the enemy was hidden in the bush, well-concealed and completely invisible as we flew by. We relied on directions from the ground commander.

Smoke grenades were also very useful as a point of reference. The grunts had smoke. We had smoke. It was a simple matter to pop the pin and toss a specific color for a specific meaning. Red for marking danger, yellow for landing and marking the location of this or that, and purple or bluish-green for all others. But, for the most part the choice of colors was limited to what was left. The meaning of the smoke color was usually decided by the "team that had the ball." The "receivers" were simply informed what it meant.

During late June, I was promoted as Special Fourth Class (E-4)[37]. Rank was displayed on the shirt, never the flight jacket. I had one shirt left to have the rank sewed on when we were informed about a change. Cloth rank insignia was no longer to be used. We were switching to metal, olive-drab pin-on style rank insignia. It was easier, except the pins (one on each collar) would need to be removed for laundering. The 1st Aviation Brigade unit patch, the name and US Army tabs were also being changed to OD, which meant the old ones had to be removed and new ones sewn on at our own expense. The pilots began using OD flight helmets, but we kept the white ones for a little longer.

---

[37] My first DD Form 214 incorrectly shows my promotion date to E-5 as June 30, 1967. At the time, I didn't care.

A few more guys with more flight experience were transferred into our company from other units. As it turned out, we were also learning how strange some of those guys were that had been in combat for months longer. One of the guys new to the Rat Pack, A-Jay, was from California. He was a draftee and older than most of us, probably about twenty-six. I would consider him to be the quintessential Californian: lofty, don't take things too seriously, and groove with the music.

After we got back from missions, refueled the ships and such, we'd gather around the last one to finish and help out if necessary. Then, we'd all go into the company area together. One day, A-Jay wanted to stay behind, alone. He told us he wanted some "time to think." We gave little thought about his staying behind, but it just seemed odd for some reason. Maybe he wanted to reflect of the day's events. But, as I recall, the CA we were on was uneventful. It wasn't until months later that I learned that "time to think" was a coy euphemism used to separate oneself from non-initiates of smoking weed (a crime), thus allowing oneself alone time for deep, THC-induced thought and reflection.

We were naïve. Nobody I knew brought up the subject of marijuana. I never knew if A-Jay smoked weed or not. But, the phrase "time to think" would prove to be more common than I imagined among the stoners.

We were very busy flying, so much so, that being in the company area during the day was very rare for my gunner and me. When we got back to base we still weren't done. As the crew chief, it was my responsibility to go over the ship to check for proper oil levels, damage from wear and tear or bullets and shrapnel, pull the post-flight and daily inspection, update the log book and refuel the ship. When all that was done, I helped the gunner clean the weapon systems and rearm the ship. Usually, the pilots left us as we took care of these post-flight chores while they went into operations to debrief, get briefed about future missions, and then onto the officer's club for a beer or two-fingers of Scotch to de-stress.

The amount of time we flew each day was entered on a Dept. of the Army form 2408-12, referred to as a "dash 12." This form was turned in to operations at the end of the day where individual records of flight hours would be updated accordingly. Being in a combat zone, every 25 hours of combat assault flight time (whether engaged with the enemy or not) qualified for an Air Medal for meritorious service. To the best of my knowledge, none of us individually kept track of our own flight hours. We trusted the system and had no reason to think otherwise. To be honest, the number of hours we flew was not important to many of us. We knew we flew a lot, and that was just part of being on a flight crew in Vietnam. Trust the system and wait for written orders.

My first Air Medal was from the period of March 23–May 8, 1967. Twenty-five combat hours in six weeks? That's an average of about one and a half hours per day; or, four hours per week. It seemed wrong. Really wrong. I was flying combat assault missions much more than that. I was sure the records would catch up and the clerk would adjust accordingly. Heck, we were all new and learning things that should have been addressed when we were at Bragg. It made sense that the clerks were learning, too.

I didn't complain or make any sort of inquiry. It wasn't really important to challenge them. My motivation was not to be awarded a medal. I wanted to fly because I enjoyed doing so. I enjoyed traveling in an armed-to-the-teeth gunship. I liked the prestige, even if it was only self-perceived. I liked the adrenaline rush that came with combat action, having a mission to accomplish with a degree of teamwork that was unlike any other I knew. I liked the comradery we shared, our brotherhood-in-arms being nurtured with each mission.

I had plenty of time to think and didn't need to stay behind, alone, after a mission. I trained myself not to succumb to boredom. Keep alert, at all times. Think of something, think of your mission. One of the primary goals, if not *the* primary goal, of a gunship is to draw enemy ground fire away from the slicks dropping off grunts into the LZ, and to provide close air support wherever and whenever needed. We wanted the VC to shoot at us, not them. Gunships were heavily armed: mini-guns capable of shooting 3,000 rounds a minute; a front-turret grenade launcher capable of firing up just over two hundred rounds per minute; air-to-ground rockets capable of firing all at once, or one at a time; and a door gunner on each side of the ship armed with an M-60 machine gun capable of firing about seven hundred rounds per minute. Badass? You could say that.

Like Tom and Babe, crew members left our unit and new guys arrived. My gunner changed due to the infusion process. The one I started with was shipped out, replaced by a guy named Zack[38]. I'm not sure how he got assigned to the Rat Pack. He told me he had been riding with the slicks and requested the Rat Pack when a vacancy occurred. Wary at first, I kept an eye on him and helped him along in the chores of reloading the ammo, cleaning the forty-mike-mike, and what to look for when we were in the air. During the first couple of missions, we saw very little action. A few rockets were fired as suppressive precautions at suspected VC locations, a little side action with our M-60s, and these missions went without a hitch. Zack was going to work out fine.

But, I was wrong. I quickly learned he did not seem to have a clue as to what to do during a hot combat assault. During our last mission together, we were heavily engaged with enemy ground forces. Our rockets and forty-mike-mike were getting a workout. We were taking fire from the right side of the ship. Me, on the left, had the slicks and troops on my side and had to hold my fire. As we made passes of the hot LZ, Zack didn't fire a shot. Not hearing anything from his side, I looked at him to check on his well-being. Was he hit? No. Was his gun jammed? No. His M-60 was just resting on his lap, not even pointed at the ground. He sat there looking down at the ground. The troops were being inserted in the LZ. The slicks were lifting and banking to the left due to intense ground fire coming from the tree line on the right. That tree line was at our three and four o'clock position. Red smoke rose from two locations, tossed by the grunts to mark target areas and reference points.

Zack, wake the fuck up. Look down and fire, I said to myself. The radio was blaring on all frequencies. The grunts were taking fire. We were taking fire. Our A/C was talking to Rat Six, located somewhere over the AO. We were moving low and fast.

I lost it.

As we passed the LZ and banked around to have another go, I focused my attention on Zack. Maybe because I was scared of being shot down, I cursed at him as loud as possible, but not through the intercom. I didn't want the pilots to hear me chewing him out for sitting on his ass. He turned and looked at me with a blank stare. No explanation, no comment, no retort. I ran my eyes up and down. Was he hit? I didn't see any red and

---

[38] Not his real name. I cannot, for the life of me, remember his correct name.

he didn't make any move towards his body that may have given me a hint of his being wounded. He just sat there.

As luck would have it, that was our last run at the tree line. We remained on location in case we were needed. Zack didn't move. I couldn't see his face as it was still turned away and his darkened sun visor was down. I didn't know what to do. Should I switch on the intercom and notify the A/C that Zack froze? Maybe he didn't, maybe it was something else. I didn't know what Zack's problem was, and didn't know what to do about it. So, I sat there, stewing for a solution.

When we landed, he kept to himself as I was doing my paperwork waiting for the fuel truck to arrive. I was biding my time and collecting my thoughts about the best way to confront him. Expecting him to be busy doing his work on the ship, I looked up and saw him walking off towards the company area. He didn't say anything about going, and wasn't done with his work. When I finished my job and his, and returned to the company area, I got some food in the mess hall. He wasn't there. After I ate, I went over to the EM[39] Club. Not there, either. He wasn't in his bunk when I returned to our tent.

The next day, Zack was not on the flight line as we were preparing for another mission. I had a new gunner, Richard Brauher. Zack was no longer assigned to my ship. In fact, he left the Rat Pack and I never saw him again. Sarge never told me why he was gone except that he was transferred.

Whenever we flew, we were looking for trouble. I guess it affected our attitudes, as we began to think of ourselves as invincible—though we never verbalized that. We became good at what we were doing. We kept to ourselves much of the time. The Rat Pack was different from the other platoons. We were like the shotgun rider on the stagecoach, the bodyguard for celebrities. We had our own mission, uniquely different from the slicks.

Aside from flying there were some extra duties to pull. Spec Fours and below pulled guard duty. I did it twice, one time as a roving guard where our ships were parked, and the other time at a perimeter bunker.

---

[39] Our Enlisted Men's Club, a/k/a EM Club, was reserved for Privates up to Spec Fours, and was essentially a bar serving 3.2 beer, sodas, and chips.

Spec Fives became the sergeant-of-the-guard. We were made aware of the possibility of infiltration of our base by the enemy. The guys that had infused into our unit shared some experiences they had with VC Sappers[40]. Concerning our aircraft, the VC were known to remove the fuel cap, drop a grenade in with the pin pulled but handle taped closed, and put the fuel cap back on. Similar to a delayed timer, the glue on the tape would eventually dissolve from the fuel and the grenade would explode. To counter this, we began to scratch a small mark to match a point on the fuel cap to a point on the cap-housing. In that most of the re-fueling was done by the crew chief, he knew where the marks lined up. If it was not, he also knew there was a good possibility that it had been tampered with, possibly by a Sapper.

Like almost all GIs, I also had KP (kitchen police[41]), but only pulled that duty twice during my tour. Just before I became a Spec Five and no longer eligible for this detail, I was trying to prepare some hot water for tray cleaning. It had been raining hard earlier, but stopped. I was having difficulty lighting the immersion heater[42] outside of the mess hall. The fuel, dripping down drop-by-drop into the receiving compartment at the bottom, would not ignite. After maybe five unsuccessful minutes of careful dropping a lit match into the submerged heating element, adjusting the fuel drip to no avail, I decided to look down. I saw a small puddle of liquid, fuel, maybe water, too, and five or six 'dead' matches. *Why isn't this thing igniting?* I asked myself. It was time to watch where the next match landed. The matchbook was almost empty. There were two left. I had to be careful. I dropped one and watched it hit the fuel and ignite. The quick blast of intense heat and fire singed my eyebrows and the front of the hair on my head. That was the last time I ever pulled KP.

Sarge informed me I was selected to go before the E-5 promotion board. Perhaps he was afraid I was going to blow up the mess hall the next time I had KP? He assured me that wasn't it, and that a few of us had been selected. We didn't know what to expect. So far, all of our promotions

---

[40] A Sapper is a skilled NVA or Viet Cong soldier trained to penetrate heavily fortified perimeters undetected. Once inside the base they would attack with satchel charges, rocket-propelled grenades, etc. to cause as much damage as possible, then disappear into the night undetected.

[41] Being assigned duties for one day at the mess hall; washing trays, tables, filling beverage containers, washing pots and pans, peeling potatoes (if available), etc.

[42] A metal heating element fueled by drops of diesel fuel that fed a fire at the bottom of the unit submerged in a barrel of water.

were automatic, E-2 through E-4. I suppose each also required some type of recommendation, but I wasn't sure and didn't care as long as I got paid at the end of the month. Was it expected for us to study for the promotion board? What type of questions were they going to ask? Was this a mere formality? We didn't know anything.

Sporting starched short-sleeved khakis, a fresh haircut, and spit-shined shoes, we went to where our battalion headquarters was located. One by one, we entered a room alone. Seated in a chair in front of a table with one lieutenant and two NCOs, each of us answered the questions posed by the board. A few days later our promotion orders came through. If I was a grunt, I would have been a buck sergeant. But, as it were, aviation units did not have buck sergeants, per se. I was a new Spec(ialist) Five.

On July 2, one of the slicks in our unit received fire from a VC sniper as the ship was lifting off from an LZ. The bullet hit the legs of both pilots, rendering each unable to pilot the ship. The story is legend. Under enemy fire, the crew chief, SP/5 Larry Mackey, immediately took control. He got the A/C tilted back in his chair and removed him from the seat. Without any hesitation, he took over the flight controls and flew the ship to safety and landed without causing further harm or damage. Due to his heroic actions and unexpected skill under fire, he was being recommended for a Silver Star—with one condition. The battalion commander wanted Larry to be his crew chief. The rumor-mill was spinning out of control. If he declined the offer his award would be downgraded to a Distinguished Flying Cross. A couple days passed. I didn't know Larry that well, but he was one of us from Bragg. He felt a strong sense of loyalty to the 187th and wanted to continue flying with us. He did not want to leave the 187th and did not want to crew the commander's ship. So, he forfeited the Silver Star in lieu of the DFC that was awarded to him unceremoniously.

On July 7, the company had its first fatalities. Major Charles Sauer, Captain Thomas Derosier, Spec Four Ivra Tatum and PFC Paul Simon were on a single-ship "cold" mission to deliver supplies to an American forward observation post near Minh Thanh. The flight there and back, including the unloading of gear, should have taken no more than a few hours. By late afternoon, they hadn't returned. There was no radio or transponder communication at all. A search party of a few slicks and a gun team were immediately dispatched to follow the flight path filed earlier by the A/C. We found the slick on the ground, or what remained of it. It had crashed and burned beyond recognition. Magnesium-aluminum alloy, the stuff helicopters were made of, burns very fast and very hot. All that remained in the bush were the gray ashes of what was once four men and their helicopter. The mystery of what caused the crash was never solved.

The next evening, we had a memorial service in our company area for the four men. As was customary (but new to most of us), four bayonet attached M-16 rifles were placed muzzle down on a makeshift platform. Polished boots were at the base, and a flight helmet was placed onto the butt-end of each rifle. The company commander, platoon leader, and a chaplain spoke and offered their condolences.

Without a doubt, we came away knowing we had a dangerous occupation. That crew could have been any of us. We knew them from Fort Bragg. They were our brothers. They were just here the other day, talking about missions over beers at the club. Now they're gone. Fairness? I don't think anyone thought about that. I know I didn't. But, it left me emotionally numb. I had to stifle my emotions and continue on. There was a war to be fought. No time for tears. No time for grieving. Push on, soldier.

From that day on, I knew that there were no guarantees. Everything could be going smooth and perfect. You could be enjoying the good weather, the beauty of sunrise, or sunset, and having a comforting sense of brotherhood and camaraderie. In the air, the feeling of flying was unique to all other sensations. It made one feel free, like a bird. No stink, no mud, no bugs. It's habit forming. And, just like that, you could die in an instant. You never knew when or where, but it could happen any time.

In July 1967, we learned through the *Stars & Stripes* newspaper that race riots were taking place in Detroit. I knew of no one in our company who was from Detroit or had relatives there except for me, so news of the riots was taken very matter-of-factly. Race riots, in a northern state? The idea was so incomprehensible that it didn't make sense. I knew of the racial tensions in the South, and riots, dogs, firehoses, and police clubbing victims. My mind could not accept the concept of that sort of thing in Detroit. We didn't have that problem in Chicago, at Fort Bragg, and not in

Tay Ninh, either. We all got along. Was it just a protest march run amok, or was there actual fighting involved? The term *race relations* had not yet entered our vocabulary.

There wasn't time to really think about it, though, as the days were very busy. I was still flying a lot of hours, starting early in the morning and getting back to the company area by six or seven o'clock, then working on the ship and cleaning the weapons; same-old, same-old. The pilots would tell the mess sergeant to keep some food for us in the mess hall. So, we'd eat late, go to the enlisted men's club and maybe grab a can of beer for twenty-five cents, and go to bed. No time for anything else. Get up early the next morning and do the same thing again. We did not have days off unless our ship was in maintenance or no missions were scheduled (a rare occurrence). We worked every day of the week. The concept of weekends and holidays had no meaning to us.

On August 7, Sarge scheduled me to fly with Spec Five Harold Hawk, who was the crew chief of another gunship. His gunner was either sick or away on R & R, and we were out of spare gunners. This would be the first time I flew on a gunship with mini-guns and just as a gunner. He and I got along well and found some humor in our situation. His ship, not mine. We got that clear.

We started early that morning. Hawk and I carried the M-60s and mini-guns to his ship, he did his pre-flight, and waited. The pilots arrived and the aircraft commander did his pre-flight inspection. Hawk and I got briefed that we'd be working with the 199th Light Infantry Brigade in an AO about seven miles north of Saigon. At their own briefing, it was revealed the LZ was expected to be hot, a contingent of VC had been spotted. Therefore, two fire teams were going.

Soon, we were all buckled in and the rotor blades were at idle speed. Sitting in our spot, waiting as the slicks were getting started, one by one. It was time.

"Clear left," Hawk said as he panned his side for nearby obstacles, finding none.

"Clear right," I said as I did the same on my side.

The A/C pulled pitch and off we went, following the slicks that rose in formation. I had never flown as a gunner at the right side of the ship before. Getting the M-60 adjusted on my lap, and the belt of ammo draped over my leg, felt uncomfortable. It felt, well, backwards. Being right-handed, at least it would be easier to shoot from the twelve o'clock to the four o'clock field of fire. Past that, this was going to be tricky.

A short time later the slicks landed in a field to pick up the grunts. Again, we lifted off beautifully. Airborne, we flew in formation like a flock of geese. Once we got to the LZ, the other fire team would take the left flank and we would take the right. The voices on the radio droned on. The faintly heard rhythm of the rotor blades dulled my senses. Even at our altitude the air was warm and humid. The wind rushing inside the open cargo doors was steady, no ripple. My eyelids grew heavy.

Being so exhausted from the last few days, I allowed my eyelids to close, just for a second. But not before I scanned the skies for other aircraft. We were clear. I'll close them, just for a second, just enough to get the burn out. I wasn't accustomed to the warm air rushing in from the *right* side of the ship. It felt good. Comfortable. The sunlight, bright and warm, slowly crept over my knees and legs as I sat there, sensing a slight turn of the ship, tired eyes burning and being not too difficult to remain closed.

The whine of the transmission and engine, so familiar then, just behind the bulkhead behind me, faded. The main blades, rotating in perfect alignment, like gliding on glass. The voices on the radio frequencies droned on, steady talk. No one excited. Very business-like. I still heard them, but the sound was getting softer. The blades, engine and transmission engaged in a rhythmic, hypnotic discourse. I was slipping away, unknowingly and without intention. My eyes stopped burning...

WOOSH! **WOOSH!** I opened my eyes really quick-like. I was alert immediately as the second rocket from the pod on my side, trailing the first by a nano-second, left its tube on the way to a ground target. I must have fallen asleep, but the adrenaline kicked in.

"We're taking heavy fire from our right flank," radioed one of the slick pilots.

"Chalk Three to Chalk One, Charlie's running up to your four o'clock," came another voice over the radio. The slicks were on the ground.

"We're hit. Cyclic's loose. Chalk Three's bailing out. Mayday, Mayday."

I looked past Hawk towards the ground, just a glance, really. Five slicks were in the LZ, grayish smoke coming from two of them.

"Alright, boys," our A/C spoke through the intercom. "Keep an eye out for friendlies on the left."

We continued the assault. Our air speed increased as our nose lowered some more. We were on our gun run. A third rocket followed the second. **WOOSH!** Going in.

Looking down, still at treetop level and traveling fast, I saw only one man on the ground at first. We were about a hundred feet in the air. The guy was directly below me, wearing a khaki uniform and pith helmet. He was running in the opposite direction from where we were headed, towards our five o'clock. I quickly dropped a smoke grenade to mark his location. Seeing some movement on the ground, I fired. As we passed the LZ, still at treetop level, I was able to see, through the branches, four other men in beige or khaki uniforms running this way and that. I kept firing my M-60 toward the ground movement. At treetop level, I observed fire-pits and cooking pots rested on what had to be metal tripods. We must have interrupted their lunch. More slicks approached the LZ on our left as we banked to the right to make a quick orbit around to begin our second pass.

Coming back, I noticed, peering through Hawk's side, smoke still coming from the first slicks at the LZ as the grunts were jumping out. Four slicks were immediately hit and stayed on the ground. The blades on one ship stopped, the others still rotating. Crew chiefs and gunners on the ground, dismantling M-60s from the pole mounts. Still on their right flank, at treetop level, we banked hard right. There was a lot of chatter on the radio. The crews of these slicks have to be airlifted out. Their ships were damaged too severely to fly out. Other slicks approached the LZ. One or two were taking so much ground fire that dropping off the grunts was aborted.

A little further on were four .51 caliber machine guns. I caught only a glance of them, really, hidden beneath tree branches. I wasn't sure exactly what they were. The barrels were connected to a mobile platform (the rust-colored and aged metal construction made me think it was a Japanese weapon left over from World War II). As we flew overhead, another gook was running to it. The few cooking sites I could see were abandoned, as were the campsites and unattended pots of steaming food. We were still receiving intense ground fire. More ships were damaged. I initially shot at anything, moving or not, at the ground below me.

We came around for our third pass.

Time slowed down, and I was able to focus on small details. My movements became purposeful and deliberate, though not consciously made. The belt of ammo fed into the left port of my M-60 without any problem. The beat of my machine gun steadied as I lit up tree branches, clumps of vegetation that appeared out of place, and anything else that looked like camouflage.

WOOSH! Another rocket let loose. **BRRRRRR, BRRRRRR, BRRRRRR**, loudly went the mini-guns in short bursts. Chatter on the radio, mostly yelling back and forth, punctuated by the calm commands of somebody taking charge and directing the recovery of crews. More slicks being summoned to the LZ to recover crews and grunts.

The LZ was in chaos. Charlie had taken cover in well-concealed bunkers and tree limbs. They became almost invisible. I continued firing into the wooded area beneath us. I was firing in tight arcs, avoiding the areas where I didn't see anybody. As we ended our third pass and banked to the right, I saw another set of .51 calibers between the leaves of trees with two guys in khakis standing nearby. I continued laying suppressive fire, aiming at those guns and surrounding area on the ground. I had nearly exhausted the 2,000 rounds in my ammo box and had maybe 30 rounds left. We could hear some rounds hitting our ship, but only after we stopped shooting. We couldn't tell the amount of damage, but the controls still functioned.

One of the slicks landed in the LZ to pick up the stranded crews. It received heavy enemy fire as it tried to lift off, and never made it out of the LZ. It plopped to the ground and all aboard spilled out like ants leaving an anthill. Radio transmissions quickly indicated the crews were okay for now.

The mini-gun ammo was nearly depleted and we were out of rockets. It was time for us to leave to rearm and refuel. A fire team from another assault helicopter company was called in to take our place. The wooded areas were saturated by our lead. More slicks arrived and successfully airlifted the crews out of the LZ. So far, we had lost five slicks, all burning brightly on the ground. Upon our relief's arrival, we left the area.

When we landed the ship, the A/C kept the rotor blades at idle speed. Hawk took a hose from the fuel bladder to refuel the ship while I checked for obvious bullet holes around the ship. There were a few in the tail boom and engine cowling. Until we shut down the extent of damage could not be completely ascertained. We got back in and hovered over to the ammo site. The peter-pilot, Hawk, and I quickly reloaded the rockets, mini-gun ammo trays, and our boxes of ammo. The A/C remained seated inside and in control of the ship, again at idle speed, monitoring the radio and keeping informed about the LZ and mission. When we had finished and climbed aboard, the rotor RPM increased and we began to lift off.

With the extra weight of all the ammo and fuel combined with the heat of the mid-day, the ship vibrated violently as we began to take off. He aborted and landed the ship, shutting her down not twenty feet from where we started. Hawk and I jumped out and worked to release each pilot from their armored chair as the rotating blades slowed.

When the blades stopped the A/C and Hawk climbed up to inspect the rotor head for damage, while the peter-pilot and me checked elsewhere on the ship for damage. I opened the tail boom cowling. The tail rotor shaft was intact and undamaged. Instrument caution lights did not indicate any engine problem. Looking up, I saw massive bullet damage to the rotor head dampeners, push-pull rods (one nearly severed), and blades. Hawk had to Red-X[43] his ship. We're lucky not to have crashed at the LZ. I climbed up top and inspected the extensive damage to the rotor head. We were definitely out of the mission.

A slick picked us up as Hawk's ship was scheduled to be airlifted back to base. We spent the night at Cu Chi and were able to compare notes. Out of fifteen helicopters, thirteen had been hit, damaged or destroyed. A few remained on the ground at the LZ, unable to fly. Airlifting

---

[43] When the aircraft is deemed not airworthy, the mechanical symbol is a red "X", also to be entered on the ships daily log. To remove the red X, the problem must be corrected and a technical (tech) inspector must sign off on the repair(s) made. Unless that is done, the ship must not be flown.

those ships out by *Shit-hook*[44] was deemed too dangerous. Command decided to call in F-4s[45] to destroy those ships at the LZ.

Word circulated fast among us. We had landed in the middle of an NVA regiment. The LZ was no longer accessible due to the vast presence of the enemy. As our crews left their ships in the LZ earlier, they grabbed what they could considering the circumstances; the pilots their maps, records and such; the crew chiefs and gunners removed M-60s and as much of anything else from the ship. The grunts had formed a perimeter the best they could while the crew stripped their ships. Allowing the ship radios, avionics, and any other gear left behind from getting in the hands of the enemy was not going to happen. They quickly loaded onto slicks that hovered nearby to pick them up. Although a few grunts were wounded, we lost no one and had only a few in our company wounded. It was a miracle none of us got killed.

Hawk's ship was shit-hooked back to Tay Ninh for repair. We spent the next day in our company area back at Tay Ninh, licking our wounds. Beyond the slicks destroyed, we were informed many more ships had serious damage from bullets and shrapnel from RPGs[46] and required major repair. The crews from the day before were gathered together. Brigadier General George P. Seneff, the commanding officer of the 1st Aviation Brigade, arrived at Tay Ninh with his entourage. We had been gathered for an awards ceremony. On this day, it was very cloudy, almost a deep foreboding gray.

While we were in company formation, a number of us were called out and stood shoulder to shoulder in a long, straight line. Still at attention, we were told the gallantry and heroism displayed during the mission of the previous day was unprecedented by any aviation company in the Brigade. The General, walking from one soldier to the other, pinned onto each chest the medal(s) earned: five Silver Stars, twenty-three Distinguished Flying Crosses. A few men received the Air Medal with a "V" for Valor.

---

[44] Chinooks, or Boeing CH-47 twin-engine, tandem rotor heavy-lift helicopters with the capability to airlift a UH-1 Huêy.
[45] Phantom Jets operated by the Air Force based at Bien Hoa.
[46] Rocket Propelled Grenades

I was 19 years old, not old enough to vote or drink alcoholic beverages in the States. But there I was in Vietnam, with a DFC pinned to the left pocket of my well-worn and faded jungle fatigue shirt.

Chapter 5

Pacification

Dick Brauher and I got along very well, and worked together as a team extraordinaire. When the opportunity opened, since our ship was in the shop for repair, we both decided to go to Japan for R & R.

Once in Japan, we were offered various destinations within the country to go. For no particular reason, we chose Atami, located in Shizuoka Prefecture, a coastal resort and favorite vacation spot for Tokyoites. We got two rooms next to each other at the hotel and then pursued our own sightseeing interests in town, usually meeting for breakfast in the hotel restaurant the following morning. Local women were very receptive to American men, and both of us took advantage in our own way.

During the middle of our five-day vacation, I ate lunch alone at my table in the hotel restaurant. There were two other tables used, both by Japanese couples, for lunch. The room was dimly illuminated. Only the light from the windows facing the street filtered inside. The restaurant seemed to me to be very reserved, very proper in etiquette. People at the others tables spoke softly. I began to understand the polite and gentile nature of the Japanese, respectful of others, not wanting to offend. But, my peaceful reflections were rudely interrupted by loud voices coming from the hallway, just outside of the restaurant doors, near the elevator.

Entering the restaurant, still speaking loudly among themselves, I realized the group of about twenty were speaking English. They were older, middle-aged Americans, wearing gaudy clothing: brightly colored, Bermuda shorts on fat men; flowery low-cut blouses on the women, showing off the faux pearl necklaces nestled nicely in their ample cleavage; and oversized bags and purses filled with more than one could possibly need on a trip. I couldn't help but think of them as ugly Americans. I saw them not as compatriots, but as strangers. I ignored them the best I could.

To this day, I remember thinking how embarrassed I was. Behaving as if the world was at their footstep, as if the room belonged to them. It seemed to me that they had no regard for the other people in the dining room. The contrast between them and the quiet mannerisms of the Japanese was stark. I finished my meal and left.

The following evening, I was walking along the sidewalk a few blocks from the hotel when a Japanese man, about thirty and with a scruffy three-day-old beard, approached me. He asked, in fairly good English, if I would be interested in speaking to his students who were learning English. For the first time in my life, I didn't think I could trust a civilian, especially this man. Yes, he was wearing a white shirt and tie loosened at the collar, gray trousers and shined shoes. But his true motive? I wasn't sure. I politely declined. He offered again, sweetening the deal with a dinner. No, thanks. But, I offered to walk him to my hotel lobby to see if any Americans there would be interested. He agreed, so we walked back.

In the lobby were three guys also on R & R. The man made his pitch and two of the three took him up on his offer. Away they went. The next morning Dick and I saw those two guys in the restaurant. I asked them how it went, and they told me how much they enjoyed themselves. The Japanese man taught English in high school. He had them speak candidly and casually in English in front of the class with the teacher making a few comments to the students in their native language, explaining or emphasizing one point or another. Their experience was a resounding success. Before the evening was over, the class hosted a small traditional Japanese dinner, complete with sake.

For most of the five days, Dick went one way and I went another. We did share dinner one night, seated on cushions surrounding a four-foot by four-foot table no more than eighteen inches off the floor. The communal food was placed in the middle for all to share.

On the last day of our R & R, Dick and I were approached by a swarthy-looking man who wanted to set us up with his "escorts." We politely refused, and told him that we were leaving that afternoon. But he didn't believe us. Apparently, in his line of work, he got that kind of excuse all the time. We couldn't get rid of this guy, so finally we told him to have the girls meet us at our rooms at eight o'clock. He wanted a downpayment of half the overall cost up front, but that was not going to happen and we told him so. We parted ways, and Dick and I promptly left the hotel. We had a good laugh at that guy's expense on the way back to the airport.

When we returned from R & R, reality hit. The war didn't stop and people were still being moved around. The last of my good friends from Fort Bragg, Don, had been transferred to the 188th Assault Helicopter Company at Dau Tieng. As with Tom and Babe, I didn't get a chance to him bid farewell.

It was a week later that word about Dau Tieng came to our attention. The 188th company area and the airfield were directly across the road from a known VC-controlled village, and therefore off limits to the Americans stationed there. We heard the 188th had been attacked by VC at night, beginning with a mortar barrage and ending with a ground assault. *Oh, shit*, I thought, *Don's there*. I did everything I could think of to find out if he got hurt. Eventually, I learned they had no fatalities. And, he apparently had not been seriously wounded, if at all. Information about the attack and losses trickled back to us.

Numerous Hueys were destroyed during the attack. Mini-guns were used by the Americans at the perimeter to fight off the invaders. The next day, their company commander was relieved of duty. No news is good news, as they say. For the first few days after the ground attack, we learned of no injuries sustained by any of the former 187th guys were transferred there. As the days wore on, no further information was provided and soon, that incident faded into history as we kept busy with our own missions.

Dick and I continued flying missions as soon as we got back, seemingly never-ending hours of flight time. The routine was replayed day after day. The days of the week blended together, but we always knew the calendar date for our paperwork. I often wondered whether the mission of the day would last a few hours, or into the night. Would the LZ be hot or cold? Sometimes we knew in advance, sometimes we didn't. It all depended on if the A/C told us or not. Sometimes we would be told the Vietnamese name, or the hill number, of the mission's location, which meant virtually nothing to us. We didn't have a map of the area, only the pilots did. It wasn't as if we could go to the PX and get a Rand-McNally map. But, soon enough, various names, locations, and landmarks became increasingly familiar.

On August 30, ten slicks made three trips into a hot LZ. We were told where, but as usual the name was forgotten by the time we got airborne. The pilots, keepers of the map, knew we were going to Phu Hoa, a village east of Cu Chi. Like all the others, this one was located in the middle of nowhere.

It began like any other mission. The grunts were taking fire from multiple locations in the bush[47], three of the four sides of the LZ, as soon as the slicks dropped them off. As the firefight continued, our fire teams went in search of the VC. Contrary to standard operating procedures, we flew slowly at treetop level in order to flush out the enemy. It was nerve-racking to concentrate your eyesight into the trees and ground, looking for any hint of enemy activity. Focus on the ground, refocus when looking up to check for other aircraft, then do it again and again.

Smoke grenade at the ready, any visuals of VC activity would be answered with red smoke to mark the spot. We found a few men hiding in tree limbs, a few more hiding in bushes and tall grass. As we drew their fire away from the slicks and grunts on the ground, Dick and I peppered the enemy locations.

Crews of gunships did not take prisoners. We killed or maimed the enemy, unless the command orders stated otherwise. We did a lot of killing and maiming that day. When the mission was over, most of our slick and gunship aircraft had been damaged. Only one of our men was wounded. We stopped counting enemy casualties after the VC KIA number reached twelve. Most of their wounded were taken away by their comrades, but our grunts captured a few.

Here's the frustrating thing. It was usually noisy inside the ship while flying. The flight helmets helped reduce the high-pitch whine of the jet engine just behind the bulkhead, wind rushing past the open cargo doors into the cabin, and the roar of the rotor blades spinning just six feet or so above us. These helmets, with the cushion-style all-encompassing ear protectors inside, were pretty much all we used. Some guys (though very few actually) also wore earplugs. The more protection for your ears, the more difficult it was to hear the radio or bullets striking the ship.

---

[47] A term used by GIs to describe heavy vegetation. The Military Occupational Specialty (MOS) for infantry was 11B, Eleven Bravo, or Eleven Bush.

During a mission, additional noise comes from many different sources. Radio transmissions blast instructions and/or reports from three different frequencies, let alone crew-generated communication via the ship intercom. Then, too, when weapons are being fired from the gunship, the noise increases dramatically. When I'm shooting 500-700 rounds a minute from my M-60, it is nearly impossible to hear a single bullet fired by the enemy hitting the ship. We learned firsthand that adrenaline peaks during moments of danger, and to expect it to happen. One physiological result is the suppression of some noises, and the amplification of others. So, knowing the enemy is there because you were shot at was not that common. Unless, of course, Charlie was actually seen.

To make matters worse, the VC were famous for hiding beneath small, expertly camouflaged lids, leading to small bunkers or a tunnel entrance. Keep in mind when a well-concealed sniper is aiming a rifle at you, for example, all you are apt to see is the front end of that weapon. The image may be no larger than 3 inches wide by 4 inches high. It would be devoid of any shiny metal that could have helped it being spotted while flying by at 300 yards. If we saw people on the ground, were they friendlies or not?

We couldn't always see the enemy, we couldn't always hear the enemy, and we were not really sure if the enemy was even there or not. If we were lucky, we'd see the *star*, the very bright star-shaped pattern of exhaust gasses, muzzle blast, when the bullet leaves the barrel.

So, this particular mission on August 30 the grunts searched the area and found numerous dead bodies and their weapons. They attributed us with silencing numerous enemy positions. From our point of view, seeing the enemy was extremely difficult as they were hidden everywhere possible. It was only luck and suppressive fire that saved the day. The pilot's vision of the ground is limited to their front and partial sides. They were strapped in tight, inside bullet-resistant sliding panels on the out-board side of their protective seats that restricted head movement to the side. They could not see the ground directly below, or behind. The value of door gunners on each side provided the necessary observation.

Also, flexibility of fixed weapons was limited. Rocket pods could only be aimed by positioning the aircraft straight to the target. The mini-guns and grenade launchers had a degree of flexibility, but more to the front and forward sides of the ship. It was up to the gunners to take care of the sides and rear.

There were times when we could not return fire. In a *pacification zone*, for example, if we saw the guy shooting at us with his AK-47 or RPG, we'd have to call it in first before we could shoot back. While we waited for clearance, we'd increase our altitude to get out of range, but still close enough to keep an eye on the bad guy. From experience, we knew it could take up to twenty minutes to get an answer from headquarters. This was the order, and to break it would mean court martial.

Why get clearance to shoot back, you might ask, instead of just returning fire? Some areas were politically sensitive. Pacified areas had become a key strategy. By driving out the VC, we could allow the South Vietnamese people to live their life in as much peace as possible. I wasn't involved in this on the ground, and really didn't know how successful it might have been. But, in some areas the VC were able to return, intimidating the locals to cooperate by threats of harm or kidnapping. Even so, the reasoning behind holding fire in these pacified areas was that as long as nobody got hurt, our command (and their bosses) did not want any fatalities, on either side. Maybe it was back-room deals and political promises that had to be kept, and we were unknowingly part of the deal.

As a crew chief of a gunship, though, I knew nothing about the backroom deals, plans, and strategies of the higher-ups. I'm sure our military had deals with politicians, or at least had deals among themselves to ensure the illusion of success for political and/or career enhancement. Political favors are as common as mosquitoes in a swamp. After all, what the military wants (e.g. additional troops, supplies and munitions, and approval for a larger military budget) the politicians had to approve. And what's in it for them?

On a sunny morning days later, we escorted a flight of five slicks into a cold LZ. Each slick had roughly seven or eight grunts. After they were inserted the slicks left the AO, but one fire team of gunships remained, us. We stayed at their request to provide cover and protection for the guys on the ground as needed. The grunts split into two equal groups to flush out suspected VC from hideaways within the moderately vegetated, but expansive AO. I was listening to the ADF through the headphones inside my flight helmet, enjoying the day at work, while scanning the terrain for Charlie.

The sky was clear. The sun was warm. We were not getting shot at, nor were the grunts. It had all the makings of another boring mission. Keep an eye out for any other ship in the sky. Scan the trees and underbrush for hidden VC. I looked over the M-60 resting on my knees, supported by the single bungee cord, adjusted perfectly so that the free-weight of twenty-five pounds or so felt more like a pound. I admired the modification of the gun. The original butt-plate had been switched to one made by the sheet-metal shop. It was a small, rectangular box opened at one end that fit snuggly inside the armpit, much better than the bulky one the factory provided. The bi-pods had been removed from the end of the barrel to reduce air drag to enhance maneuverability in shooting and to lessen the weight of the front-end.

I felt very comfortable with the gun on my lap. The belt of ammo from the box, draped over my left knee, was checked routinely for misalignment and to make sure each round was properly seated into each link. If not, just one out-of-alignment round could jam the gun when fed during firing. That was what you did when flying around all day. Make sure you're ready for anything. Pay attention to detail. Count the days before going home.

In an instant, my daydreaming ended. The ground commander's FM broadcast indicated they had found and captured a few VC, but one escaped. Of course, at the time we were orbiting the AO of the other group. We were asked to divert from our present location and assist in their search for him. From a distance of perhaps a half mile away, it didn't take us long to get there. When we arrived to the last known location, we immediately saw the dark auburn trail of muddy water, in contrast to the pale brown translucence of the rice paddy. It was the type of trail one would leave if running through a foot or more of water over a muddy base. The A/C radioed our findings to the ground commander. This trail could not be easily seen from the ground, so it was no surprise that the grunts asked for our help to track down the escapee.

Hovering about a hundred feet high, we followed the muddy-water trail to where it ended abruptly in a thicket of reeds. It was about seventy-five yards away. I saw the scantily clad young man crouching low beneath the surface of the water. He was breathing through a reed. His face was skyward. He had no weapon. We were almost directly over him. My orders were to fire a few rounds to make a circle around this guy. We wanted to encourage him to stand up and surrender, rather than be shot and killed. I did as I was instructed by keeping the circular pattern of bullets hitting the water at least two feet away from him. It worked. He stood up, dropped the reed and raised his hands in surrender. Within minutes, the grunts arrived and took him into custody again. Our brief mini-mission accomplished, they gave us the okay to return to where we were before to support the other group.

It wasn't quite fifteen minutes later when we got another call for assistance from the same guys as before. The same prisoner had escaped again. Could we help out and search the area for him? Well, of course. This time, the escapee did not travel via rice paddy. I guess he learned his lesson the first time. There was no trail to follow. We only knew the direction he took when he escaped from his captors, and we began our search.

Not too far away we found a man prone on his back atop of rice paddy dike. His clothing suggested this was the same guy as before. His arms and legs were positioned in such a manner that it would appear he was dead. He did not twitch a muscle as we hovered over him from about thirty feet up.

The A/C asked, "Alex, can you see any blood?"

There was no evidence that the guy had been shot. "No," I said.

"Does it look like he's dead?"

I keyed my mic-button again. "Hard to tell, Sir."

Still hovering over the body, a minute passed. The A/C said, "Put a round in his leg. See if he flinches."

We were not more than fifty feet away. I couldn't miss if I tried. I let go with a short burst. One round hit the inside of his left thigh.[48] Reflexively, both of the man's hands went immediately to the site of the wound. He was not dead, but now he was wounded and not going anywhere on his own. The wave of crimson red from his leg grew. A few

---

[48] This was the second unarmed man I shot in Vietnam. With this one, I felt no remorse whatsoever. Many CAs had occurred since that first kill, with some body counts to my credit. Killing became easier.

grunts arrived, administered first aid, and remained with him while a Dust-Off[49] was called to get him out for medical attention and interrogation.

The Dust-Off left. We did, too, to refuel nearby. About forty minutes later, we were back and continued to provide close air support. I lit a cigarette and prepared myself for another hour or two of boredom.

Days passed. One day was much like the day before. We were on duty twenty-fours a day, seven days a week, three hundred sixty-five days a year. I thought less and less about home. I'd get the occasional mail from home. Mom would write, or rather type, a few letters to me. Barb kept writing on a regular basis. Every time her envelope was handed to me by the mail clerk, like a bloodhound I'd try to detect the scent of perfume. And, every once in a while, her envelope did have a pleasant smell to it. But, was it perfume? Was it from contact with other envelopes that were perfumed? Or, was it just the clean smell from back in the world, from Barb's home where she lived with her family.

A few more days passed. After a grueling combat assault at a hot LZ, we returned to Cu Chi to rearm and refuel. Two other gunships arrived at the same time so we waited. When it was our turn, we went to the ammo dump first, reloaded our rocket pods, 40mm grenade box, topped off our wooden ammo boxes, and got more smoke grenades. Then, we hovered over to the fuel bladders. The fuel bladder reminded me of a fat octopus on the ground, large and round with long arms. This octopus only had six arms, though, so maybe it was more like a bloated cockroach.

With our ammo fully loaded and fuel topped off, we lifted off. The A/C pulled pitch, lifting the collective stick. We were about six to ten inches off the ground when he moved the cyclic stick to the right. We moved a few feet. Then, a bump. The right skid struck a rut in the ground. Tire tracks in the hard, dried mud caused the ruts to be deeper and higher than usual. The ship tilted slightly to the right. The A/C corrected by moving his stick to the left. It was too much. We began to tilt to the left. He corrected that by moving the stick to the right, hard. Again, too much and too late.

---

[49] A Dust-Off is a UH-1 helicopter used exclusively for medical evacuation.

The ship was tilted to the right and forward slightly when one of the two honeycombed wide blades first struck the ground. I watched as it broke upon impact, splintering into small and large chunks of material flying off in all directions. The abrupt stoppage and the torque caused the ship to roll to the right. My gunner and I walked through the roll—very casually, I might add—inside the ship until it stopped, resting on its top, belly up. We got out of the ship to release our pilots, still strapped in, from their armored seats. I found the door handle awkward to open, upside-down, but we got them out.

Fuel was squirting up from the belly fuel valve. Our ship, full of JP-4 and ordnance, would become a devastating explosion if it caught fire. We cleared people away. Five minutes passed. Nothing happened. Our ship simply died right there. The main rotor mast was bent and the rotor head broken. The blades were broken. The tail boom seemed okay. But, this ship wasn't going anywhere soon except for major repair, if possible. Otherwise it was good for parts. Grabbing our gear, we left that ship for the last time and headed home, courtesy of one of the slicks.

I filled in here and there as a crew chief since my ship was red-Xed. My responsibility for that aircraft ended when it went to 3rd and 4th echelon maintenance for repair. The guys in the maintenance platoon, civilian technicians, and other specialties would decide if it could become airworthy once again.

I never found out. My days were numbered, unknown to me at the time. As with Babe, Tom and Don, I was being transferred to another unit with a few other originals from the 187th at the beginning of September 1967. I had been with the company for a year and was one of the originals. But many of my friends had gone and my ship was down, so leaving the unit at that time was not so hard.[50]

---

[50] While assigned to the 187th AHC, we had participated in two campaigns: Vietnam Counteroffensive, Phase II and III. Our company had earned the Vietnamese Cross of Gallantry with Palm (Unit award) and the Meritorious Unit Award.

Chapter 6

Bien Hoa

Without so much as a formal sendoff, a few of us were transferred to the 190th Assault Helicopter Company in Bien Hoa (pronounced: *Ben Wah*). We quickly became aware of the fact that this company was relatively new in country. Our billets were newly built two-story barracks. We had a concrete-block shower and latrine with porcelain fixtures. Gone were the sand bags and tents. Compared to Tay Ninh, the base at Bien Hoa was like a resort town, and the company area fit the surroundings. The U.S. Air Force was at the other side, Tan Son Nhut Air Base, which was also used by the Republic of Vietnam Air Force.

Here, town was accessible to the GIs, no pass required. Guys could go into town wearing jungle fatigues or civilian clothes; it didn't seem to matter. Weapons were not worn here. Most of the people had their M-16 rifle locked up in their company arms room. Military police guarded the front gate separating the base from town, a distance of the width of a two-lane, hard-packed dirt road.

Processing into the company, I had put $600 into the orderly room safe. This seemed like a lot of money, and it was. We were paid in cash on a monthly basis. Except for going to Japan on R & R, I had no place to spend it while I was with the 187th. I delivered my 201-file[51], flight and medical/dental records by hand. Being a six-month in-country veteran of a gunship, I was assigned to the gun platoon, called the Gladiators. The platoon sergeant was Staff Sergeant Tom Emerick.

The ship I was assigned to had mini-guns and two pods holding seven rockets each. The mini-gun ammo trays could hold about 6,000 rounds. Crewing this UH-1C was the same except for the mini-guns. I wouldn't have any problem getting used to that, though, and it would be nice to fly as a lead ship once in a while.

A few pilots from the 187th were infused into the 190th as well. Because of that, it was a smooth transition to fly missions with my new unit. My new gunner was an original with the 190th and had some CA flight

---

[51] A written record of assignments, dates of important events, awards and training, etc.

time under his belt already. It was just a matter of learning how to work with each other, and it went well.

I heard one of our slick pilots from the 187th, Captain Billie Presson, was killed while in an LZ from a bullet wound to his head. He had been an A/C of a slick and well respected among his peers, but I knew him only by reputation. The slick was on the ground, just for a minute or two, enough time for the grunts to jump off. During that time, a well-trained sniper to took aim and fired. It was all over that quickly.

Snipers were a continuing problem for both grunts and helicopter crews. During one mission, early on at Bien Hoa, we were helping a company of grunts that were taking fire from what they deemed to be a sniper, maybe two or more. Concentrating our search efforts to where Charlie was reckoned to be hiding, we did not find them. We had no specific area to lay suppressive fire, as the AO was too large. Keeping in mind that a sniper is trained to be well camouflaged and to shoot very carefully and accurately, it came as no surprise that sniper(s) remained invisible to us. After all, part of their mission is not to be found.

As we flew past one specific area, the sniper took a shot at our wingman (the second gunship) striking the back side of the helicopter. The grunts heard the shot as they were moving forward, stealthily searching for the sniper's whereabouts. The sniper fired again. Was this a second one? A firefight on the ground began targeting the sniper, who in turn fired back at them one bullet at a time. Soon, one sniper was killed, and two Americans were KIA during the process. They were still taking fire and needed every man to move forward. Time was of the essence. They would not leave the KIAs behind unattended, and could not spare one or two guys to stay with them until picked up by a slick. The company had to move, and move now.

The A/C told me to make room on the floor in the back, but for some reason, I didn't hear the FM radio communication from the field. My gunner and I moved our spare M-60 barrels and ammo boxes, placing them on top the mini-gun ammo trays. We were on final approach to land in the AO near the place where the two KIAs were. This was *highly* unusual for us; we never picked up our dead compatriots in the heat of battle. That was the slick's job. But that day we did.

We landed just long enough to take the KIAs aboard. We remained at full RPM. Having a fully armed gunship on the ground in hostile territory meant we were a prize target for the VC. We knew we had a large bounty on our heads. Our ships and crews were not invincible; just ask Cpt. Presson. For the moment, I felt what it was like for the crews of slicks, and I didn't like it at all. I wasn't scared, but very, very alert.

One KIA was slid, very carefully and face up, onto the floor space in my ship. By the actions of those who carried him, I knew this dead man was well regarded and one of their own.

His brown eyes were wide open. His head was on my side of the ship, facing up. I looked at him. He was the first dead person I had ever seen close-up. As we lifted off en route to the base, I couldn't be sure if he was really dead. I didn't see any blood on his skin or clothing. He didn't blink, just stared straight up. Should I touch him? Should I slide my hand over his eyes to close them? What if he wasn't really dead? What would I do if he twitched? Was I confident enough to render first aid if he was still alive? Hell, maybe he really is dead. The guys in his company told us he was. I really didn't want to touch a dead guy to find out for myself.

As we pulled pitch and left, my mind drifted a bit as I wondered where this guy was from. Here was a man, alive just hours before, now dead and within arm's reach from me. His family had no idea what was about to occur to them during the next few days. At that very minute, they were probably living their normal routine: working, shopping, visiting friends and relatives, having fun, laughing, joking, or eating dinner. I didn't know what day of the week it was, but maybe they were in church.

I tried to imagine what happened to him, and what was about to happen to this guy once we got to our destination. Would he be put into a body bag? Maybe he would be put into a morgue and kept cool until it was time for him to leave country. What about his Purple Heart? Who gets that? His wife? His parents? Did he die a heroic death? Would he receive a Bronze Star for valor? Maybe a Silver Star? Was it possible he did something really heroic and would get the Congressional Medal of Honor, posthumously? And there he was, on my floor staring up.

As we flew back to base, I forced myself to steal a glance at him every so often. I did see his nametag on his well-used, weathered and almost worn-out faded jungle fatigue shirt, but my eyes couldn't read his name. Very strange, I thought. Seeing each letter, I could not make them into a word, a name. It was as if his soul could not accept his demise and by preventing the name being said, his death would be delayed somehow. But, yet, there he was, motionless. He was a black man in his early twenties, dark complexion, very short black hair, and had a clean-shaven round face. He seemed to be stocky in build, but difficult for me to guess his weight. His head was about eight inches away from the edge of the door on my side, and it appeared his scruffy jungle boots were about the same distance to the other edge at my gunner's side. That would make him about five-foot-ten.

The flight back seemed quick enough. Where we went, how he was removed from my ship and by whom, and what we did afterwards, I cannot recall. It seemed that time stood still that afternoon during the flight back. Did we resume the mission where we left off? Or, did we go back to Bien Hoa? It felt like a fog at the time, and does now too.

Warfare in 'Nam was not constant. For us it was like waking up in the morning to go to work. Wash up, shave, comb your hair, brush your teeth, select a well-pressed and starched set of fatigues from your wall-locker to put on. Check your boots, if needed put on a quick coat of shoe polish to make them shiny and black. Go to breakfast. Check your watch. Was there enough time to wait for breakfast to be served at the mess hall, or just enough time to gulp a cup of coffee drowned in milk to cool it off? We didn't have paper cups to take the coffee with us. Styrofoam cups didn't exist. Gulp and go, or not; the choice was yours to make if you were running late.

In the fall of 1967, it seemed I flew on missions at least every other day at a minimum. Our platoon was kept so busy that making the morning formation was rare. We never had work details assigned by the first sergeant. It seemed so *Mickey Mouse*[52] to have to play Army with all the trimmings: inspections, detail assignments, standing at attention or "at ease" for what seemed indefinite periods of time. Most importantly, I preferred to avoid the chance of being assigned a detail. As a Spec Five, I would be responsible to make sure the detail was completed correctly.

---

[52] A term we used to describe petty-assed crap. An example would be during an inspection; the NCO or officer might find a loose threat on your uniform and chastise you for that mistake. From a military point-of-view it was to encourage fine attention to detail; but, from a troops' point of view it was ridiculous.

But, then, half of us were Spec Fives, anyway. You never knew who your platoon sergeant would pick. I looked forward to having an early flight mission. Avoid the company formation at all cost.

On any given day, we'd work on the ship to complete whatever maintenance inspection was required. Or, we'd fly off on a mission, almost never knowing how long it would take until we were released and returned to base. We also never knew how bad it might get, or if we'd return dead or alive. It was this daily uncertainty that was most annoying, so I learned not to give it much thought. I thought about A-Jay and the 187th when he wanted to be left alone to think, or get high. Did he think about dying, that maybe that day could be his last? He wasn't new in country like many of us were. He'd seen as much combat as we were about to. Assigned to a gunship, every mission had the potential of being the last mission. Now, months later I understood why he wanted to be alone to think; to either consider or forget about one's imminent mortality and/or getting stoned and putting your fears to rest. Being dead was so close at hand.

Here, at Bien Hoa, getting high by smoking grass[53] was an open secret. Not many did, and getting caught with as little as a seed or stem was enough to get you six months in jail. More and more I heard of guys who wanted to be alone in their "thoughts." It seemed so innocent putting it that way. *Yeah, Sarge, I'll catch up to you in a minute. I just need a few minutes alone to think—about dying today for no good fucking reason. (Pass the doobie.)*

From my point of view my daily hopes and dreams centered around getting back in time for chow, hoping there was mail waiting for me, and maybe have a beer and catch a movie. If none of these, then maybe I needed to write a letter. After all, postage was free going out. The requirements were to put your name, rank and serial number, unit with APO[54] SF (San Francisco) number for the return address. Mail coming to us needed a stamp, but at domestic rates.

Life at this base was very close to stateside duty, except we were in a combat zone and received combat pay. As far as I knew, every GI in Vietnam received combat pay because we were in a combat zone. It wasn't

---

[53] A reference to marijuana.
[54] Army Post Office

predicated on actually being in combat. It didn't seem fair. There was no difference in money if you actually engaged with the enemy, or if you stayed in an air-conditioned office somewhere pushing papers from one side of the desk to another. To me, combat pay should be reserved for those who actually earn it, not by those who receive it by default. We risked our life and limb on a daily basis while the REMF[55] didn't risk a damn thing except being bitten by a mosquito and contracting malaria.

The word got around that another of our pilots from the 187th died. On October 11, Captain Ellis Bailey was the A/C of a slick that had somehow crashed into the water. His crew and passengers escaped, but he was caught in his armor-plated seat and drowned. I had not heard of him before and, sadly, his death had no impact on me. I was becoming calloused. My days were filled with kill or be killed. Nothing else mattered anymore. I was getting really good at my job, so were my buddies. It got to the point where we didn't give a shit about anything or anybody outside of our own personal AO.

Trouble was brewing in I Corps (pronounced: *eye-core*) near the DMZ[56]. A decision had been made by higher command to split our company up, temporarily, for a few weeks. The slicks were going to Duc Pho and the guns were going to Phu Bai. We left Bien Hoa (in III Corps) during the end of October and expected to return in about 45 days.

It was a cloudy day when we left. The flight of aircraft flew north. As we gained altitude, we ascended through the underside of the dark, cloudy ceiling into brilliant sunlight. At 8,000 feet or more, the heavily vegetated, bomb blasted, pot-marked landmass of Vietnam disappeared beneath the topside of fluffy white clouds. For just the moment the war had also disappeared. Accustomed to my ship being heavily armed, I didn't dwell on the fact of it being a *gunship*. I knew from ground level we were just a few dots-in-the-sky, barely noticeable. But, from where I sat, we were in an open-air cabin, just the four of us fellow crewman, each with our own job to do and honed level of skill forged by numerous hours of close combat. None of us were FNGs[57], and I was proud of that fact. I

---

[55] Rear Echelon Mother 'Effer.'
[56] De-Militarized Zone
[57] Fucking New Guys, inexperienced, new to the unit, not knowing shit from Shinola (shoe polish).

didn't know anything about Phu Bai, but I knew once we got there, we'd kick ass and take names.

We were flying in Heaven. Above us? Nothing but brilliant sunlight and pale blue sky. I felt the smile of God, Himself. I was at peace. Who cared where we were going? We kept the cargo doors open. The wind, cooler than at ground level, felt refreshing. Flying at high altitude, in a loose formation, gave me a sense of pride. We were invincible. Nothing was going to happen to any of us, I just knew it.

At Phu Bai, it was back to grubby living standards after the relative luxury of Bien Hoa. In many ways, it was worse than Tay Ninh. We lived in a tent with a sandy floor, slept on cots, and used our steel-pot helmets to hold water to shave and wash up. We were positioned at the perimeter of the base, secluded from other American units but somewhat close to a U.S. Special Forces compound. It became our responsibility to defend this portion of the base perimeter. An old trench, lined with sandbags, near the perimeter wire would be our protection. But nothing ever happened here; all was quiet. We provided support to the Special Forces, U.S. Marines, and ARVNs as needed.

The ARVNs piloted the Sikorsky CH-34s, older Choctaw model helicopters, like they were baby-buggies. I once marveled at their adeptness of jockeying them in position to pick up troops along Highway 1 in Phu Bai. By contrast, American pilots were orderly, safety-minded, and gave wide berth to other ships nearby so as to prevent rotor-blade strikes. One morning, I witnessed an ARVN flight all in a line, nose to tail, with about ten to fifteen feet separated each, except for one. A large space was left, large enough for one CH-34 to fit inside. That space remained for some time while all their ships were kept at idle speed, waiting to leave. From behind us came one of their ships. I always thought of these helicopters as appearing as distorted, oversized grasshoppers. That beast of an aircraft flew over us fast, at a height of maybe a hundred feet, towards their line. With a hard right-pedal, pull-back on the cyclic stick, and push down on the collective stick, it abruptly slowed and eased ever-so-gently into the empty space, taking its place among the others. Amazing. As we sat in our ships close by, we watched the maneuver with awe. It was so contrary to flight protocol we knew so well, and it took us by surprise.

Any other time, any other place, some commander would chew out the pilot flying that bird.

We also worked with the U.S. Marines[58]. Their gunship aerial techniques and battle methodologies were slightly different than ours, being more restrictive while ours was more aggressive. On a few joint missions, the ground forces requested pinpoint close air support from the Marine gunships, as it was essentially their AO. Each time, they had a reason not to oblige. They had to call it in and get approval. They were low on ammo. They weren't allowed to go below a certain altitude. The circumstances required a heavier form of air support, maybe fixed-wing.

On one mission towards the end, the commander on the ground got fed up with excuses, heard time and time again. I heard him transmit on his FM radio, "Forget your ass. Send the goddamn Army here. I know they'll do the job." Frustration, fatigue, and weariness probably got the best of that man. But, my image of Marines being so gung-ho and badass was knocked down a peg or two.

From the Special Forces compound, we were able to gain access to a wide variety of personal weapons. All we needed to do was select what was available and sign it out. I chose a Thompson submachine gun, the kind of machine gun used by gangsters in Chicago. It was heavier than what I expected, weighing slightly more than ten pounds. With it was one 20-round magazine holding .45 caliber ammo. I used it once on a mission and was very disappointed by the painfully slow rate of fire. Definitely not what I remember from the gangster movies I watched when I was younger. I turned it back in a couple days later. Another guy signed out a Browning Automatic Rifle (BAR), and yet another signed out an Uzi.

One evening some of us decided to play poker with a few of the Marines. Of course, passing a bottle of booze from one guy to another, or drinking a few beers was almost a requirement to participate. We gathered in a tent near the flight line and the game was on. One of our guys, Ray, had earlier signed out the Uzi and had it with him. Inside the dimly lit tent, the alcohol started talking. He accused one of the Marines of cheating. Or did the Marine accuse him? It didn't matter much, one way or the other. They went outside to settle things. It was dark except for the reflection of

---

[58] Third Marine Expeditionary Force (MEF), HQ in Da Nang, AO in Phu Bai and Khe Sanh, etc.

110

the light inside the tent and from other living and work areas some distance away near the runway. I, as well as some others, went outside, too, just to make sure things went fair.

For some reason, and after a few nasty and insulting words were exchanged, Ray lifted the Uzi that was hung over his right shoulder by a sling, and a round discharged. He shot his own foot and fell to the ground. The Marines fled like dogs going after a fox. We administered first aid and took Ray to the dispensary. After we dropped him off we never saw Ray again. Word came down that he was hospitalized and shipped to Japan for further medical attention. The incident was never reported to our platoon sergeant or any of the officers, as far as I knew. I believe Ray explained the hole in his foot as an accidental discharge while cleaning the weapon.

We had some down time one day in mid-October 1967. Our platoon sergeant signed out a three-quarter[59] and a jeep and put the word out that he was headed to the third largest city and cultural capital of the country, Huế (pronounced: *Way*). It was once the capital city of Vietnam from 1802 through 1945. Just a few miles away, the city was non-militarized and seemed a safe and interesting destination. Responding to his invite a number of us volunteered to go along. To me, at least, it was a chance to goof off with Sarge's blessing. We didn't know at the time that Huế was sometimes known as an Imperial City, the seat of Dynasty emperors. It had a 19-century Citadel, the first western-style hospital built during 1894, and a large Catholic cathedral. Catholic? Who would've guess that? The Catholic church was a result of the French influence many years earlier.

It was a one-afternoon excursion, but visiting Huế made me realize that there was a community of Roman Catholics in Vietnam. My impression had been that Vietnam was a nation of Buddhists. In III Corps, flying all over the place, I never saw one church, not one Cross, no image of any sort that would suggest even one Christian existed in this country. There was absolutely no reason for me to think otherwise, until I visited the Cathedral in Huế[60]. It was the most beautiful, most out of place building I had seen in Vietnam.

---

[59] M-37 Dodge ¾-ton truck 4 x 4.
[60] From what I heard, the North Vietnamese Army destroyed the church during the Battle of Huế which took

Our visit there was extremely peaceful. I saw no military bases or evidence of contemporary military equipment, except for our jeep and three-quarter. Wide open spaces, buildings untouched by conflict and war.

The A Shau Valley (pronounced: 'A' as in 'at'; shaw), couldn't have been more opposite. This was an extremely remote, narrow 25-mile long north-south valley located in Thua-Thien Province, at the northwest corner of South Vietnam. The area had a bad reputation due to its isolation, heavy concentration of the NVA, and extreme vegetation. Elephant grass carpet the mile-wide bottom. Thick-forested mountains flank the valley on each side, some as high as 5,000 feet. A U.S. Army Special Forces camp was to the south, two miles from Laos. The Ho Chi Minh Trail, an NVA infiltration and resupply route, was just across the border and closely monitored by covert Green Berets. We were given a mission to support their operation. My ship was one of two gunships that went.

Flying through this valley, I could only pray that we didn't crash or be stranded in the mountains on either side. There are ample hiding places for the NVA to take potshots at anything flying within range, oftentimes with deadly accuracy. The legends of that place were well known to us.

The heavy, dark cloud ceiling was low. That day it was threatening to rain and the temperature cooled to around 45 degrees; very cold by Vietnamese standards. It felt as if nature was warning us not to go. Because of the low ceiling, we flew at a lower altitude than what we would have preferred. But, the choice wasn't ours to make. Almost like a consolation prize, the A/C allowed us to close our cargo-bay doors during this flight to help keep us warm. It gave me a sense of protection against the NVA, concealed behind the thin, magnesium-aluminum alloy door, but of course the Huey itself presented a large target to any would-be sniper. It really didn't matter if my door was closed or not.

Thankfully, we arrived unscathed. When we landed atop a knoll adjacent to the camp, there were three guys standing around a fire pit wearing their green berets and Tiger fatigues[61]. With our ships shut down,

---

place from January to March, 1968.Thousands of innocent people were killed by the communists.

[61] Camouflaged fatigues were not generally worn by the U.S. military. The exception was the few who were imbedded with the Vietnamese and Montagnard ground forces, such as the Green Berets and MACV. Tiger fatigues, uniquely Vietnamese, had a distinctive tiger-stripe pattern.

it was oddly quiet. The surroundings were heavy vegetation of three-layer canopy (except for this camp site). It was still very cloudy, but no rain. No birds, no animal sounds. We all gathered at the oversized fire pit, and the pilots spoke with the team commander while the rest of us stood around the fire getting warm.

Ka-BOOM! The sound of a single, loud explosion came from down the hill. We took cover, the eight of us, while the Special Forces guys stood around. From behind one of the logs that had been dragged, some time before, to the campfire for seating, I looked up. The SF guys, still standing around, hadn't moved. Seeing them, and hearing no more explosions, I slowly came out of hiding. The others did the same. They started to laugh, informing us it was one of their own, river fishing in the ravine. He used C-4[62]; it was easier that way. Soon enough the guy from the river came up the hill carrying a line of fish. I didn't know one fish from another, but they were at least a foot long each.

We got a quick lesson on how to clean, fillet, and debone. The fish were cut into squares and placed into the frying pan with potatoes and onions, each cubed to about an inch and a half. I never did figure out what liquid these were frying in. Now, *this* was lunch in the field. In my nineteen years, that was the best lunch I had ever eaten so far.

While in the A Shau Valley, we did not engage any VC or NVA at all. If it wasn't for lunch, the trip would have been a waste, if anybody asked me. But, no one did.

At least two NVA divisions[63] surrounded the base, pinning the Marines down above. By mid to late October we arrived to provide air support. As our fireteam approached, we aligned our flight path to the airstrip. A damaged C-130 airplane that had been pushed off the runway at one end, on the opposite side of the runway from where the Marines were set up.

I couldn't help but notice the intricate complex of trenches and bunkers as we were getting closer to the ground. Marines were positioned everywhere in trenches. Only sandbagged bunker roofs and numerous an-

---

[62] A malleable plastic high explosive having the texture of modeling clay.
[63] Approximately 20,000 troops.

tennae stood above ground level. This place was dreary and well-fortified. The clouds were dark and heavy, with an elevation of maybe fifteen hundred feet above sea level. Barbed wire was strung everywhere. I noticed a few occupied two-man machinegun positions along the perimeter. The surrounding hills were said to be filled with NVA probing the wire at night and lofting in a few artillery or mortar shells day or night.

We landed and made our way to operations. While we were walking there was a fly-by of a C-130 cargo plane along the airstrip. Landing here for these large planes had been temporarily suspended due to the damaged plane and susceptibility to enemy fire. From a height of 500 feet above the landing strip, maybe twenty large crates of supplies were pushed out, each suspended by a large parachute as it floated to earth. Their aim was good. None landed outside of the perimeter wire.

In a way that was out of the ordinary for us, we left our flight helmets in the ship and kept the barrels attached to each of the M-60s. Our steel pots were left at our camp in Phu Bai. It was not unusual for us to fly without bringing along those helmets. We kept our M-16s with us as we were escorted to the inner sanctum of their company area. Soon enough I was walking in trenches dug four feet deep in a zig-zag pattern, lined with sand bags and dark brown weathered steel corrugated panels and repurposed lumber from ammo crates as supports on either side. Squeezing past stationary Marines and having reached our destination, we remained outside the operations bunker. Our pilots went inside to discuss, as I surmised, how and where we could be best be used to help them. Operationally, it didn't seem to me we'd have much of an impact here.

We waited. My eyes were wide with excitement and anticipation, flooded with the sights and sounds of an experience I had never known before. Trench warfare. Red dirt. The enemy just outside the perimeter. Planes not permitted to land because of conditions too dangerous. Grunts everywhere, dirty, tired, and, no doubt, wishing they weren't there. And us, in our relatively clean uniforms and carrying rifles rarely used in combat. I imagined their message to us from the looks I saw from these men: resentment that the Army was there to help the Marines; envy that we would soon leave them at that hilltop outpost; jealous that we were aviators and they were grunts; and maybe self-pity knowing that one, or a few of them, may die in the hours or days that follow. Talk about feeling like a fish out of water. We were definitely out of our comfort zone.

When the pilots emerged from operations, we headed along the trench line toward their mess hall. Hungry and looking forward to some Marine food, I thought we were going to eat. It didn't occur to me their rations may have been limited. We passed the enclave they used as a mess hall and squeezed past the few Marines waiting in line to eat, careful not to get too dirty, as we headed to the flight line instead.

While walking along the trenches, my imagination ran amok. For a fleeting moment, I envisioned myself in an Army trench, somewhere in France during WWI, on a cold and cloudy day. Fifty years later it was same old shit. The weather was just is as God intended! It was, after-all, the monsoon season[64] in northern Vietnam. The type of dark, wet, sloppy, and cold miserable conditions that knows no boundaries, no political sides, no good people, no bad people.

We prepared to leave. As the rotary blades surged past idle speed, I climbed in my ship and strapped in, tightly. The question gnawed at me: why did we come here? Secured once again in my flight helmet, M-60 on my lap and being plugged in to the many communication channels, that question lingered as we lifted off. We were headed back to Phu Bai. Our mission in Khe Sanh came to a close without a shot being fired.

In retrospect, I can only guess that the purpose of our mission was for our senior pilot to personally deliver top secret battle strategy plans to the base commander at Khe Sanh. The hand-to-hand (or voice-to-voice) transfer would negate any likelihood of it falling into enemy hands, especially considering the ominous build-up of enemy forces just outside the perimeter. From my perspective, it was the calm before the storm. Hundreds of Marines and more than a thousand enemy forces would be killed in this immediate area during the ensuing winter months.

Back at Phu Bai, days passed with more routine missions. Though the storm was brewing at Khe Sanh it faded from my mind as our I Corp routine took another turn. Long Range Recon Patrols (LRRPs; pro-

---

[64] October to mid-December.

115

nounced: *lerps*) were used quite extensively in the greater Phu Bai area. These were specially trained guys (about the same number of a squad of infantrymen) who would be secretly inserted into known enemy territory. A method of insertion was to use two or three slicks flying one behind the other at a distance of maybe a quarter mile apart. If the LRRPs were in the first ship, in the best of circumstances it would land quickly and the troops would get out as quick as possible while slick number two flew overhead. Waiting for slick number three to pass, the first one would pull pitch and follow it. From a distance, the noise of the helicopters flying at treetop level seem to be unbroken. Unless observed there was no way to know that one of them had landed for a few seconds. It was a good technique. In the worst of circumstances, the slick wouldn't land, but hover low enough for the LRRPs to rappel down a rope.

The LRRPs were inserted into an area mainly to find and observe the enemy, and report. They could be in the boonies for days or weeks at a time. Aside from ARVNs wearing camouflaged Tiger fatigues, and Americans embedded with the Vietnamese, they were the only other guys I saw wearing camouflaged uniforms and exposed skin on a regular basis. They usually did not wear helmets or berets, but floppy green *boonie-hats*. Stealth was the name of the game for these guys. Move slow, undetected. Wait. Remain silent. Watch. Report. Blend in. Don't get caught. Don't get seen. Don't get killed.

On occasion, we would be called if the LRRP team was in trouble. Sometimes Charlie got too close for comfort, or engaged them in a firefight. If this occurred, they'd called for help. It was essential to get there fast, maybe extract the LRRPs, and hotfoot it out of there. Too many times we'd hear one of them whisper on the (PRC-25) radio their location, or that of Charlie. It was difficult enough to understand what was being transmitted, what with the usual noises inside the ship and other radio traffic. Of course, the quietly whispered transmissions from the guy on the ground could only be understood by concentrating as much as humanly possible above the constant whine of our jet-turbine engine and spinning rotor blades.

To complicate matters, Charlie would often be shooting at the LRRPs, the gunships, or the slick getting into position. We had many of these missions, some during the day, some at night. They were seldom easy. Sometimes the enemy was so close to the guys he couldn't talk for fear of being overheard. He could hear us through his handset, but would respond by clicking the mic button in order for him to remain as quiet as possible. The pilot would ask yes-or-no questions. The guy would answer with one click for 'yes', and two clicks for 'no', or visa-versa; whatever they agreed to.

For me, the inherent danger in this type of mission was working very close to the enemy location. It was dangerous for us, but even more so for the guys on the ground or the crew in the slick. I was safely strapped in, my M-60 ready to engage. My bottom-side protected by a chicken-plate[65] attached with safety-wire beneath my 18-inch x 18-inch metal-framed nylon seat. I wore a zippered flack-jacket and flight helmet. Most importantly, once there, we would fly in an orbital pattern around the extraction point, searching for Charlie on the ground. At least we were moving.

As far as I was concerned, the people in the most danger was the crew of the slick. To extract the LRRP team, they had to hover above them, exposing themselves to enemy fire; sitting ducks as the winch was lowered to the ground and the men were snatched up, one by one, into the safety of their rescuer.

The last point about working up north was the reputation of the Koreans. We rarely, if ever, heard about them down south. We liked to think of *ourselves* as badass with all kinds of military support available to us most of the time. Not even close. Some of the Marines at Phu Bai spoke about the soldiers of the Republic of (South) Korea (ROK) in II Corp, south of them. Now, the ROKs had a well-deserved reputation of being badass. Their AO was from Cam Rahn Bay to Qui Nhon along the coast, mostly. It seemed the Americans in this area were very familiar with them, and stories about them were in abundance. Maybe, in part, it was propaganda to scare the VC and NVA. I heard that the ROKs would capture and interrogate their prisoners without mercy. They used the enemy as practice for their martial arts moves. Supposedly, all ROK troops were Black Belt of some degree in Tae Kwon Do. If Charlie died while in captivity, as well

---

[65] Originally designed to be worn beneath the flak jacket for added protection. Pilots often wore them as designed, but the crewmen in back often did not due to it being heavy and cumbersome.

as those who died in battle, the bodies would be hung on the ROKs' perimeter fence, near the gate, as a warning (or trophy?).

As far as I could tell, none of the other allies in 'Nam came close to being as ruthless, as BADASS, as were the ROKs. Either they hated the Vietnamese with a passion, or hated the fact that they were fighting communist forces in a hot, humid, godforsaken country like Vietnam instead of their own. I'm glad they were on our side. Of our many CA missions, we never worked with the ROKs. They were in II Corp and that was an AO not assigned to us.

Chapter 7

There's No Room for You

It was early November when we returned to Bien Hoa from Phu Bai. My gunner was transferred out. Douglas B. "DB" Meckling, a transferee from the 188th Assault Helicopter Company, arrived to our company and assigned as my gunner. We bonded pretty quickly after I learned from him that he and Don, my buddy from the 187th, were in the same gun platoon.

DB filled me in on what I had heard months before about the 188th. About a week after Don's arrival, their unit was attacked[66] by mortar and small arms fire at the base, primarily in the area where the helicopters were parked. Nearly every helicopter had been damaged, a majority of them beyond repair. During the attack twenty-five Americans were wounded. Mini-guns, removed from damaged gunships, were set-up at strategic locations along the compound perimeter to repel VC ground forces. Don was not wounded and fought heroically to help defend the base. The Hueys, most having recently arrived from the States, for convenience had been parked in a straight line to enhance maintenance, refueling, re-arming, etc. Easy pickings for enemy mortar crews. The firefight lasted most of the night and by morning, the VC were repelled.

Their company commander, Maj. Bobby Wofford, was relieved of duty the next morning for not obeying orders from his commander to disperse the ships at night. The rumor-mill said the battalion commander had strongly suggested to him to disperse the parking arrangements of the ships to prevent just this type of damage. Each helicopter had a value of $250,000, not including after-market add-ons like weapon systems and radios. So, anyone could understand the economic impact of any one ship being destroyed beyond repair, let alone twenty-some.

DB was from Long Beach, California. He had a heavy, dark mustache that I was very envious of. My feeble attempts to grow a mustache did not result in a thick "womb-broom," as we used to call it, but DB's was exquisite. He also had a reel-to-reel tape recorder and a good selection

---

[66] June 24, 1967; about 11:00pm.

of music. Up to that time, my music preferences had been mostly pop and folk music: Mamas and Papas, Elvis Presley, The Beach Boys, Joan Baez, early Beatles, and so on. DB's music was different. He liked Jefferson Airplane, the Rolling Stones, and later Beatles stuff like *Sgt. Pepper's Lonely Hearts Club Band* and played it on his expensive looking reel-to-reel tape recorder quite often. I had never heard music like that before. His music grew on me very quickly.

One of Jefferson Airplane's songs was called "White Rabbit." It was wildly popular among the newer guys just arriving in country, and it was one of DB's favorites as well. At the end of the song were the words, "Be a head." I didn't know what that meant. Was it, "be ahead" as in strive for success? Or "be a head" as in... what? DB explained that people who smoked marijuana would achieve a certain mental mellowness afterwards; a *high*. Because the sensation was felt more in the head, the term "head" became a colloquial term for people who got high. It was one of many songs at the time that slipped positive references to drugs and the mind-expanding culture past the censors.

DB's friendship would not be the same as I had with Tom, Babe or Don. They were more like brothers. I had not been in combat with them: same company, yes; same platoon, yes; same AO, maybe; same CA mission(s), no. But the four of us did cut our teeth in the Army together and palled around daily for not quite ten months. Babe and Tom were loveable risk-takers and sidekicks. Don was more reserved and I think his personality more closely matched mine. Or rather, I tried to match his subtle intelligence, patience, and maturity.

DB was a few inches taller than me, and a few years older at 24. We worked well as a team because our work ethic was very similar. He was not afraid of getting into a firefight with Charlie. For a Californian, he was a down-to-earth kind of guy, very likable. I found DB also liked to be alone, occasionally, just to *think*; just like A-Jay back in the 187th. They were both from California, so maybe there was something in the water. Initially, his smoking grass was not a consideration. I was too naïve. Even though he was drafted into the Army, taken away from the surf-and-turf at Long Beach, his attitude was admirable, never complaining; not once. By all accounts, DB was a very mellow fellow. I liked that about him. As we worked together, day after day, our trust in each other grew. So much so that he saw me as no threat when he first smoked grass in my presence.

By no means was he gung-ho about the Army. He hated formations and BS details, and didn't take kindly to the Mickey Mouse-ness of the military. He stoically put up with poorly organized or executed plans. DB had a sense of sophistication about him, maturity, and deep-thinking.

Though, technically, he worked for me and I outranked him, we had more of a partnership. I did not have to tell him what to do, nor did I find it necessary. In many ways, he was like a mentor to me. I respected him, and it wasn't just because of his full mustache that I wished I had, too. If I had an older brother, it would be him. We were like two peas in a pod, a well-oiled machine, or some other analogy for near perfect team-work and harmony.

DB and I smoked cigarettes; no cigars, no pipes (a lesson I learned from basic training), just cigarettes. A lot of the other guys did too. On this base, they were not free. A pack of twenty cost twenty-five cents. Usually, we each bought a carton of ten packs at the Air Force base exchange (BX) for $2.50. But, one of the guys in our small group got hold of some strange, roll-yer-own, fatter than usual Vietnamese cigarettes. Maybe it was DB, I don't recall. After work and chow, he'd share them with us once in a while; usually at the end of the day when we walked over the Air Force side to see a movie.

They were quite a bit different from American smokes. I don't re-call the brand, or even if they had a brand name. I probably wouldn't have been able to pronounce it anyway. Each cigarette must have been hand-made. They were quite popular because I've seen older Vietnamese men and women in the fields and rice paddies smoke the same type of ciga-rettes. The smoke reminded me of the distinctly sweet and slightly acrid odor of burning leaves at home during late autumn. After a few drags from these cigarettes, a slight numbing sensation takes hold mostly between the ears. Topics of discussion become funnier and laughter is easy. Some-times, at inappropriate times. The war, witnessing death and destruction too often, unable to identify the enemy most of the time, and not knowing if you'd survive the day for a nation that was becoming increasingly hos-tile to us could be wrapped up in a tidy little box and figuratively put away for an hour or two while you enjoyed your cerebral magical mystery ride. But, then again, what do I know?

Each mission we flew was potentially our last. If Charlie wasn't shooting at us, there was always the rare threat of mechanical failure with the ship. The loss of four crewmen at the 187th earlier that year was never forgotten. The cause of that crash had never been determined, but it was sudden and unexpected. Looking at my ship's weapons systems, I couldn't help but be reminded each time that our job was to draw the fire away from the slicks and grunts on the ground. Our job was to be the target. In a way, every mission was a rendezvous with the Angel of Death.

We also knew it could take just one, well-placed shot to knock our ship out of the sky, quickly and efficiently. Our transmission housing held gears that were very fragile to abuse. In school, we learned to be extremely cautious with the transmission. Do *not* hit it with a ball-peen hammer under any circumstance. It could shatter the delicate fit of the gears meshing inside. If a hammer could do that, what damage could a bullet do? If the gears broke, the transmission would freeze immediately. If that happened, the rotor blades would stop abruptly. Without rotating blades, the ship falls to the ground like a rock.

More times than I care to admit, I thought about falling out of the sky and what it would be like. Something could always go wrong. We could have a malfunction with the mechanics of the ship. I worked hard to ensure that didn't happen. Do everything by the book. No shortcuts. In the back of my mind I knew the transmission could freeze, the main rotor blades could break, maybe an explosion inside the cargo area. What would it be like to fall *and* be on fire? Magnesium-aluminum alloy burns very hot, very fast. I had witnessed Hueys burning when I was with the 187th. If seeing that wasn't a motive to make sure nothing went wrong, I don't know what would have been.

I tried not to think about crashing, but the thought crept in from time to time. The rush of wind, constantly pressed against my body and uniform from the front, would stop as our forward airspeed came to a halt. A certain stillness would overcome. The other radio transmissions would fade inside the flight helmet so that the words of the A/C were clearly heard as he transmitted "Mayday, Mayday", quickly adding his call-sign and our location. No one else talking as distant objects on the ground rush up, unrelenting, not slowing down. Spiraling out of control.

Are we too high? How hard will the landing be? Can we make it? How much time do we have left? Will I die? Will any of us die? Will it hurt? Will the ammo explode? What about the JP-4? The self-sealing fuel bladder could take a bullet or two, but what if it tears? My thoughts went back to the moment, months before, when Captain Derosier's ship crashed, killing all aboard. What was going through their minds as they hurled to the ground?

Wake up. No time for daydreaming.

Bien Hoa was a safe space. It had not been hit for approximately five years by the time we arrived from the 187th. People who did not venture away from this base only heard about the war. From a support role, they each did their job. Taking the blue-colored Air Force bus from our side, driven on well-constructed roads, it was difficult for me to remember we were in a combat zone as we travelled to the Air Force side. Our barracks had no sandbagged protection. It was rare to see a bunker except along the base perimeter. It was also rare to see anybody carrying a weapon of any sort. (Remember, they were all locked up.)

The perception of being in a combat zone, I suppose, is an abstract concept—especially for guys close, but not close enough, to somebody trying to kill them. They'd start their day wearing nice, clean, starched fatigues, polished boots; not getting dirty enough to change clothes for the next day. For a few, travelling off base meant a trip into Bien Hoa, to Saigon or Long Binh, rather civilized and safe areas by bush standards. Though neither DB nor I knew of anyone personally, we heard some American GIs were actually married to Vietnamese women, had a family and lived in town off-base. How did they do that, extend their tours time after time? I never found out. I was too busy fighting the war.

Oddly, fighting the war was very much like going to work. We'd go somewhere, shoot and destroy something, fly escort, or whatever the mission was; then, return to base after work. It was almost like the war-for-a-day I used to play when I was much younger—choosing sides, building forts, assembling weaponry, play and going home for dinner—but with live ammunition and a not insignificant chance of death. The dichotomy of war and peace was present in my mind every day. We knew of guys who would be assigned an M-16 when they arrived to the unit, secure it in the arms Conex, and never see it again until he out-processed at the end of his tour, twelve months later. The front gate of our base, being adjacent to the Vietnamese civilian population in town, was guarded by the Army's military police, but people were basically waved through coming and going without being searched or providing ID. If you were an American, it was a free pass to enter, or so it seemed.

Access to town was very limited for DB and me. We were just too busy to go. As a result, we never got the chance to blow off some steam in town. On our base, the Air Force BX during the day was a popular destination. Not so much the enlisted and NCO clubs. At the BX, there was a huge selection of high-end 35mm cameras, reel-to-reel tape recorders, civilian clothing, record albums, etc. From our company area, somewhat near the front gate of the Army side of the base, we could either walk to the BX, or take a bus. I did both from time to time. During the evenings, a few of us went to the Air Force movie building for free entertainment on the silver screen.

When we walked over there, and if the hangar doors were open we could see from a short distance the super-secret, high altitude, black jet-plane used for reconnaissance missions. It might have been the U-2, or something very similar. Even though the mere existence of this plane was often denied by officials, the ground crew had to open the hangar doors every so often. This plane was huge. The wing-span must have been a hundred feet wide, but the fuselage was very narrow.

While our schedule and missions kept us in the war most days, there was little reason for me to go to town anyway. I gave it a lot of thought, actually. Going there for female companionship would be a lot cheaper than going on R & R for a piece of ass. I just had this feeling of foreboding whenever I thought about going there. I couldn't put my finger on it, but it was real. Maybe it was a lack of confidence, or inert danger ready to spring open the very minute I crossed the gate into town. Because town was "safe," we were not permitted to carry weapons with us unless we were there on-duty. How many VC lived in town, anyway?

In true Army fashion, I believe some on-duty "assignments" were created to enable some of the guys to take advantage of the perks found in the town of Bien Hoa or at the base in Long Binh. Ice cream trucks, dental clinics, large restaurants, snack bars, an Olympic size swimming pool, a driving range, college extension classes, and a bowling alley were just some of the luxuries one could find at the Long Binh base. The only time I had an opportunity to go to Long Binh for "pleasure" was when my ship landed there for the pilots to deliver some material. DB and I had about 30 minutes of down time, so we stopped one of the roving ice cream trucks nearby for a little mid-day snack.

On December 7, one of our young pilots, a *wobbly-one* Warrant Officer who had also been with us in the 187th, was killed while inserting ARVNs into a hot LZ near Phu Loi. I had seen WO1 Charlie Wilcox around about both at Tay Ninh and Bien Hoa. I remember him as a very likeable guy, serious when it came to his job of flying, and a young man with a promising future. I heard about him getting hit while we were flying on the same mission. Of course, his name was not broadcast over the radio, nor was his condition revealed. For that moment, he was the Whiskey India Alpha (WIA) who was being flown to the field hospital at Long Binh.

About a week later we went on a mission I'll never forget. Before dawn, DB and I woke up and went over to the mess hall to grab some chow. For me, it was usually a cup of coffee. We jumped onto the three-quarter and headed to the flight line. One crew at a time, we were dropped off at each of our ships. We began our daily routine as we unwrapped the mini-guns and stowed the ponchos into a side compartment of the ship. With flashlight in hand, I completed my own pre-flight inspection. Standing on top of the ship, inspecting the rotor head and push-pull tubes and bearings, I saw the pilots approach our flight line and called out to DB and me that they were on their way.

Our A/C pulled his pre-flight while the pilot came around and gave DB and I a quick briefing about the mission. We prepared to go.

"Gooood Mooorning, Vi-et-naaamm," came the greeting over the armed forces radio network I listened to from my helmet at oh-six-hundred. We heard this guy on the radio just about every morning. He was a DJ in Saigon, an Air Force guy, who seemed happier than we thought he should be. But, we didn't give him much thought. He was pleasant to listen to, and played good music. He was not controversial, except for the fact he was just too happy, and we were not.

Remaining in the revetment[67], I listened to the music. We sat there at idle speed (low RPM for the rotor blades) and waited. I was deep in thought. We didn't talk much as we waited. I'm sure each of us were lost in our own thoughts, or just listening to the chatter on the radio as one A/C was chit-chatting with another A/C elsewhere on the flight line. I kept my eye on the horizon as the sky's darkness transitioned into the increasingly bright predawn hues.

The sun was up. The sky clear and temperature a balmy 80 degrees at oh-six-thirty. We remained in the revetment, at idle speed, waiting patiently as each slick left to hover to its chalk position and wait for the others to fall in line. At the command, the slicks lifted off one-by-one and we followed. A short distance away, the flight, still in formation, landed briefly in the midst of an open field. Segregated squads of infantry each waited to hop into each ship. We orbited the pick-up zone during this process, which didn't take long at all, until the last of the grunts were aboard.

Once airborne, the earth seemed so tranquil. We first travelled along the populated areas of Bien Hoa, then rice paddies. Then over the edge of Saigon and finally to open fields, pockmarked with bomb craters, some large, some small. Sunlight from the morning sun reflected from the water inside each crater, creating brief flashes of light.

Eight slicks in formation were on final approach towards an open field. I adjusted the boom-mic on my flight helmet, making sure it was positioned properly, and lowered the tinted eye-shield from its retracted position for protection from the sun's glare and any debris from ordnance. As each bird landed, we were approaching the LZ along the right flank. Friendlies were on my side of the ship, preventing me from firing any further than 10-15 degrees out from our lower vertical position; and then only if I saw an immediate threat. I had to be mindful of ricochets hitting our guys. Otherwise I'd drop smoke.

---

[67] A protected helicopter parking enclosure in the shape of an "L" designed to prevent shrapnel from damaging the ship or others nearby, depending on the location of the explosion.

The LZ was hot. Almost immediately the flight was taking fire from the right flank, beneath us. Within seconds the grunts jumped out and spread into their protective formations. As each bird become airborne once again, our mini-guns cut into the tree line in front and to the right in long bursts. **BRRRRRR, BRRRRRR, BRRRRRR**. The rockets launched into suspected enemy locations in the bush ahead. **WOOSH, WOOSH, WOOSH**. DB fired his M-60—**tat, tat, tat, tat, tat, tat**—into the heavily wooded area on his side of the ship. We completed the run and made a hard-right bank. The centrifugal force pushed me deeper into my seat. I was looking at nothing but blue sky from outside my door as we were in at least a 60-degree banked position, my side up. The blades sang out their tune: **WOMP, WOMP, WOMP, WOMP**.

"I'm hit, I'm hit. My neck." Our peter-pilot reported on the intercom he was shot.

As I got up to examine and treat his wound, I stole a quick look at DB. **Tat, tat, tat.** Pause. Nothing. Against a backdrop of various green hues, he had stopped shooting. Hunched over his M-60, I witnessed the frantic moves of his left upper arm and elbow moving in desperation. He was struggling. We were directly over enemy positions, shooting at us with everything they had to kill us. He ripped his Nomax flight glove off his right hand and tossed it aside. Time stopped. I weighed my options of what to do first. It seemed I had all the time in the world, yet no time left to decide. It felt as if we had stopped in mid-air, at an angle with DB's side down.

At this point I knew two things: the pilot was wounded, and our starboard side was unprotected. Both spelled trouble.

We had no suppressive fire coming from his side of the ship. The mini-guns could not be used because the peter-pilot was wounded. Rockets were impractical because of our position. I swear, time seemed to literally change. It seemed to take hours between each passing second while we hung in mid-air as an up-close-and-personal floating target for the enemy gunners.

Our ship was vulnerable. Holding the M-60 butt-plate with my left hand and the barrel pointed out, I trusted the bungee cord to hold and moved forward to check the peter-pilot. He had already placed his handkerchief on the wound and it was becoming very red very quickly. My right hand reached out, grabbed his hand and handkerchief, and I saw his direct pressure on the wound as being sufficient for the time being. I looked to my right. DB was still struggling. With these two events occurring simultaneously I had to make a choice, and make it quickly.

As far as I could tell, each was potentially a matter of life and death. Save the pilot's life if his wound was more serious than I perceived, or protect the ship from being shot down. I decided the pilot's wound would have to wait. Being shot down at close range needed to be avoided at all cost. We were about a hundred, hundred and fifty feet off the ground, so essentially, we were too close for comfort.

We took another round into the cabin, striking the ceiling.

I considered each thought in a split second as it arrived, and acted on it a split second later. I cannot explain how the time slowed to a crawl, but it did.

I removed my M-60 from the bungee cord. Carrying linked ammo in my left hand and my weapon in my right, I moved over to DB's side. He was still working to unjam his gun. We exchanged an instantaneous glance of acknowledgment to each other and I saw what I perceived to be fear and desperation in his eyes. Dragging my belt of ammo closer with my left hand, I began firing into the trees. We were about one hundred feet above the treetops, close enough to focus my eyes through the branches and onto the ground. I spotted gooks in khakis running to various areas beneath us, only to be suddenly hidden by vegetation and not emerging from the other side. I saw three to four bright *star bursts*[68] emerging from the ground, and those became my immediate targets.

I fired, frantically spraying bullets as quickly and accurately as possible into as many targets I could find.

After what seemed like minutes, but could only have been frantic seconds, and *still* in our steep bank, DB successfully un-jammed his gun. Both of us fired into the underbrush where enemy positions stood. Two M-60 machine guns firing from the same side of the ship. Devastating.

---

[68] Due to flash suppressors at the muzzle end of a weapon, gasses from a discharged bullet appears to be flash of light. Because of the configuration and looking directly at it, the flash with four to five points appears as a star burst.

As we rolled out of the bank and got out of range, he got close to me and asked (loudly, not using the intercom), "Did you see that quad-fifty down there?"

I said I did, though actually I did not know for sure.[69] I don't know why I gave him that answer.

Something happens during battle. Events occur quickly, sometimes simultaneously. Everything is observed, yet not much is seen. Adrenaline affect the senses in ways that are difficult to explain afterwards. Time seems to stand still, yet we know it really doesn't. Cognitive abilities are either hindered or enhanced. Responses to stimuli rely on training and experience. Memory, both short-term and long-term, have a way of suppressing the horror and acceptance of danger. You might be scared shitless, but never admit that to anyone, not even yourself. Right?

I turned back to the peter-pilot. Lifting his crimson blood-soaked handkerchief from the right side of his neck, the wound seemed serious, but not fatal. The bleeding had stopped. I redressed it with a couple 4 x 4s from the first-aid pouch I tore down from the cabin wall right behind him and applied pressure.

The A/C radioed in the pilot's condition and informed Gladiator Six we were departing the AO, en route to the nearest medical facility. We were safe and his wound was under control. Taking the time to catch my breath while applying direct pressure to his wound, I looked forward and noticed the bullet hole in the windshield, directly in front of him. The round came in through his windshield just above the nose cowling. It had to have happened during the first stage of our gun run, not while we were banking right.

We dropped him off at an area medical facility. Three medics arrived with a stretcher to carry him in, but he declined. The last time I saw him he was walking away with the medics. As we headed back, we learned the NVA had occupied the immediate area of the LZ, hence the heavier weapons.

Back at Bien Hoa, the A/C made his entries in the logbook, grabbed his gear and that of the pilot, and headed towards operations to

---

[69] Somebody credited me with silencing several enemy gun positions.

file his report. DB and I remained to get the ship ready for the next mission. We had taken two rounds in the upper tail boom, one in the cabin ceiling, and one through the windshield. Further inspection revealed the bullet that came in through the front had continued to the bulkhead behind my seat and left a 7.62mm size hole behind where my head would have been. Had I not been bending forward at that time, that same bullet would have killed me. God and my guardian angel were watching over me, for sure.

After we checked the ship, I pulled my daily inspection while DB started cleaning the mini-guns. The rocket tubes were reloaded, the ammo trays were refilled as were our own ammo boxes, and waited our turn for the fuel truck to refuel.

Finished, DB and I returned to the company area at about six o'clock and dropped off our gear, then headed to the mess hall for chow. While we ate, we discussed the events of the day, but not too much, surprisingly. We decided to see a movie afterwards.

Our path to the Air Force side took us over a small shallow in the ground. Two wide, 540 rotor head used blades (the kind on UH-1C ships) had been placed side by side, forming a bridge to walk on. For the number of times we walked on this bridge, not once did we see where either one had been damaged. Of course, our inspections were in passing. We did not look underneath, did not inspect the bearings where the blade attached to the rotor head, and didn't really care. We just came to the conclusion that it was probably the most expensive footbridge in country, considering the value by the inch.

Passing it from one guy to the other, we shared one of those Vietnamese cigarettes as we walked across the large, vacant area separating our side from Tan Son Nhut. When we got to the building where they showed movies, it was already running. I didn't pay much attention to the plot, the name of the film, or the actors involved. Somebody spoke and I began to daydream. Mentally, I was somewhere else, not in Bien Hoa, not in Vietnam. Not anywhere, but everywhere. How close had I come to being killed that day? An inch? We were so close to being shot out of the sky. The ship could have exploded, killing all of us. Or, we could have crashed and been taken prisoner. The events could have ended the day very differently. We denied the Angel of Death his prize.

We learned early on in our tours, don't dwell on death. It could be hazardous to your health. Except for our pilot getting wounded, no one else got hurt. I was just glad to put the day to rest.

Here's the strange thing: When I recall that event, it was as if I was watching it from a position behind me, a little to my left at times, a little to my right at other times. There are only three times I remember seeing it through my *own* eyes: inspecting the pilot's wound, looking into DB's eyes when I first got to his side, and searching for enemy positions.

One of the guys in our barracks was going to go on R&R soon, but was short of money. He was one of our crew chiefs and I knew him. I agreed to lend him some money and he could pay me back at the end of the month on payday. It was a handshake deal, and that was all we needed to make it official. I went to the orderly room and got access to the money they placed into the company safe for me when I first arrived, taking out half of it for the loan.

According to the Army rumor-mill, the NVA had been trying to kick some serious American ass up at Khe Sanh. American strength had been building for weeks, peaking at five thousand including the support guys dedicated to saving that post. Yet, the NVA managed to ambush and kill twenty Marines on patrol near a hilltop defensive position[70] about five miles northwest of Khe Sanh. Intel would later note a buildup of NVA forces of armor units, infantry divisions, and artillery preparing to invade south of the DMZ. Estimates figured there were 30,000 NVA troops in the area, give or take. After days of enemy movements and incursions, Khe Sanh's outer perimeter had been breached after NVA heavy mortar and rocket fire preceded infantry movements. The Marines were fighting for their lives. I wondered how many of the Marines we bumped into a few weeks before were now dead, wounded, or scared shitless.

Meanwhile, back in our neck of the woods, we were about to get a taste ourselves.

On the morning of January 30, 1968, DB and I posed for a picture with the ship. We hadn't taken a picture together to show the folks back

---

[70] Officially known as Hill 881 North.

home, so I climbed into my seat with an M-60 on my lap and a belt of ammo carefully draped over my left thigh. DB was on the ground in front of me. That photograph is one of my most prized possessions. Funny thing is, once it was developed I never sent it home to show the folks.

At the time, I didn't believe my family knew exactly what I did in Vietnam. It was intentional. I didn't tell them much other than I flew in gunships, and that everything was fine and I was doing well. Of course, I did brag about the DFC, but offered no details as to what happened. My promotions were obvious due to the return address on the envelopes. I figured by telling them what was what, it would force me to face the dangers and my own mortality. I didn't want to approach those subjects. They were very personal, and if I wrote home about it too much, it would make me think about it too much. I was quite content in my little world made up of adrenaline, excitement, and bravado.

A mission that required one fire team only was sent to an area outside of Saigon for a search and destroy (hunt and kill) mission. My ship was the tail on that team. Before we took off, I had grabbed some Willy-Pete[71] grenades and some empty Mason jars. Were these grenades intended to be used to burn something up, or to produce smoke? It didn't matter to us; either way they would work.

The Tet Holiday Truce was about to begin, but there were indications that the VC were growing in numbers locally. We were ordered to hunt them down and destroy any VC and/or materiel.

We were looking for enemy bunkers and/or positions. Our lead ship was about a quarter mile ahead of us, and both of us were flying at treetop level. Our flight path was not a straight line, but somewhat of a serpentine pattern. The lead ship would go to the right of the imaginary median line of travel, then slowly turn back to the left crossing the median line, then turning right again, crossing the median line, and so on. We followed the same method, but ours was opposite theirs. In other words, where they were on the right side of the median line, by the time we got there we'd be on the left side. All the while, the peter-pilot, crew chief and gunner were searching for targets.

---

[71] White Phosphorous is a highly flammable, fiercely burning chemical substance. It produces a white smoke that is easily seen.

We found a string of half-buried bunkers, positioned 75 to 100 yards apart. Fortunately, they were more or less in a straight line for us. We saw no one nearby, neither enemy nor non-combatants. Tree lines were at a distance and the ground vegetation was minimal. The entrance 'hole' for each was easy to see from our cruising vantage point.

I'm not sure what the lead ship was going to do in order to destroy these bunkers, as I was busy preparing a Willy-Pete to drop into the bunker entrance as we flew by. Now, let me explain. White phosphorous is very dangerous. Like hand grenades, there is no room for mistakes. When the pin is pulled, the handle flies off. After a four second delay, it explodes. If it is thrown from a helicopter flying at 80-90 knots or so, the explosion will occur about 30 feet below the tail boom. I know because I tried this once with a regular grenade. The shrapnel will deploy in mid-air, essentially causing no damage except as falling metal pieces when they hit the ground; maybe clunking somebody on top of his helmet.

Here's where the Mason jar comes in. The Willy-Pete is the shape of a cylinder about seven inches long and two and a half inches wide; similar to a smoke grenade. With the handle still attached, it fit neatly into the mouth of the Mason jar. By inserting it all the way in, pulling the pin will not release the handle. It was held tight by the glass sides. When this was tossed down from the ship, you want to be careful not to strike any portion of the ship's structure (skids, rocket tubes, mini-guns, etc.). When it strikes the ground, the glass breaks, causing the handle to snap off and the grenade to detonate. With proper timing, the jar will hit the bunker, or close enough to cause some damage.

I knew this was very risky. Because of the danger, it was a method used very rarely and only in special circumstances. In this particular outing, I did manage to hit two of the bunker entrance ports. And, no, the pilots were not exactly in cahoots with my technique.

As far as we were concerned, a truce was to begin at midnight that night because of the Vietnamese Tet[72] holiday. A seven-day military truce had been arranged months before to cover the period of January 27 through February 3, 1968. It was a time for the ARVNs to go on holiday leave, and many did. In the weeks leading up, the cease-fire was whittled

---

[72] Lunar new year holiday.

down to three days beginning January 31. Going on that search and destroy mission was our last chance to find and destroy something of military value before the truce was set to begin. Command hadn't talked about that truce much, at least down to our level in the chain of command, but in the back of our minds were knew for weeks it was coming up soon.

We returned to base about 1700 hours. Passing overhead, I noticed the streets of Bien Hoa, just outside our base, empty of civilians except for a few. There were, literally, only three people in the street. Usually, the streets were jam-packed with Lambretta scooters, crowds of people, old model cars and trucks. Not that day.

I keyed my mic and said, "Ah, Sir, it looks pretty empty down there. Looks like something's up."

"I was thinking the same thing," the A/C replied.

While we were in the mess hall later on, Sgt. Emerick came over to our table to inform us that we and the other crew we flew with earlier that day would go back on duty at 2000 hours. The primary stand-by team had already been scheduled. We would be the second back-up team until released. Operations had received word that the VC might stage an attack that night.

We got our gear, jumped on the three-quarter, and headed out to the stand-by shack. It was the first time I was inside this building as it had been recently constructed for our platoon. We spent so much time off base on missions that we didn't know it had been built and didn't know who built it. It was actually pretty nice. Inside were four cots and four small wooden chairs surrounding a 3' x 3' aluminum card table. Above the table was a single light bulb connected to an outlet on the ceiling. A smaller table near the wall supported the crank-style field phone. Sixteen of us sat or stood around, some just outside of the building, talking, playing cards, smoking cigarettes, and shooting the breeze—just waiting for the word to scramble us into action, or release us.

Things were quiet. The only noises I heard were the muted conversations of the other guys around the shack, the hum of a generator somewhere in the distance, and the occasional loud roar of a fighter jet taking off from Tan Son Nhut. The dark sky was decorated with occasional glowing bright spots, flares, floating to the ground oh-so-slowly at different intervals.

At midnight, we received a call. One of the pilots answered, listening for a few minutes. After a short pause, he said, "Okay," and hung up the field phone.

"What's the status so far?" another asked.

Looking at our A/C, he said, "You guys are released."

About five minutes later, Sarge drove up in the three-quarter. Leaving the primary team there, we returned to the company area. The time was about thirty past midnight.

It didn't take long for me to get settled. DB and I bunked down on the second floor of our recently built wooden barracks. Closest to the only second-level door leading to the exterior stairs was Sarge's own cubicle space, then me and DB in the next shared space, and so on for the other guys in the platoon. Each metal framed bed, tented by a mosquito net, was on the floor. No bunkbeds here. It was a long day. I dozed off quickly.

"**Get up**," somebody yelled out from down the hall, but it didn't seem loud. *Did I hear that right? Am I dreaming? Am I late?* My eyes opened at the sound of hurried foot-steps, shuffling down the aisle, towards me and the exit door.

"We're getting hit," shouted someone else as they walked very quickly past my bunk on their way towards the door. "Everybody out. NOW!" The figure ran down the stairs, followed by two or three other guys. **Whoomph!** An explosion someplace at a distance.

I got out of bed quickly at the sound of explosions. Nothing too close, it seemed. What were they, mortars, rockets? Hard to tell, not that I could. Expecting the next explosion, I waited. Nothing. Getting out of the barracks was imperative. We knew, from basic training, the closer to the ground, the safer we'd be. DB was up as well. Men were rushing past us in the narrow aisle towards the only door to get out. We waited for a space to jump in and join the others.

No time to get dressed. DB, me, and three others guys paused at the top of the stairs, just for a second. I looked at my watch, the time was 0305 hours. All the exterior lights were on throughout the entire area.

Whoomph... Whoomph.

I heard a couple muted explosions, and a few seconds later a couple more.

Whoomph... Whoomph.

These explosions were off in the distance, maybe at the perimeter or at Tan Son Nhut.

The pale-yellow illumination from numerous flares, each independent and floating slowly to the ground, provided an eerie imitation of daylight. **Tat-tat-tat-tat-tat** went a machine gun somewhere, maybe at the perimeter; again, at a distance. When we reached the last stair, and stepped onto the ground, I took a few steps.

A hugely bright yellow and red ball of fire appeared off to my right, not fifty feet away, instantly. I don't recall hearing the explosion. The fireball must have been at least twenty-five feet wide, and seemed to be at the same height as the top floor to our barracks. Then, everything went blank.

I found myself on the ground as I regained consciousness. My first conscious thought was that my head was ringing, as if I took a hard punch to the head. Whatever it was landed across the road at the corner. It looked like maybe the water tower had taken a hit. More explosions, louder and closer than before. **Whoomph... Whoomph...** Hugging the ground, I prayed. A spiraling sound in the air preceded the next explosion. They sounded close. I decided to stay down and dug in deeper for dear life. I pressed my body as far as it could go into the ground, which wasn't very much. I wanted to melt into the dirt. I knew instinctively each round would finds its fateful target. We had no bunker.

They made a certain, distinct sound as they flew overhead, a swirling, spiraling sound like metal cleats skidding some distance on a smooth concrete floor. No matter how low I tried to get, it was still too high above ground as far as I was concerned. Feeling overly exposed and in a very dangerous position, I stayed where I was. **Tat-tat-tat-tat-tat-tat**; again, near the perimeter, **tat-tat-tat-tat-tat-tat**. Machine gun fire, probably an M-60. A minute or two later, another explosion.

During a lull lasting a couple minutes, using the light of flares and a few lightbulbs nearby, I raised my head and looked around. The other guys, who had also been knocked to the ground, were picking themselves up. As we crouched and quickly made our way to the corner of our barracks, I saw a fuel truck revetment, probably a hundred feet away, take a hit.

Whoomph.

The truck within the 55-gallon barrel and sand-bagged enclosure didn't explode, but it caught fire.

One of the guys asked loudly, "Where's the bunker?" I didn't know. I never saw one on base, especially in our company area. This was REMF-ville, no need for bunkers except what was required for IG inspections.

We had no weapons with us. In that sense, we were all naked. Unauthorized personal weapons were prohibited. The M-16s and M-60s were locked up in the company arms CONEX. The mini-guns were with the ships on the flight line. We weren't issued the .38 or .45 caliber handguns; they were reserved for the officers. The stand-by ships had weapons, but they were probably in the air. Standing there close to the building, we were without our clothes, steel pots, flak jacket, and boots. Just skivvies. If the VC came running around the corner of the building next door with his AK-47 blazing away, we'd be shit outta luck.

We assessed our situation and tried to decide where to go. I looked down and saw the right side of my boxers[73] dark with blood. It seemed as though I had been wounded by shrapnel on the right side of my abdomen, which was also covered in blood. But, surprising to me, there was no pain whatsoever.

Whoomph. Whoomph.

---

[73] It was all I was wearing at the time.

More explosions. A few seconds later, more. We didn't quite know where to go. **Tat-tat-tat-tat-tat-tat** sounded the perimeter machine gun again.

We needed to do something, anything, and do it quickly. We quickly discussed our options. Should we stay, or go? One of the guys remembered there was a bunker somewhere close to battalion headquarters, about 300 yards away. Checking among ourselves, two other guys had been wounded, but so far none seemed critical. We were all ambulatory.

We decided to go, one after the other, to the bunker. I took the lead, running off in a zig-zag pattern like I'd seen in the movies. In retrospect, you only zig-zag when somebody is shooting at you, not during a rocket and mortar attack. I wasn't thinking too clearly, it seemed. I felt alone, so looked back expecting to see the other guys right behind me. They weren't. Where the hell were they? I'm by myself here. Did they get hit? Did they go somewhere else? Did they stay put? I didn't see them anywhere. I didn't stop running. Should I go back? No. I decided to continue forward to find that bunker. At a short distance, I saw it—or at least I hoped I did.

I was right. It was a sandbagged shelter about twelve feet wide by twenty feet long and four feet tall. An open, but protected doorway was at one end. I knelt down beside a man who was also crouched outside the entrance.

"Why're you out here?" I asked him.

He said, "Somebody inside told me it was too crowded and to wait outside."

"Bullshit," I said as I started to crawl inside.

A husky voice from inside said, "You can't come in, there's no room for you."

Well, okay then. So, I stopped and crouched next to the guy outside for a few minutes.

Whoomph.

Another explosion.

Whoomph.

Then another, louder and closer. Scanning the area, flares dangled beneath small silky parachutes barely noticeable, each one having a slow, back and forth swing like metronomes. Shadows of buildings, vehicles, and so on danced, ever so slowly, along with the beat. Using that artificial daylight, I checked my side a little more carefully. The bleeding stopped. It didn't appear worse than before. I still didn't feel any pain except for the sole of my left foot. I looked down and saw what appeared to be a two-inch diameter burned spot near the arch on the sole of my left foot. I must have stepped on a piece of hot shrapnel when I was running.

A couple minutes later the same husky voice called out, "Anybody out there get hit?"

"Yeah, me," I replied.

"Well, get in here," he said. I crawled in on my hands and knees due to the low door overhead. Surprisingly, only three men were inside, all on their butts, two leaning against one wall and the third leaning against the opposite wall. One of them checked my wounded side with a flashlight and left.

Within a few minutes two other guys arrived with a stretcher. I didn't recognize anybody. They helped me get on just outside the door-way, and carried me away a short distance. I looked around when they stopped and saw they had taken me to a tent. A tent? There, in the battalion area? Where'd that come from? Who put it up? Why? How long had it been here? I never saw it in our area before.

Inside the makeshift triage tent, two lightbulbs provided just enough light to see clearly. Three or four guys were wounded and the others were treating them. It was a little crowded. Two guys helped me off the stretcher and propped me against the wall. Sitting upright, another guy noticed the blood and looked at my side. I began shaking uncontrollably for at least a few minutes or so. Was it because I was scared? I no longer felt in imminent danger, almost calm, though I still hadn't seen anybody with weapons of any sort to protect us.

We're being invaded. None of us had a weapon. They were locked up in an arms room somewhere. This was bullshit of the highest order.

Whoomph.

Another explosion punctuated my predicament. "Can you breathe okay?" the guy asked.

"Yeah, I guess so," was my scared and shaky reply.

"I think your lung's punctured," he informed me as he began to apply and tape to my side a 6' x 6' gauze and plastic covering.

I sat there for no more than a few minutes after getting bandaged. They placed me back on the stretcher and carried me out to a waiting Huey. I recognized the crew chief as being from my unit.

"Nothing like being taken care of by your own." We traded smiles but he was all business. I appreciated that. A couple more bandaged guys came aboard, stepping around me as I lay there on a stretcher on the cabin floor. We lifted off.

A short flight later we landed in Long Binh at a medical landing site. Still on the stretcher, I was taken into the building and transferred onto a gurney. Medics inside parked me in one of the brightly lit crowded hallways where I waited for a time. A nurse came by to look at my wound and hook me up to an IV. She was pretty. It must have been no longer than a half hour until I was wheeled down and parked and on the other side of the hallway.

Before long I was surrounded by nurses. Young, pretty American *round-eyes*[74]. One of the nurses adjusted the IV while two others cut off my skivvies with scissors. They said they were checking for additional wounds. Feeling exposed? Yes, but they were good looking and I didn't care. It didn't last long. One of them with a syringe approached and plugged it into the IV. Quickly, a pleasant warm numbness overcame me. I felt *very* relaxed just before I lost consciousness.

---

[74] A term we used for "American" women (with round eyes) as opposed to the Oriental women we were accustomed to seeing in Vietnam. No disrespect was ever intended to American women, or any other, with an Oriental ancestry.

Chapter 8

DEROS

I woke up the day after Tet, February 1, finding myself in a recovery ward, clean and sterile. I had been out of it for about 36 hours straight. Looking to the left and right, all the other beds, also clean and fitted with white sheets and a light blanket, were occupied. A large 8 x 8 gauze was taped to my right abdomen, but nothing done to what I thought was a burn on the bottom of my foot.

At my request, a nurse cleaned and bandaged the foot, and then I went back to sleep. After a while the surgeon came in to examine his work. It was the first chance I had to see what he did. There were no stitches. He was going to let the open wound heal without sutures because of the amount of flesh that had been removed. The shrapnel did not penetrate deeply enough to require stitches, just nicking a rib or two. It apparently tore its way past me. I was lucky.

The next morning, Sgt. Emerick came by to visit. He filled me in on what had taken place. Saigon was under attack. One of our gunships fired a rocket into a room at the American Embassy where Charlie had taken position. The NVA and VC had attacked many bases in country. Our unit had no fatalities yet, but quite a few were wounded. DB was okay.

Our base had sustained much damage from the heavy mortar and rocket attack. My ship had been hit[75] significantly by shrapnel. Maintenance was deciding whether to repair it or cannibalize it for parts. Our barracks had taken three direct hits and would require rebuilding. It was estimated that at least 150 rocket and mortar rounds had struck the Bien Hoa airbase alone, with an additional 45 or so other Allied bases hit by the NVA and/or VC. The Long Binh ammo dump had exploded. We had been caught totally by surprise by the intensity of the assault.

I was shipped to the hospital in Cam Rahn Bay for convalescence. An entire crew of an armored personnel carrier (APC) had been wounded and shared the same ward as me.

---

[75] A photo taken by Willis Long captioned "190th AHC hangar next to 573rd maintenance hangar following Tet 68 mortar attack. (68)" may be found at the 118ahc.org website, entitled **TET 1968 (Battle of Bien Hoa) January 31, 1968** showing my stripped down and damaged UH-1C inside the hangar.

Day after day, just lying in bed. I mostly listened to the APC guys. After a few days, I started to walk around with the plasma bottle on a stand. As the days slowly passed, sheer boredom crept in. There was not much to do. No radio, no TV, nothing. There wasn't much reading material, and the magazines we had, like *Life* and *Time*, had been read many times over. We had no phone. I wrote a letter to Dad, but I could not remember Mom's address. Everything I owned was back in the barracks, the address book included. I had no money, but learned the Red Cross could provide a small stipend to get by.

With five bucks from the Red Cross, and after confirming some information about me, I left to return to my ward. On the way, there was a small crowd of convalescing GIs standing in the narrow hallway, each wearing his hospital gown. I think there were maybe six of them, crowded around a short, heavy-set man wearing civilian clothes. As I got closer, I recognized him as Mr. French of *Family Affair*, a TV program back home. His actual name was Sebastian Cabot. I was surprised at his height. He was shorter than I; maybe five-foot-five. He was here on a USO[76] tour, greeting the troops. I was within a foot of this TV celebrity, the closest I've ever been to one. He was signing autographs, talking with the guys, and just being a friendly guy as I slid past and continued my way through the hallways. I was not inclined to wait, and had no interest in getting his autograph.

Leaving Mr. French and his admirers, I returned to the ward. One of my APC ward-mates mentioned to me a lieutenant colonel from the hospital came in to present each of them with a Purple Heart. He left mine in the top drawer of my bed stand. I found it right away and inspected it. My name was engraved on the back.

Near the end of three weeks, the doctor wanted to send me to Japan and then back to the US, but I had about a month to go before my DEROS[77] and I was adamant in convincing him I needed to get back to my unit. My request was approved. Besides, the real reason was I wanted to recoup $300[78] I loaned to one of the guys some days before so he could

---

[76] United Service Organizations, providing help and raising morale for service members and their families.
[77] DEROS: Date Eligible for Return from Over Seas.
[78] The calculated worth of the dollar from 1967 to 2016, considering inflation based on the Consumer Price Index indicates $300 during 1967 is equivalent to $2,156 in 2016. It doesn't seem plausible.

take his R&R. Payday was supposed to be January 31, so I expected to be repaid as promised.

Soon after arriving back at Bien Hoa, I headed to the company area and signed in. I caught up with DB later on. He showed me our ship, still parked in the hangar since the day after Tet, peppered with hundreds of shrapnel holes, missing salvageable parts that had been removed to fix other ships. He was filling in as a gunner on another ship. Our platoon sergeant had been removed and assigned to the maintenance platoon. Rumors were rampant as to the reason why. But from what I understood, whatever he was officially accused of doing was still under investigation. Let it suffice to say he just didn't fit in with the other men in the platoon.

I learned our barracks had been hit three times by mortars and rockets. One of our serious casualties was the guy I loaned the money to. His bunk was also on the top floor of our barracks at the other end of the building, in the corner. I was told he stayed behind to put his boots on when we started getting hit that night. He was directly beneath where one round had struck the corrugated steel roof. One of his knees sustained serious damage from shrapnel. The entire reason for me returning to Bien Hoa had gone to Japan. I could empathize with him, if his wound was that bad. And, I believed that it was, notwithstanding the fact the docs wanted to send me to Japan for the comparatively small wound I received. He was probably just as short in-country as I was at the time, but more seriously wounded.

Our relatively new wooden barracks was still standing. Except for a few areas that were damaged, it remained sturdy. DB and I went inside; me to get my stuff or whatever was left, and DB to pick up some of his stuff, as well. I grabbed my flight jacket, still on the bed after three weeks, noticing a multitude of shrapnel holes. I stuffed it into my duffel bag along with the rest of my gear. DB told me he'd been keeping an eye out to make sure none of my stuff went missing.

Word travels fast, especially bad news. We heard the guys at Khe Sanh were getting clobbered by the NVA. Up to a thousand rounds of NVA artillery hit the base and surrounding defensive positions in one day alone. Marines were getting killed in the double digits, daily. It had gotten so bad that B-52s, alone, dropped tons of explosives in the hills surrounding the base over a period of nine weeks. That's a lot of ordnance.

Within six months, the siege at Khe Sanh, the battle of Hué, and the Tet Offensive by the VC and NVA at so many bases in Vietnam were wake-up calls, proving we weren't quite as invincible as many believed. Suddenly the realization hit: we were fighting a real, honest-to-God war. They were out to kill us, and were doing a pretty good job. We could actually lose this war.

Things in our company area were quite chaotic. A number of guys had been wounded, some seriously, so we were low on manpower. The gun platoon was down one platoon sergeant with no replacement. If the crews were not flying, they were maintaining the ships and helping build bunkers. It was a huge project as command wanted a bunker for each building. We slept in Quonset huts with single cots at each side. There were a few mortar attacks during the next few nights. Most seemed to be on the Air Force side of the base, but a couple were close by. On one occasion, after being awaken to get to a bunker, I was too tired to move and went back to sleep on the floor.

The orderly room wasn't much better. Flight records were not being kept up-to-date, at least for the time being. Other records that should have been forwarded to higher command by the usual routes and methods were being sent by alternate methods—trucks instead of helicopters. They had new reports to figure out: equipment damage reports, requisitions for materiel emergency resupply, re-allocation of personnel, attrition reports, etc. More paperwork, less people.

The war just got real to these guys, especially the REMFs. All of a sudden, they were wearing steel helmets, flack-jackets, web-belts and attached gear. Nearly everyone had his M-16 and a few 20-round magazines of ammo within reach.

During this time, I was essentially an unassigned crew chief with no ship to crew and no platoon sergeant telling me what I should or should not be doing. Through no fault of my own, I was grounded. I checked around to see if I could fill in as one of the crewmen, but they didn't need anybody at the time.

My side still hurt from my wound, more so if I bent one way or the other. The burn on the bottom of my left foot healed, but it was still tender, especially if it twisted around. My hearing was not up to par, but I wasn't deaf. Not wanting to complain, I kept a low profile to stay on flight status. Before Tet, I would work tirelessly on my ship and help with the weapons system. But, at the ripe old age of twenty (and just by weeks), my current inclination to find something constructive to do and to seek out a responsible role within the somewhat chaotic surroundings wasn't happening. I reasoned it this way: If the doctor at Cam Rahn Bay had his way, I'd be in Japan or maybe on my way back to the world. They hesitantly approved my request to return to Bien Hoa. But only I knew it was just to collect my three hundred bucks and the rest of the money I had remaining in the company safe. Nothing heroic. I had only a few weeks or so to go, anyway.

The bunker-building details were in full swing. As I assessed the progress that had been made in our company area and what still needed to be done, I did what every "good" soldier does: wait to be put to work, never volunteer. There wasn't much more that needed to be done. During the four months before Tet, I participated in the company morning formation less than five times. Since I returned from Cam Rahn, they didn't have any at all.

As far as I knew at the time, Dau Tieng was the only aviation base where Charlie actually attacked by ground forces, at least until Tet. I was not aware of the large numbers of the NVA in our area and their assaults on the base perimeter. The full scope of the attacks since Tet had not sunk in. It was impossible for me to grasp the seriousness of our situation. Being a part of a flight crew, my world revolved around flying in support of ground missions, responding to emergencies, hunting and killing. The mentality of those assigned at Bien Hoa, and especially those who stayed on base were softened by the comforts of home. The war was always somewhere else. Then, BAM, all of a sudden, war came knocking at their door.

Tom, my close friend from East Boston, was assigned to the 118th AHC just down the road from us. I had seen him once months before when I first arrived. Since I now had very little to do, I went over to his company area to look him up. I found him, alive, but he seemed different. To me, he looked worn out, exhausted. I could see that thousand-mile stare in his eyes. He was busy, but no longer flying much. He seemed to be coping as best he could. We spoke for twenty minutes or so on the street that connected our company areas. He had to get back to work and we parted, promising each other we'd let the other know when we got our orders to leave country. Our DEROS date was fast approaching.

It wasn't a week later when Tom came over to my area, and we compared our orders sending us home. We were leaving on the same date. In fact, we'd be on the same plane. I didn't see him again until we were both in Long Binh waiting to leave.

When I out-processed from the 190th, I was handed my flight record form. This documented the dates and number of hours I flew, and categorized them as CAs or not. The clerk told me he wasn't able to do anything with it considering the circumstances. I was to take it to my next assignment and turn it in to the operations sergeant. It'll be processed there. *Well, okay*, I thought. What else was I going to do? From the company's safe, I recovered the rest of the money I had put there for safe keeping months before.

Some lieutenant loitering in the orderly room gave me a hard time about it.

"Where'd you get that money?" he asked.

It was three hundred dollars. I didn't know if he was joking around or not.

"What do you mean 'where did I get that money', Sir? I had it when I first signed in months before from my old unit."

He was worried about the biggest problem in the battalion, drug dealers. Could I be one of them? They didn't know who or how, but it was a problem. He seemed satisfied at my answer.

Besides, it was common knowledge among the troops that marijuana was as easy to get as going to the corner store for a bottle of milk back home. Vietnamese were known to package it disguised as factory-made, name brand American cigarettes by the carton. It always surprised me, watching from my ship's revetment, seeing some GIs coming back on base through the front gate carrying a small paper bag with a carton of American cigarettes sticking out the top. The MPs didn't seem to challenge anyone bringing cigarettes *into* the base. Did they actually believe cigarettes were cheaper in town than at the BX?

My bag was packed, all my files in a thin Samsonite attaché case I bought at the BX, and orders in my hand. It was time to go. No big farewell, no party, no celebration. I didn't even look up Sgt. Emerick to let him know I was leaving.

After a month leave and travel delay, my next deployment was going to be to West Germany, assigned to the Third Infantry Division (Mechanized). It was the same division my dad served with during World War II. I had seen the division patch on his Army uniform hanging in the front closet for most of my life.

Tom and I met up in Long Binh. How odd that we came to Vietnam together, got split up during the year, met up again, and here we were: leaving Vietnam together on the same *freedom bird*[79]. We were scheduled to board the bus at Long Binh in the dead of night, but delayed due to a continuous yet unpredictable pattern of incoming mortar and rocket attacks at Tan Son Nhut. We were all dressed up with nowhere else to go.

While we were waiting in a room of 45 or more guys, we heard the distinct swirling sound of an incoming 122mm rocket. Having heard many lately, there was no mistake. Everyone dived to the floor, instantly, waiting for the explosion. Nothing. We were still alive. After a few minutes, Tom and I got up from the floor and dusted ourselves off. The other guys did the same.

One guy asked, "What happened? Was it a dud?"

Somebody else asked, "Did anybody hear it go off?"

Another man, closer to the door, yelled, "I did it. It was me." Most everyone turned his way. "I slid my bag across the floor."

The floor was concrete. The four metal *feet* on the bottom of his bag, sliding on concrete only about ten or fifteen feet, sounded exactly like an incoming rocket, a sound we were all too familiar with of late.

---

[79] A term used to describe the airplane taking soldiers back to the World (home, USA).

Some of us started laughing. Others cursed him out. Our nerves were on edge. We were so close to leaving, and yet, so close to getting clobbered by an incoming round.

We well understood that an attack on the airport was the only thing standing in our way. Was our freedom bird going to get cancelled? Will we be stuck in country for another night? In our situation, we were very vulnerable. No combat gear, no weapons, no real leadership that we could tell that would make us into a fighting force if things got worse.

It was about 1:00 am or so when the bus arrived. Except for the color, it was very similar to a school bus. It was either dark green or blue, hard to tell at that hour. The duffel bags had already been loaded, so all we had was our AWOL bags and anything else we carried. We boarded the bus, but didn't move. So, we sat and waited.

"Tan Son Nhut's getting hit again," someone in front of me said as the word passed from front to back.

We waited some more. Tom and I sat together, just like we did when we on our way to Vietnam. We were each lost in our own thoughts, as were almost everyone else on the bus. I looked out of the window, seeing the buildings, street, lights everywhere; wishing we would go soon.

With a pneumatic hiss, the brakes released and the mechanical double doors closed. We were on our way. The bus ride was uneventful. A few flares lit the sky some distance away. Otherwise, everything seemed quiet—oddly quiet. I wondered what happened to Babe, Don, Jack and the others. They should have been with us. After all, we all arrived on the same date; we should be leaving on the same date. Deep in thought, I realized Tom and I were very lucky. I had to believe the others were alive and well. It didn't want to think otherwise. This had been one hell of a year.

I was happy to leave, but I realized I was actually going to miss Vietnam. Although my two ships had been severely damaged, neither was a result of poor crew-chiefmanship. I would miss flying, most of all. Flying, not to acquire flight time, but for a reason, a mission, a purpose. Armed to the teeth, my two gunships were my home. I never felt safer and more secure. And, I trusted my crew with my life time and time again. We kicked some ass, that's for sure.

As the bus travelled down one street to another, leaving Long Binh, along some vacant hard-packed dirt road towards Bien Hoa, I tried to anticipate going home to my family. I couldn't. Instead, I sat in my seat quietly, as did nearly everybody else on the bus.

Passing through fortified gates and armed sentries at the Tan Son Nhut airbase, we were taken directly to the *freedom bird*, dropping us off at the base of the mobile stairs. One by one, we climbed aboard. Tom found two adjoining seats and we sat together, just like old times.

The stewardesses were all round-eyes, young and good looking. It didn't take long for the plane to fill up. I didn't keep track of the time as we waited to take off, but it wasn't long before we were rolling. As the wheels came off the ground, nearly everyone aboard yelled out loudly in joy, and relief. So far, we had made it out alive and were on our way home. Slowly, it got quiet. The lights in the cabin dimmed. One by one, each of us took a snooze, as this was probably the best opportunity for a good rest that most of us had had in months.

On the way back to the world we stopped in Hawaii to refuel. Tom and I got off the plane to stretch our legs a bit, as did most others. I stayed in the gated area while Tom ventured off to pick up a souvenir from a gift shop. A few hours later we arrived at Travis Air Force Base, near San Francisco. We were bused to the out-processing point.

Most of us heard stories about GI's returning home from Vietnam being harassed by hippies and anti-war protesters, being called derogatory names, spat upon, and generally not making us feel warm and fuzzy about coming home. But, I was not a witness to that experience. Even as we arrived to the airport in San Francisco, still in uniform, to connect with civilian flights home, no demonstrators crossed my path. I looked for them. I wanted to see exactly who they were, what they said, and how they acted. I was ready for them. I was young enough, still, to not consider the consequences of kicking some hippie's ass. It just didn't happen to me.

A group of us, about six, waited together for our individual flights home. The only guy I knew was Tom. The others were newfound friends, returnees from Vietnam just like us. We sat together in an area close to a bar with couches and a short table in between. The waitress came over. Each of us ordered a beer. She looked at us, scanning each face and asked me, only me, for ID. I looked young for my age (and still do). I wasn't sure what the legal age was in California, but I knew I wasn't twenty-one, of course. But, maybe I could pull this off by at least going through the motions of her checking and maybe saving her job.

When she examined my military ID, and noted I was underage, she apologetically told me she couldn't sell me a beer.

Too young? Sure, I understood the law. But, after nearly a year in Vietnam, not as a REMF but as a combatant, I figured she could bend a rule. *Hey, girl, look at my ribbons. Look at my wings. I just returned from a combat tour in Hell.* Damn near getting killed how many times—ten, twenty-five, fifty? I lost count. Being wounded by our nation's enemy with scars for the rest of my life didn't mean shit. Treated and respected as a responsible adult in Vietnam and Japan, but not here in this dinky lounge? Really? I suppose, next, you're gonna tell me I can't vote[80], either.

"Okay, fine. I'll have a soda, maybe a ginger-ale." Totally embarrassed, I avoided the glances of shock and dismay from those around me.

"She wouldn't sell you a beer?" asked one.

Little did I realize at the time that being denied a beer at the airport was going to symbolize my return to the States. I went over to Vietnam as a kid, naïve and inexperienced. With each passing mission and near-death episode, my outlook on life matured exponentially. My mind and behavior had changed, though by appearance I had not except for ribbons on my chest that were placed in a certain order. To non-vet civilians, they didn't mean a thing except for how many and how colorful. Maybe they could recognize one, maybe two, but usually not all. To the military, ribbons told a story. They revealed where you were, what you did, and how you were recognized. They didn't mean a thing to that waitress.

Tom abruptly changed his order to two beers, making sure I wasn't left out. While we were waiting, we were shooting the breeze. It was as if we all had known each other much longer than the hour before when we first met. We were all enlisted, Spec Fives being the highest rank. While we were exchanging general information about where we were stationed in 'Nam, what our job was, where we were going home to, and our plans

---

[80] The legal age to vote in local and national elections was twenty-one. I knew I couldn't vote.

after that, the beers arrived. Tom slid the extra beer over to me. The waitress passed us a couple times while serving others, but said nothing to me about the beer in my hand.

Tom and I were the only aviation guys there. Three were infantry, one was a truck driver. We sipped our beers as the stories flowed. They were 'no bullshit' stories and rang true. We didn't have to prove a thing to each other. We were all brothers, no matter what our skin color.

One of the infantry guys had a few photographs he wanted to pass around. As my time came around, I looked at the black and white photos with interest. One of the photos depicted the severed heads of four Viet Cong soldiers placed next to each other on a log. An American soldier, wearing jungle fatigues and web-gear, kneeled at each end, cradling his rifle. The heads, each with a cigarette in its mouth, and the grunts faced the lens when the cameraman took the photograph.

It was gruesome. I wanted it to be shocking to my senses, but it wasn't. My mind tried to imagine the minutes and hours prior to the time the picture was taken. Were they in a firefight? Were the gooks already dead when their heads were removed? Who came up with the idea to do this? It was obviously against Army Regs to cut up a dead VC, let alone take his head off. Wasn't it?

It reminded me of one of our missions. Months before, we had landed in an open field waiting to be called back to the AO. A squad of grunts passed our ship, haggard, dirty, and wearing full field gear. My impression was they hadn't had a good night's sleep or hot meal in weeks. The rucksack of one caught my attention as he passed me no further than a foot away. This grunt was short, maybe five-foot-six. He was wiry, didn't weigh too much. His facial expression was blank, tired I supposed. I stopped him to ask about what I saw attached by a cord to one side of his pack.

"Ears", he told me. "The left ear of every gook I killed. Souvenirs. Got fifteen, so far."

He forced a smile as he looked at me. Or did he merely look through me at nothing in particular? It was hard to tell. I had nothing to say to him. After all, what could I say? He left to rejoin his squad.

Four heads on a log? Ears on a string? For some strange reason, I didn't find these atrocities as offensive as I would have expected. Had I changed that much since a year earlier? And I still can't even buy a beer!

Tom's flight was about ready to board, so he had to leave. We said our good-byes. He was off to Boston. I still had an hour or so to go for my flight to Chicago. One by one, the others left, too.

I called home to let them know I was on my way. Hurray! Call Dad when I land in Chicago.

My journey to O'Hare Airport was ordinary. It had been less than forty-eight hours since I left Vietnam. It was night. The plane wasn't full. Many empty seats were here and there. In my row of three seats, I was the only one, so I sat next to the aisle. I had a better view of the stewardess for our section of the plane. They really know how to pick them, you know? Beautiful women, all of them. Not one wore a wedding or engagement ring. What were my chances of getting a date with one? Zip! Why even try? I dimmed the overhead light and tried to get some shut-eye.

Still in uniform, I prepared, mentally, for the onslaught of war protesters to attack. Setting my plan in case they were there, I rehearsed the words I would use: "Bring it on, asshole." How many would there be? Would they be aggressive, or just standing there with their signs? I had nothing to be ashamed of. I did my job. Nobody back home knew what I did or didn't do. Maybe I should just ignore them.

Being hyper alert, I was ready. I'd be on my own, doubting anybody would lend a hand if a fight took place. So far, we returned from Vietnam one-by-one to no official recognition, parade, or welcome home party. I sensed there was nothing special about us, so why expect to be treated special?

Chapter 9

Still No Room

When I got to O'Hare, there was a crowd waiting to greet the passengers stepping off the plane. Regular people. Families. As I entered the building terminal, I saw a few groups of people hugging and kissing, clearly missing that person who had just reentered their lives. No protesters. No anti-war signs. Nothing. From the baggage claim area, I found my duffle bag. No protesters there, either.

Soon after I called, Dad, Cathy, Scott and Janie met me at the airport. I could tell they were just as happy to see me as I was to see them. Standing on the sidewalk, just outside of the terminal, each of them switched off to take a few pictures with me wearing my Army overcoat. I kept my smile going, but I wasn't sure if I was *happy* being home.

I didn't know what it was, but I lost something of myself during the past year. It made adjusting to the tranquility of home somewhat difficult. Years later, I would later learn that the U.S. casualty rate in Vietnam during 1967 was slightly over nine thousand—an average of roughly 173 per week, or about 25 a day. So far, it was the highest number of fatalities we suffered since we got involved in the war. I had survived. I was not going back. Germany would be a piece of cake. Then, I'd be a civilian with no obligation to the Army. My two years of active reserves were wiped out by the one year of combat duty.

I came back with a greater appreciation for Vietnam. I saw her people, suffering; her terrain, chopped up by untold number of bombings; her villages, primitive but habitable; her cities, crowded; and, her economy, struggling to survive. I had flown from very close to the DMZ to south of Vung Tau; from the Cambodian and Laos borders to the Vietnamese shores of the South China Sea. I knew of good men who died; not close friends, but known by face, name and reputation.

A lot of people back home didn't seem to understand our war. We went to Vietnam to fight Communist aggressors, honoring our SEATO obligation. The South Vietnamese, we were told, didn't want to be controlled by communists of any persuasion—Russian, Chinese, North Vietnam, whatever. The North Vietnamese Army, to many civilians, meant nothing. Every country has an army. So what? It's not a war, they'd say. It's a civil war. We have no business being there in the first place. The big, bad superpower against the poor, little underdogs of Vietnam. Of course, the VC tried to kill you. You invaded their country. What would you expect? The American public seemed to be totally oblivious to the fact regarding the other four nations that were in Vietnam honoring their SEATO obligation.

I had a lot of awkward conversations. People were curious—some of them, at least —but I could tell each one was trying to fit my responses with their own perception of our involvement's justification for being there. Short-lived conversations usually went something like this:

Them:	Me:
"Where've you been?"	"'Nam."
"When did you get back?"	"A week ago."
"What did you do there?"	"Flew in helicopters."
"Was it fun?"	"Yeah."
"See any action?"	"Yeah."
"Did you kill anybody?"	"Yeah."
"Did you get drafted?"	"Nope, volunteered."
"Why?"	"Seemed like a good idea at the time."
"Would you go back?"	"Nope, don't think so."
"Why not?"	"Once was enough."
"Do we belong there?"	"I think so."

Not exactly stimulating conversation. The follow up questions were nearly the same in each conversation. It was predictable and bothersome.

"Got any good stories?"

Well, where do I begin? Which story would you like to hear? Which would I think most interesting to take up our time? Which is better for me to share? Do I really want to share something with you that is very personal to me? Would you even understand me if I told you, or would I have to explain myself every other sentence? How can I put into words things that my mind can't really understand? If I tell you, will you think I'm some kind of lunatic? You almost had to be to do some of the things we did over there.

On top of it all, we had to relive our experience via TV news. We left the war behind. But, the media kept bringing it back to us every evening. In the name of "free speech" and the "public's right to know," censorship of televised coverage of the war didn't exist, unless it fit the narrative of some yet-to-be discovered hidden political agenda. Graphic images of men fighting and dying, in real life, were broadcast night after night. Perhaps the most graphic depiction of the brutality of this war was the public execution of a Viet Cong officer by the general of the South Vietnamese National Police. Of course, the story behind the VC's crime was not broadcast to American audiences. *That* was censored. The VC had killed one of the general's men, a national police officer, as well as the man's family. The general heard the evidence, passed summary judgment and sentence, and carried out his execution. Why on a public street in Saigon? Maybe it was a warning to other VC in the area, or to Ho Chi Minh in Hanoi.

The public was outraged. It did not make for good TV, that's for sure. People saw that general, pointing a .38 caliber revolver at the other man's head, the shot, and the victim crumple to the ground. The public naturally assumed that if a high-ranking police officer could do that, what did *we*, having much less rank, authority, and public exposure, do over there?

Suddenly people wanted to know if the stories they'd seen on TV and read in the papers were true. On the other side of the coin, some people seemed to try their best not to bring the subject up. They didn't want to hear or think about it. One side, asking too many questions, ready to pounce and debate the validity of the war; the other side, nothing.

I couldn't get away from it, no matter how I tried; until I learned to retreat into my own little world. It was safe there, I was in control. Nobody in or out unless I said so. Dad didn't press for information. He'd ask a question here and there, but carefully. I appreciated that, though I really wanted to unload.

If that wasn't enough, the daily body-count was broadcast on the TV news each night. March 7, 1968 marked two years since I enlisted. Forty-some men died[81] in Vietnam that day. By the end of the next six days, seven days total, three hundred and some Americans died[82] from combat action in Vietnam or from wounds sustained from the war. Walter Cronkite, David Brinkley, Chet Huntley, and others seemed all too eager to share this with the public. Were they trying to fire-up the American people? Did it fit into the grand scheme of scaring people to juice the ratings?

Boys were getting killed over there. Parents urged their sons to go to college. Get a deferment. Protest the war. Burn their draft card. After all, what parent wants to send a son off to war, knowing the casualty rate was in the double-digits, daily? Nope. The media was against what we believed to be true, and we didn't know why. If Walter Cronkite said something, people listened. But, I, and many others in my unit, saw a different set of circumstances in Vietnam. A lot of us bought the government propaganda that the South Vietnamese government needed us, and we were willing to risk life and limb for that belief.

One day, Dad wanted to show me off to his co-workers and asked me to wear my uniform. When we arrived at his office, he took me on a twenty-five-cent tour of the building. One of his office guys gave me a five-dollar bill and a complimentary pat on the back. On the way home, Dad told me one of our close neighbors, a classmate from high school, Ted Sturtevant, was killed in Vietnam just the previous month. I didn't learn of the circumstances causing his death, only where.

After the first week at home, nobody wanted to talk about Vietnam, and it seemed nobody wanted to listen. I felt like a fish out of water. Dad continued to work while I was home. It was going to be a long, three-and-a-half-week delay before I left again for Germany. I tried the best I could to fit in. It was useless, compounded by the fact that just a few days before I was in Vietnam waiting for a lull in a rocket attack to board the plane to leave. And now, here, it's almost the same as when I left a year before.

---

[81] www.vietnamwarcasualties.org/index.php?page=directory&dd=03/07/1968.
[82] *Ibid.*

Cathy, always a pretty good stepmom, helped me get caught up on a few events that occurred while I was away. The race riots in Detroit involved thousands of National Guard and police to protect life and property. Forty-some people were killed, three hundred or so injured and over a thousand buildings destroyed by fire. Other race riots had taken place in Alabama, California, Minnesota, New Jersey, New York, Washington, D.C., and Wisconsin. The Reverend Martin Luther King, Jr. had denounced the Vietnam War. Anti-war protests took place in New York City, San Francisco, Washington, D.C. and the Pentagon, numbering in the tens of thousands of people at our nation's capital alone. Cassius Clay[83] refused to be drafted into military service as his way of protesting against the war, and ended up going to prison. While there, he changed his name to Muhammad Ali.

Closer to home, a number of tornadoes struck the western suburbs of Chicago, killing more than thirty people. The infamous serial killer of eight Chicago nurses, Richard Speck, was convicted and sentenced to death in the electric chair.

President Johnson had his hands full with the Civil Rights Movement, his War on Poverty, and the Vietnam War. Notwithstanding the President's efforts, anger among blacks spread nationwide. In many cases, the counter-anger among whites rose exponentially. Many people in my neighborhood took on a negative attitude. They were fed up with the riots and the criminal activity on the streets of Chicago, fed up with the daily updates of the war, fed up with knowing the nation they grew up in was changing for the worst, and fed up with hippies and student protests, draft-dodgers, and so on. They didn't protest, *per se*, but the general attitude of my neighborhood was changing.

I was known around the neighborhood as the nice young kid who could draw. I was seen as a do-gooder; I didn't swear, didn't smoke, didn't get in trouble with the law, and didn't hang out with the "wrong crowd."

"He's in the Army nowadays?" one neighbor asked, "Didn't know that."

"He was in Vietnam?" I heard someone ask another.

---

[83] Famed heavy weight professional boxer.

Then, the whispers and talk behind the back: *Was he a baby-killer? Did he see any action? Did he kill anybody?* Nobody knew a thing about Vietnam except what they saw and heard on TV. But they knew, in the back of their mind, what movies and stories told them about previous war veterans coming home. *Watch him, maybe he's gonna wake up from a bad dream and hurt somebody.*

I couldn't help but sense I was being watched, surreptitiously, for any noticeable change of behavior. Then again, maybe it was all me, watching myself. I couldn't comprehend any possibility that I had changed. It was them, not me. I wanted to cry out for help, but no one was listening.

Dad's attitude was no longer lofty as before, in terms of politics and race relations. I sensed a different kind of anger had found its way in; no doubt influenced by current events and commentary from Cathy. She grew up in Alabama, with almost no interaction with people of color, and had a hot, Irish temper that was kept in check 99% of the time. I never considered her a racist, though, and she never gave me cause to.

Still, all the racial strife made my sense of isolation more keenly felt. I never experienced any type of racial animosity in the Army. From my point of view, skin color made no difference from one guy to another. We were all green. We worked together, lived together, fought the VC together, and drank together. Yes, for the most part they stayed with their own and we stayed with ours, but that choice was not, as far as I knew, borne of animosity. It was more of a culture preference. People tend to stay with their kind, comfortably.

My social life wasn't any better. I lost touch with Deb from Bellwood, and I tried connecting with an old flame from high school but it didn't take. Gary Schultz, a friend from high school, used to come over during our senior year and we'd play some war-strategy-themed board game quite a bit, but he had moved away from Addison. My childhood friend, Jim, next door, was away at college. Skip Hall was around, but he was more of a good acquaintance than a really close friend. Was he still dating my cousin? Having lost touch with Mom and my two siblings in Michigan, I also lost touch with my cousins in Villa Park. I was sad about that, and too embarrassed to look them up. It had been so long since the last time we were all together.

Mom had written to me while I was in 'Nam. Her letters were always typed rather than handwritten. She worked as a secretary and I understood it would have been much easier to type a letter from work that to sit at home and write one out longhand. But, I recall thinking how impersonal that was. To me, a person's heart is shared in a handwritten letter, not one typed. Maybe that played into it, but I had no interest in visiting Mom during my leave. Besides, how would I get there and back? Borrow Dad's car? That was not going to happen. I could hitchhike or take a bus or train. I could have figured a way, but I really didn't want to go.

My emotions about our family situation had not changed much, even after two years in the Army. In my case, distance did not make the love for my family grow. By that time, Steve and Sue seemed more like distant cousins rather than close siblings. Dad's input didn't help, either, with his sly remarks about the "Michigan camp." To bury the raw emotions about the absence of half of my family, I tried my best not to think about them. At one level, I blamed Mom for the divorce and her husband, Bill[84], for them moving out of state. And I blamed Dad for his insecurity about losing loyalty from me and Scott.

With the last of my leave ahead of me, what was I going to do? The Veterans of Foreign Wars post in Villa Park was not accepting anyone for membership who claimed Vietnam as their combat tour. It wasn't as if I really wanted to join the VFW, I just thought I could get a beer there, forgetting that I was underage. I was leaving for Germany soon, anyway. But, it would have been nice to go inside, buy a beer (if they'd let me), and trade war stories with some other vets, maybe one or two my age. But, you needed to be a member to buy a beer inside the post.

"Vietnam is not a war," they said. "Try over at the American Legion."

The American Legion didn't interest me. I had earned the right to belong to the VFW. It was exclusive. The American Legion wasn't, except for veterans serving when no war was being fought. Or at least that's what I told myself. Mostly, it was my attitude that prevented me from going over there and picking up a membership form. My recalcitrance was a product of war, of combat action being a daily routine that stopped abrupt-

---

[84] Vice president of automotive services with K-Mart Corporation. His primary responsibility was operations and logistics for K-Mart gas stations.

ly that night in Bien Hoa. To me, the American Legion was for guys who hadn't gone overseas. It was for the guys who spent their "Vietnam era" at places like Fort Sheridan, Illinois; Fort Campbell, Kentucky; or, any other place in the world that was safe and secure. At the time I believed it was for those who never knew the sounds of battle.

Try as I might, fitting in was impossible. The words from that night during Tet came back to me: "We're too crowded. You can't come in. There's no room for you here." Just like squatting next to that bunker door, back home I felt like I was still waiting to get inside. The only difference was nobody *back in the world* asked if I was wounded.

Dad's car was available to me during the evenings. I drove around town, went to downtown Chicago to find some nightlife, but found none where I thought I could afford. My search for getting a buzz was getting desperate. So, I'd end up going to a movie theater alone, not really watching the movie, but just sort of sitting there, trying to be entertained, trying to forget what I had been through. Where were all the single women? Not one single girl ever went to the movie while I was there. I know, I checked. Strangely, it seemed people my age had vanished.

During one of my early forays into the evening hours, I stopped off at a drugstore uptown to buy a pack of cigarettes. The store was empty, almost deserted except for the only employee I saw. She was standing behind the counter. Very pretty with dark, curly hair down to her shoulders, I couldn't take my eyes off her. As we talked a little, I stole a glance up and down her upper torso, finding the curvature of her body very appealing. My glance went further down her left arm to her hand. Very quickly; I didn't want to seem obvious. And, there it was, no band on her ring finger. I studied her face. Her lips, with just a hint of lipstick, smiled as she spoke. Her lips begged for my attention. The attraction was immediate.

She was not seeing anybody. Her name was Nancy and she lived in town with her parents. That's all I needed to know. I asked her out, and she agreed. It was sparks, a whirlwind of activities together: movies, lunches and dinners, meeting parents, and talking about everything under the sun. I suppose what charm I had I laid on pretty thick, and our courtship flourished. I couldn't be with her enough. She consumed my thoughts day and night. She was a lady and I respected that about her. I kept thinking, *One step at a time. Slow and easy, don't mess this up. Don't do any-*

thing you'd regret. To the background of Frank Sinatra singing "Nancy (With the Laughing Face)", we'd dance alone in the back room of the house. It felt so good to have her in my arms.

She lived with her parents on the north side of town. We dated for two weeks when I realized she was *the one.* This was the most serious relationship I had ever experienced. Convinced I was in love with her, I told her so. She felt the same about me.

Dad and Cathy took my news about Nancy in stride. They were happy knowing I had found someone special. I talked to him about getting engaged to Nancy, and he didn't try to talk me out of it. I needed to get a ring. At my request, Dad knew somebody downtown who had a nice jewelry store, small but nice. That Saturday, we went there, in Chicago, on State Street. It was located on the ninth or tenth floor of an old office building, probably built at the turn of the century. We looked at a number of engagement rings. Most were so expensive that I nearly wanted to rethink my intent. But I found one, and Dad and I left with a quarter-karat single stone diamond ring.

With less than a week left of my leave, Nancy accepted my proposal of marriage. After a day or so, and knowing I'd be leaving for Germany soon, her mom offered to drive us to Madison, Wisconsin to make it official. Eighteen was the legal age there, her mom said to me, almost like an invitation. Very politely I declined the offer. A voice inside me said, *Don't do it.* My gut was telling me there was something wrong, but I couldn't understand what it was. Maybe Nancy's mom was just a little too eager.

Somewhere along the line, or maybe all along the line, I learned to have utmost respect for girls my age. This respect required me to observe every point of etiquette I could muster. I even treated the young woman in Vietnam and Japan with respect, though we both knew the business aspect of those short relationships. The more I respected a girl, the more I had to behave myself. And by that, I mean not saying or doing anything that I may regret at a later date, for whatever the reason.

Steve, my brother, came to Villa Park for a visit while I was home. I was so glad to see him. Two years younger than me, he had grown up. It had been, what, over three years since I saw him last? I hadn't seen or heard from him since they left Villa Park about three and a half years before. He was curious about my experiences in 'Nam, and about military service in general. At eighteen years old, he was considering his options about enlisting, waiting to be drafted, or not going at all.

There was so much uncertainty about waiting to be drafted. You lived day-to-day not knowing if your letter from Selective Service was going to be in that day's mail. If he enlisted, he would have more control of his destiny. Directed mostly to Dad, he asked what kind of work would be available for him? What type of school should he enlist for? Would enlisting be better than being drafted? What were the pros and cons?

The three of us sat in Dad's car, parked on the concrete slab behind the house, to discuss these things. We had been a patriotic family, not shirking our duty to God and country. Steve wanted part of the action, or maybe he just wanted to move out from home as I did at eighteen. He stayed for dinner that night, but then he left. I wasn't sure if he was going back to Michigan, or not. Steve looked pretty good, wavy black or dark brown hair compared to my straight, blonde hair, and standing about an inch taller than me.

Steve enlisted into the Army on March 30, 1968. He went to Fort Leonard Wood, Missouri for basic training and military intelligence school. I would not see him again for almost eight years, though we almost met under much different circumstances a year later.

I had just days left for my leave. A Special Bulletin was announced on TV. Martin Luther King, Jr. had been assassinated by a sniper while in Tennessee. I was shocked and saddened, like so many in the country. I admired him not only because of his peaceful nature, but also because of one thing that stood out in his most famous speech. Speaking about his own children, he dreamed that one day "they will not be judged by the color of their skin but by the content of their character." I really liked that concept. It was, after all, the way I was raised.

My leave in the States was over. I had to get to Fort Dix, then on to Frankfurt am Main. Nancy wanted to come along. Two days before I left, her mom made a final plea for us to go to Madison and make it official. No thanks.

"We could get married in Germany," Nancy tried to convince me.

I was able to put her off by letting her know that Spec Fives don't make that much money. Living in the barracks I was able to go from one monthly pay to another. But, if we were married and lived in town somewhere, I wasn't sure the money would stretch that far. I didn't have any married friends yet, so I didn't know about the extra pay that was available for married GIs. Regardless, I'd made up my mind to leave without her.

She offered to come visit. I told her that sounded great, that she could come visit sometime next year. I cared about her, but something in the back of my mind kept saying no. I really didn't want her to visit me there and should have told her, but I was still trying to be positive and supportive. Maybe I would change my mind after a few months. Don't burn your bridges, as they say.

Dad, Cathy, Scott and Janie, and my new girlfriend/fiancée, Nancy, saw me off at the departure gate at O'Hare International Airport. Sitting with her, I contemplated my new directions in life. I'd be in Germany for no more than a year. Engaged, I'd have to behave myself and not run around with any women I thought about meeting there. Then, there was Barb, too. I had almost forgotten about her during those last few weeks.

Nancy wasn't talking much about our future. She seemed to be more interested in me inviting her to come visit once I got settled in with my new unit. I couldn't commit to that. I didn't know what was going to happen once I arrived, let alone making plans for her to visit. Where would she stay? Who'd pay for her travel, lodging, meals, etc.? Me? Too many questions, and I didn't have any answers, or enough money.

The flight from Chicago to Trenton, NJ was quick. I checked in at Fort Dix and soon afterwards left for Frankfurt. That final journey over the Atlantic Ocean was much too quick, it seemed. I didn't have time to think of all the things that were piling up in my life. It was my first transoceanic flight during the daytime. Nothing much to look at out the window except water, and lots of it.

Chapter 10

West Germany

My initial impression about the U.S. Army in Europe was military culture shock. Back to spit and polish, in spades. It was like basic training, only worse. Fatigues and hats were heavily starched and creased. Boots shined so well that you could see a reflection of your face on the toe tips while standing straight up. Army jeeps and trucks were spotless. Everything seemed to be aligned perfectly and in proper military order. STRAC[85] is what we called it. Processing into the Third Infantry Division (Mechanized), also called '3ID (M)' and pronounced as "three-eye-dee, meck", was personal to me.

Here and there were reminders of the Nazi regime that reigned not twenty-three years before. There were a number of *bas-relief* examples of stone carved eagles, shields, and so on that were strictly Germanic style. All of the swastikas had been removed. It was almost like a constant reminder, due to the remaining blemish, that the Nazis were gone.

Soon enough, April 6, 1968, I arrived in Schweinfurt, my new duty station, and assigned to D Troop, 3rd Squadron, 7th Cavalry Regiment, 3rd Infantry Division (Mechanized). It was an aviation reconnaissance company with one UH-1D Huey and two OH-13 helicopters located in Cohn Barracks. The gate at the front of our barracks was constructed of stone and concrete. Over the arch were the remains of yet another Nazi Eagle *bas-relief.* That swastika had also been removed, maybe chiseled off, but the void remained, as did most of the eagle.

Our barracks, an old stone multi-room building, was next door to the hangar and airfield. One story I heard during the first couple days here said it was an old rooming house for German officers, while another identified it as a small hotel next to the adjoining airstrip. Either way, it wasn't important. I had my priorities straight, or so I thought: beer. A short walking distance away was the regional Rod and Gun Club. There, not two hundred yards from our barracks, was a bar and sports shop. It had a room where beautiful and expensive hunting rifles were sold. Inside the main

---

[85] Officially, an acronym for Strategic Army Corp, but widely used to describe strict behavior, sharp markings, straight lines, and smart military bearing.

room of the club were tables and chairs, a few nickel slot machines, and a jukebox.

My first night in D Troop was 'exciting.' I signed into the unit and dropped off my stuff in my room upstairs. My roommates were two other Spec Fives, also 'Nam vets. As I returned to the ground floor, I was confronted by a young black Spec Four. Because I had changed into civilian clothes, he didn't know who I was except as the new white guy fresh from the States. As I was headed to the main door to leave the building, he went out of his way to block way in the hallway. I moved over and he did it again, and again, and seemed to make every effort to initiate a fight right there.

"Hey, what's your problem?" I asked.

"You," he said. "You wuz just in the States?"

"Yeah."

"Why'd Reverend King have to die? Why'd you do it? He never did nothin' to you."

His beef? He blamed me for the assassination of Martin Luther King, Jr. I told him I didn't have anything to do with that, but he persisted. I tried to walk past him. He blocked my way again. I tried to get past him on the other side of the hall. He blocked me again. I wasn't in the mood for this shit. I pushed past him. Should I have reported him? Yes, and I did. After talking to the CQ[86] in the orderly room I learned he was an okay guy, just young. He would talk to him forthwith. I went on about my business.

The next morning at formation, that same Spec Four approached me.

"Sorry, man," he said, "I didn't know who you were, and didn't know you're a Spec Five," as he stared at the rank insignia pins on my fatigues. "I don't really blame you for King's death, but saw you and wanted to blame somebody. I've been really angry he got himself killed."

---

[86] Charge of Quarters. Usually, a soldier with a pay grade of E-5 (and usually a Spec Five) would remain awake and on duty throughout the night. Stationed in the company orderly room, he was 'in charge', beginning at 5:00 pm until relieved the next day at 8:00 am by one of the senior NCOs, or if a weekend, when the next CQ came on duty. The CQ represented the first sergeant and had a list of duties to perform.

I processed into the unit. As instructed by the orderly room clerk at the 190th, I turned in my complete flight records to the operations sergeant, an overweight staff sergeant who seemed to be glued to the chair seat. He asked me what he was supposed to do with that form. I told him I really didn't know, maybe process the information through channels? I trusted he would figure it out and take care of it. Looking at his fatigue shirt, I saw no patch on his right shoulder. And that told me he'd had no previous combat assignments.

During formation, I noticed we had probably no more than forty men in our unit. One by one, I was introduced to the other guys throughout the unit by name. If it wasn't for the name tags, I wouldn't have remembered one guy from another, except for Useless. His first name is Ulysses, but he told me everyone called him "Useless." He preferred that I call him by his nickname, though I couldn't understand why. He was a comical young man, a year or two older than me, and very pleasant.

Our troop had three aircraft, and we supported the other troops in the squadron that had tanks. Someone told me this regiment was once under George Custer's command when he was a colonel at Little Big Horn. Because he disobeyed orders and lost that battle with so many killed, the Army punishment was to never allow the entire regiment to be actively on-duty, together at one time, inside the Continental United States ever again. The regiment had dishonored the Army, and banishment was payback.

At 0600 hours, the bugle played *Reveille* over the parade ground loud speakers as the American flag was raised for the day. If you happened to be outside, the protocol was to stop walking—or, if driving, to get out—and stand at attention facing the flag. Render the hand salute until the music ended, and only then be on your way. No exceptions were permitted except for emergencies. Failure to show respect would likely find you getting chewed out by a senior NCO or officer, if you got caught. It was the same thing at the end of the day. At 1800 hours, the bugle rendition of *Taps* would play, people would render respect to the flag, and the workday was officially over.

Going into town required a pass signed by the first sergeant. Wearing civilian clothes was required. It had to be a shirt and tie, sports jacket, and trousers. No blue jeans, open neck shirts, T-shirts or sweatshirts. The gate was guarded by two GIs who were there to monitor the wearing of appropriate clothing, check the pass of those leaving and verifying active-duty U.S. military status or other forms of military authorization (check IDs) for those coming inside. Fatigues were not allowed to be worn into town, unless the man's living quarters was located there, and then only to home. For those of us in the barracks, our curfew was at midnight, regardless of our age or rank (Spec Five and below). That was the time for bed check by the CQs in each troop and accounting for all living in the barracks as being present and accounted for, and to see who was AWOL.

For entertainment, the single guys on base would go to a Gasthaus[87] (pronounced: guesthouse) in town. Other than the Rod & Gun Club next door, there really was no other local place to go for me and the other guys living in the barracks. There seemed to always be one or two German taxis waiting just outside the gate to take us to town.

The various Gasthauses ranged from full-menu restaurants to watering holes in more rural areas. Occasionally, they were in conjunction with rooms to rent for the night. From a financial and cultural point of view, it was more rewarding going to one instead of staying on base and going to the clubs. After spending all day on base, it was good to get away for a while. German beer tasted better (much better), had a higher alcohol content, and was less expensive because of the exchange rate (four Deutsche marks per U.S. dollar; and one mark per bottle of beer). It was preferable to go into town to get a beer than to buy one on base, except for the convenience factor.

The selection of beer was either local or European brands, such as Heineken from Holland. Some bottles had ceramic and metal flip-tops, while others had traditional metal bottle caps. German white wine was also a favorite for some GIs, especially with dinner. I preferred Liebfraumilch, semi-sweet and cooled. My favorite dinner, above any other, was and continues to be Jägerschnitzel (pronounced: yager-shnitzul). Also known as 'hunter's cutlet,' it is a fried, breaded veal cutlet served with fries or spätzle, all smothered in brown mushroom gravy.

We'd sit around a table, trading stories about war and women against the background music of Tom Jones, Elvis Presley, The Beatles,

---

[87] A German-style inn or tavern serving beer, wine and spirits. GIs always seemed to have a favorite one to spend their money on wine, women and song.

Donovan, Bobby Goldsboro, Otis Redding, Simon & Garfunkel, Gary Puckett and the Union Gap, Tommy James and the Shondells, etc. Elvis Presley, more so than any other American singer, was wildly popular with the Germans we met. Sometimes, somebody would throw in a polka or march to listen to, but not too often.

It would not surprise me if the hospitality we received was all show for our benefit. The Germans wanted our business. The best way to draw an American crowd was to give them what they like, what they're most comfortable with, in order to keep us in their establishment. It was a fine line, because if Americans really wanted American entertainment, they might just as well go to one of their clubs on base.

I would say that our relationship with Germans was good. The only difference between them and Americans was the language. And, many Germans spoke English. I learned that occasionally they'd play with us, pretending not to understand English. It was only later I learned English had become almost a second language for most Germans due to a large number of Americans stationed in their country since World War II.

Once, we ran across some older German men who hadn't adjusted to the fact they lost during both World Wars. We didn't speak much German and they didn't speak to us in English, but by the facial and hand expressions of anger and contempt, it wasn't difficult to understand they hated Americans. And, with a few beers in their belly, that anger got loud and threatening.

These guys, maybe one-time Nazis, almost all in their late forties and older, usually frequented certain Gasthauses. We learned to avoid those places. American GIs have been in Germany since 1945, so where to go and not go have been passed on from one group of GIs to another ever since.

During the mid-spring of 1968, I was notified by the first sergeant I was going to be the recipient of an award from my tour in Vietnam. The Squadron commander wanted to have an awards ceremony, and I was going to be one of the guests of honor. It would be held at Ledward Barracks. Well, okay, but what award? He wouldn't tell me. Could it be the oak leaves for the Air Medal? I had recently received orders for an Army Commendation Award for my year in 'Nam, but didn't get the medal. So, naturally I thought maybe that was going to be the big surprise.

The day before the ceremony, the first sergeant asked me if I happened to have a Distinguished Flying Cross medal with me. As a matter of fact, I did. He told me that they couldn't find one available to use. Most of the men in the squadron (working with tanks and trucks) never heard of a DFC, much less seen one. Because they did not have one for the ceremony, they needed to use mine. Was it for one of our pilots who had also recently returned from Vietnam? He wouldn't say. I loaned him my medal and presentation box as he told me to wait and see.

The next day, the entire squadron was present in the formation. The temperature was mildly cool and the sun was out with just a few clouds in the sky. A little extra spit-shine was applied to my boots that morning and I put on a fresh set of fatigues, starched and pressed. Each troop in the squadron lined up, present and accounted for before the squadron commander, sergeant major, and a few others stood in front of the men holding the American flag and the red top and white bottom 7th Cavalry swallow-tail guidon. The Squadron Commander said a few words about the history of our unit, of which we, the 3rd Squadron, were part. We were an aviation-tank reconnaissance unit, one of two stationed in West Germany since 1963. The nickname of the 7th Cavalry was Garry Owen, named after an Irish march tune *Garryowen*. The 7th Cavalry had seen action against American enemies over many generations, the most recent being Korea and Vietnam.

I was surprised to be the first to be called front and center. The ARCOM medal came to mind, and I thought it odd they'd start with that lower one. I went forward, making certain all of my pivots and turns were in strict military fashion. After all, the entire squadron, the commanders, and senior NCOs were watching. Once in place, I remained at attention, waiting. Two other guys were called out. As each name was called, that man left his troop formation, marched out and stood beside me to my left. The commander said something again about the courage of men assigned to this squadron being recognized and his being a proud commander.

The three of us remained at attention as the commander and his entourage approached.

While I stood there, the citation was read by one of the assistants. "The President of the United States takes great pleasure in presenting the Distinguished Flying Cross to Specialist Five Martin D. Alexander for heroism while participating aerial flight evidenced by voluntary actions above and beyond the call of duty...actions while serving as door gunner..."

The words continued, and faded as my mind took over, going back in time. A vivid picture formed in my mind. It was the day in Vietnam when ten slicks were beat up pretty bad by well-fortified enemy positions. It was a heavy firefight at the LZ. We flew over a batch of NVA automatic weapons trying to shoot them, and us, down at close range. We were sitting ducks in front of their encampment. It was the day when our pilot was wounded and DB's M-60 jammed. Almost directly above, for what seemed like eternity, I was the only one shooting at the NVA from DB's side of the ship. I only did what anybody else would have done in the same circumstance. I think so, anyway. Just trying to prevent us from being shot out of the sky. As the words were read, I visualized the scene replay in my mind. The replay was from the eyes of someone else, my guardian angel, maybe. The same angel who was with me during Tet '68, pushing me down and aside.

My guardian angel had made me lean forward, at the exact time to miss the bullet that wounded the pilot; a bullet I had no knowledge of at the time. He watched me as I tore the corner of the mosquito net[88] down and got close enough to check the pilot's wound, then taking my M-60 and belt of ammo, working my way over next to DB. He was at my right shoulder, watching, as I began firing into the treetops, aiming at the many star-bursts of muzzle flashes from the ground. Through his eyes, I remember most of that scenario.

The sound of the squadron commander's voice came back, saying, "... great credit upon himself, his unit, and the United States Army." His aide handed him the medal, my own medal, and pinned it onto my chest over my heart. I rendered the hand salute.

"Gary Owen, Sir," I said.

"Gary Owen," he replied as he returned my salute.

---

[88] Too often, the hot brass ejected from the M-60, especially from my side of the ship, would fly forward in the cabin. Some would land inside the pilot's collar, causing a burn and more importantly, a distracting reaction. The mosquito net was the right size, perforated to allow air-flow, and easily available. To attach a brass catcher to the gun would have been impractical due to the drag it would have created, and the limited amount of brass it was designed to catch.

I remained at attention as he handed me the display case and they went to the next man, from one of the tank units, in line. He read his citation and pinned a Bronze Star with "V" device on his chest. The third man received an Army Commendation Medal with "V" device. Their awards were also for heroic actions in Vietnam. Our orders and certificates were provided after the ceremony.

Okay, so I got to attach an oak leaf to that ribbon on my Class As. That and a quarter would get me a cup of coffee at the cafeteria. But, two DFCs? Wow. It is the highest aviation medal to be awarded "for heroism or extraordinary achievement while participating in aerial flight", to an officer or enlisted person. Charles Lindbergh was the first recipient. I was the only one in the Squadron who had one, let alone two. Because of that, I felt I had to downplay the award. Most didn't even know what it was, anyway. I didn't want to come across as a braggart, then, or now. It was better to fit in with everybody, being one of the guys.

Most of the UH-1 guys in our troop who were Vietnam vets had the Air Medal with a bunch of oak leaf clusters. Bronze Stars are not awarded for action in aerial flight. For heroic action, the Air Medal with "V" (Valor) was awarded instead. The Air Medal was also awarded for meritorious service, requiring twenty-five combat flight hours for each. I had been expecting my flight records to have been processed by this time. I had seven oak leaves for the Air Medal up to the summer of 1967 and I thought that low. I flew a lot of combat hours and expected another twelve or thirteen oak leaves. The orders hadn't been cut yet, maybe next time.

The Rod and Gun Club became a habitual place to go. The nickel slot machines just took my money, never paying out. The retail store within the club stocked high-end rifles, bone-handled knives and such. So, like a kid in a candy shop, I oohed and aahed to myself at the perfectly aligned weaponry, shiny metal and polished wooden stocks on display inside the cases and on the back-wall rack. Every once in a while, I remembered a request from Dad. Before I left the states, he asked me to look into purchasing a thirty-odd-six rifle for him. They were too expensive at six or seven hundred dollars apiece. That was at least two month's pay, maybe more.

Beer and the four or five guys at 'our' table always drew me back to the club. More beer, more fun. We sang along with John Lennon (of

The Beatles) whenever "Hey, Jude" was playing on the jukebox; and it was often. We made sure of that. Forget Vietnam. Forget Nancy. Forget the Army. Forget killing. Forget people with AK-47s and rockets and machine guns wanting us dead. Just forget. I couldn't so I drank some more.

We sang at the top of our voices. The more beer we drank, the louder we became. Was this our way of crying out for all the terror, killing, sacrifices, and experiences we had that no one else could possibly understand? Was this the way for twenty- and twenty-one-year-old men to act?

Taking a break from the club next door, I entered a period of social withdrawal. I found solace being by myself for a while. The cafeteria in Cohn Barracks was just a few blocks away from our barracks.

In going to and from, I would pass one particular area, a large brick-sided building that, I think, was once a ball-bearing factory during the war. More often than not, I had the strangest sensation that I had been there before. I don't mean the day before, nor the week before. I felt as if I had been there, at that location, *years* before. It was only and uniquely at that location, during daylight, when the sun was shining at a certain angle, and during warm weather that I had that sensation, many times. Walking past that building had a special meaning for me, but I didn't know what, or why.

Sometime later, the Russians invaded Czechoslovakia, a state within the Soviet bloc. On August 20, 1968, Soviet tanks and troops arrived. Martial law was invoked in Prague and in a few other key major cities to control mass uprisings by the citizens. In response, NATO forces were placed on highest alert. American forces were getting ready to mobilize if needed.

The border of Czechoslovakia is about 30 miles from Schweinfurt, so the Soviet invasion caught our attention, became very real, and potentially dangerous. That first day, our troop commander, his executive officer, and our first sergeant went to quite a few meetings at Ledward Barracks. Events were turning serious, very quickly. Our platoon sergeant, Bob Minton, remained cool, though the rest of us were chomping at the bit to get into the fight. Most of us were Vietnam vets; we should have known better than to seek out warfare. But being relatively young and having too much testosterone and adrenaline, we weren't thinking clearly. None of us had been issued any type of weapon. Not when we signed into the troop, not during this crisis, not at all. Did we have an arms room? None of us knew where it might have been.

Our daily "busy work" activities stopped. This was a big deal, and it was totally unlike our preparation for 'Nam. All of us went through formalized training with maps and manuals, learning to decipher and respond to secret classified coded messages. Our security clearances were updated, and posted in our two-o-one files. All annual leaves and passes were cancelled. The guys who were married and living with family in the surrounding areas were called back on base, to remain until further notice. In the middle of the night, we loaded essential gear in trucks and trailers, ready to move out at a moment's notice. Our vehicles were lined up. The three aircraft, ready to go. We waited.

Thirty miles is not far. It was a good thing the Soviets hadn't decided to invade West Germany. If it took us days to get our shit together in response to the invasion of Czechoslovakia, how could we have responded at a moment's notice if the Russians had actually crossed the border? So much for being STRAC. All that spit and polish, but we were nowhere near ready. Absolute Mickey Mouse. DB was right.

After a couple of days, our alert status was cancelled. The Russians stopped at the border. The United States and other NATO forces did not cross over, but we were prepared to go at a moment's notice—finally.

Only a week after the Soviets invaded Czechoslovakia, we learned there was also trouble in Chicago. At the Democratic National Convention, major riots were taking place. Fights among delegates, due to disagreements about our continued involvement in the Vietnam War, broke out on the convention floor. Anti-war protesters saw the gathering of politicians and media as an excellent opportunity to make their voices heard, both inside and out. War protesters, draft dodgers, anti-establishment college students, hippies, and just about anybody else who had an axe to grind took to the street.

Tens of thousands of people, of seemingly every color and persuasion, descended on downtown Chicago. The mayor called up 12,000 police officers and an additional 15,000 state and federal officers, including 7,500 members of the Illinois National Guard, to quell the destructive behavior of the protesters. The riot became known as the Battle of Michigan Avenue.

We heard it was televised nationwide, but we didn't have a TV to watch it. Dad might have mentioned it once in his occasional letters to me, but most of the news about the riots we read in the *Stars & Stripes*. There was almost no discussion among us about the seriousness of the demonstrations and change in the national mood about the war. From our standpoint, the riots were just one of those things that happened because of hippies, draft dodgers, malcontents, and people who were simply too scared. But we failed to realize that the national mood about our involvement in 'Nam was changing. Military thinking is so much different than civilians. More people were now in opposition to the war, the draft, and the military in general, than those who supported us. It was us against them.

Some weeks passed. We had a field maneuver at Graffenweir that lasted three days. I was assigned to one of the OH-13 helicopters that were used for recon and observation. We slept in pup tents and pulled perimeter guard. Being late September or early October, it was cold and dreary just about the entire time. As we returned to Schweinfurt, our two OH-13s flew in formation. I rode with the pilot in one, and another Spec Five rode in the other ship. The fog got thicker the closer we got to base. Neither of the two young pilots were Instrument Flight Rated (IFR), meaning they could not fly by instruments alone. We couldn't see anything farther away than two hundred meters, so we flew as low to the ground as possible, following the autobahn below. With about a half hour of flight time left to go, the density of the fog forced us down. We landed in the center of one of the cloverleaves of the autobahn, each ship about fifty-feet apart.

The lead pilot radioed our position and circumstance, requesting that a vehicle be sent to our location. The plan was this: we were staying with the ships to guard them until the weather cleared. The pilots would get picked up and one of them would return later to bring supplies; or, if weather permitted, they would both return to fly us back home.

While we waited for their transportation, the four of us gathered firewood from the adjacent woods and started a campfire. About an hour later, an Army three-quarter arrived. Both pilots approached the driver and got into the front of the truck. They left, with not a word about when to expect them back. I turned to the other crew chief and said, "Okay, this'll be fun."

Cold, damp and surrounded by a very light drizzle and thick fog, we hunkered down closer to the fire to keep warm. We were no farther away than fifty feet of both ships. No food, no water, no warm clothes besides our field jackets and fatigues. In our wildest dreams, we never considered the possibility of being stranded. We considered sitting inside the cockpit of one of the ships, but there was no heat there. The cold just goes through the spherical tempered Plexiglass front end of the OH-13. The heat only works when the ship is working, and we needed a pilot to be present for that, though each of us had received certification to start the engine at idle speed; but, only permitted when a pilot is present.

About mid-afternoon, a middle-aged German man stopped his older model black Mercedes near us. He got out of his car and began walking toward us. We didn't consider him a threat at all. He spoke broken English. After some small talk and explanation about why two U.S. Army helicopters were parked in the middle of nowhere, he told us he had something for us. Going back to his car, he took out a 'milk-crate' full with bottles of German bier from the trunk. It was his gift to us as we weathered the elements. "Danke," we said as he walked away to his car and left.

Later, the three-quarter returned, with just the driver. He told us we'd be staying the night, at a minimum. We helped him unload two sleeping bags and a case of C-Rats from the truck. He left and we were on our own once again. We stoked up the fire, threw a couple more logs onto it, ate and drank. It was mid-afternoon when the three-quarter left.

The fog was still as thick as molasses in most spots, but there were areas it was clearing. The ceiling was about twenty-five, fifty feet. At a short distance, maybe a hundred yards off, I noticed two hitchhikers walking along the autobahn. As they got closer, I pointed them out to my partner.

"Are those girls?" I quietly asked, not believing my eyes.

"Yes!" he said.

They were two young women about our age, presumably tourists backpacking to save money.

"Yoo-hoo, hello," we both yelled out. They heard us and started walking over.

As they got closer, each greeted us in English. They told us they were from Australia, vacationing in Europe. Of course, they spoke English. God's face was shining down on us today.

We all seemed to get along very well and friendly-like. They were quite pretty, but we tried to downplay that and play our hand very smooth. They took us up on our offer of beer, and we shared a few bottles. My partner and I seemed to know what the other was thinking. We had to communicate with our eyes and eyebrows to avoid scaring them off. Just play it cool. Maybe they'll decide to spend the night. We could cuddle-up in the sleeping bags to keep warm in front of the campfire. Two girls, two guys, in the middle of nowhere. Nice.

About an hour later a civilian car drove up to our campsite. It had American Armed Forces license plates. The driver emerged. He was one of our pilots who came back to check how we were doing.

"No, we're doing fine, thanks," I said. Turning towards the fire, I mumbled, "Go away," quietly to myself. The other crew chief heard me and smiled.

The pilot couldn't help but notice the two beautiful young ladies with us. We introduced the two girls to him and they started talking. He asked them, "Do you need a ride anywhere?"

"Why, yes. Thank you," one said in her cute Australian accent. And with that, they got in his car and left.

We opened another beer, sat down, and watched the flames of the campfire in silence for a short while. We sat there, sulking, wrapped in our sleeping bags, drinking our beers, contemplating our lost opportunity. I became immersed in my thoughts for a while thinking about Nancy, California where it's warm, and counting the months until I'd get discharged. What was I going to do when I got out? I didn't have a clue. Our beer bottles empty, we grabbed another and picked up where we left off before the girls arrived, shooting the breeze about any topic that came to our mind.

Around 2300 hours, the fog lifted. Stars, very bright in the countryside, filled the sky. The fire crackled and popped. It was a good fire and kept us reasonably warm while we occasionally kept an eye on the two helicopters. We decided to trade two-hour shifts so that one of us would be awake while the other slept. We had earlier gathered a sufficient amount of fire wood, and we were set for the night. Two hours on, two off. We did this twice.

I awoke to frost everywhere except for the small circle around our diminishing fire. A bed of hot embers, ash, and the last of our firewood was all we had at about 0700 hours. Both of us, awake, were zippered up, warm and snug-like, in the sleeping bags and deciding which of us was going to venture out to get more wood. Neither one of us wanted to volunteer. So, we remained where we were, keeping warm and waiting on the other. Stubbornly, we watched as the flames devoured the last of the firewood. Dawn was breaking. The sun was rising. We waited. If wishes had wings, I would have wished for a hot cup of coffee.

It was about an hour later when our pilots, refreshed, alert, clean shaven, warm, and probably full from breakfast with one or two cups of coffee, arrived. It was time to go. The ships were cranked up and we lifted off.

One of my roommates in the barracks was a quiet man of roughly twenty-three years of age. His name is Hal. He was a third-year college student majoring in English when he got drafted. He took the three-year option to enlist for a school, rather than ending up infantry. He impressed me by his studious approach to nearly every situation he faced, never complaining about anything. We shared the room with our other roommate, Jim. Because of Hal's demeanor, I don't believe he had a mean bone in his body. He always treated people with respect, even if the other person's behavior was dubious and not deserving. Though I never admitted such, I looked up to him for his sobriety, thoughtful resolve, and maturity. He never caused trouble, not once during the time I knew him.

Jim Baird and I woke up one morning and found Hal getting up very slowly. As he propped himself up by his elbows, the severe bruises about his face, neck and arms were exposed. His face was swollen, pock-marked with at least a hundred very small stippled cuts, matching those on his upper neck. His arms had a few larger cuts and scrapes like road-rash. It was obvious to us he had either been run over by a truck or tangled with a nest of angry hornets. Hal told us he had trouble at one of the gasthauses in town over the price of a bottle of champagne.

He quietly told us he had been sitting at the bar, on a stool. A woman sat next to him, and they began talking. A few minutes into their conversation he ordered a bottle of champagne. They drank and talked. When it was time to pay up, they charged him 400 DM, equivalent to a hundred US dollars. He refused to pay, insisting there had been a mistake. Two men, who Hal believed to be bouncers, approached him to encourage his compliance; no, a shakedown would be a better way to describe the situation. If he refused, they would throw him out of the building. Hal re-sisted. A fight ensued. One of the bouncers removed a small pistol and shot Hal. Apparently, the gun was not loaded with bullets, per se, but with gas emitting projectiles. Gunpowder burns caused the stippling on his face and neck.

Word of Hal's assault spread among our troop very quickly. He had gone to the dispensary during the night and was treated for his inju-ries. The medic placed him on bed rest when he returned to the barracks. Most of us reacted quite verbally, wanting to settle the score. One of our own had been wounded. We were out to avenge Hal, no matter what. I was part of the planning committee. We hastily made a plan. Working out all the possible scenarios, it was our intent to tear that place apart; teach them a lesson. The message we wanted to convey was, *don't screw with Americans*.

Word of our plan to attack the gasthaus reached our first sergeant and troop commander (TC). A formation was called just before lunch. The TC spoke to all of us, sympathized with Hal, and understood our intent. With that in mind, he restricted us to Cohn Barracks for twenty-four hours. Those who were married and lived off base with their family were con-fined to quarters for the night.

Okay. No problem. We'll just have more time to really plan this out carefully.

I remained one of the key planners of this operation. Our plan became more of a military operation, rather than a bunch of guys acting like a bunch of hoodlums. We worked out the logistics of "infiltrating" the gasthaus. Timing was important. Teams were developed and assigned certain responsibilities. One would take care of taking out their communications. Another team leader coordinated transportation for our guys, arriving and departing. We would filter in by twos and threes. By default, I became the guy inside who would start the ball rolling. Hit them hard, hit them fast, and get out. Don't get caught. It couldn't fail.

The target date was the day after our restriction to the barracks ended. We would slowly begin our infiltration, poised as customers, beginning at 1930 hours. We had fifteen guys who volunteered to go, and four of them had cars. The cars would be placed strategically so as not to have them in eyesight of the people inside. Two guys were detailed to cut the phone line first. As "point," the plan was to notify me when the phone wire was cut. That was my signal. Regarding the others already inside, my signal to them was to break the mirror behind the bar. The sound of breaking glass would start the melee. Most importantly, we decided to limit our assault to two to three minutes at the most. We would assault every male employee there, create as much damage as possible as we fought our way out. Leave the customers alone. When given the chance, the bouncers would be told why we were there. Once outside, we would disperse quickly in all directions. So, the plan was set; get in there, strike, and leave before anybody showed up to help them, put us under arrest, or both.

When the twenty-four-hour restriction was over, it was go time. Our plan was foolproof. We thought of every contingency. A few of us carried half-inch wide by three-inch long bolts, borrowed from our hangar, to stiffen the fist when fighting. Another guy had a roll of dimes. What could go wrong?

I had not been to this particular gasthaus before. It was more of a restaurant than a bar. The customers inside were eating dinner. I noticed no children as I entered, walking through the dining area. At the bar, five stools were empty. I sat in the middle, alone. One by one, our guys arrived and found seating where available. No one ordered food, just beer. The menus were perused to minimize any suspicion. One of them, pretending to use the wall phone in the corner near the bar next to me, whispered, "We're all here", as he passed by.

Not wanting to waste money, I nursed the one beer I ordered. There was no way I could drink slower that I did, sip by sip. Patiently, I waited. As I continued to wait a little longer for word that the phone lines were cut, the woman behind the bar noticed my bottle was empty and asked, in English, "Another bier?"

"Nein, danke," I said. "Not now."

I waited some more. So far, I counted six male employees, three wearing a white shirt and black tie. The others were the cook and other kitchen workers, wearing white aprons. Each one of them looked formidable: dark hair, tall and muscular. I should have ordered the second beer.

Waiting seemed to take forever. The phone line *had* to go first. It was getting suspicious (in my mind) sitting in front of an empty beer bottle for at least five or ten minutes. Politely, the bartender again offered to sell me another beer. Again, I politely declined.

Then, it happened. The lights went out. A deep, black darkness overtook the interior. It was so dark I couldn't see a thing. As the lights came back on a couple minutes later, one of the male employees reached beneath the bar, directly in front of where I was seated. I was able to see his hand pull back, holding a small black revolver. He quickly placed it into the right-front pocket of his trousers. He spoke German to the bartender. Though I did not understand a word between them, I believe I knew what they were talking about. I looked at my empty bottle of beer, as did she.

As the man with the gun stepped away, someone else stepped away from the wall phone behind me and sat down next to me. He was one of ours.

"We cut the wrong wire," he said quietly. "But the phone line's cut."

At that, I threw my empty beer bottle over the bar, striking the mirror. In a loud voice, I said loudly, "Now." As planned, all of our guys got up, targeting every male employee in the place. Fistfights broke out left and right. I fought my way out, taking the only route through the dining room. Picking my targets carefully, and stopping a few blows directed at me and one of our guys, I yelled out, "Okay, we've got to go." I worked my way to the foyer and exited the building through the main front door.

Stepping down the few steps to the sidewalk, I quickly glanced around for police. No sign of them yet. Directly across the street I saw a familiar looking small, older model station wagon. Seeing the green license plate, I recognized it as one of ours. What was that car doing there? It was too close to the building. I turned left and walked away as a few guys behind me jumped into the car and closed the doors. I hadn't gone two blocks when, in the dark of night on a vacant city street, I saw the flashing blue roof-light of a white and green Polizei (German police) Volkswagen. It was speeding towards my direction, and that of the gasthaus two blocks behind me.

I supposed it was on its way to the carnage we created. Still a few blocks away from me, it was closing in, fast. Thinking quickly, I surmised the cops would be looking for any American walking away, escaping from the gasthaus. How would I, walking alone, remove that observation? I made a one-eighty, turned around and walked back as if I was *going to* the gasthaus, not fleeing. The police car sped past me. The station wagon in front had since left. As I watched the police stop ahead, I turned around again to continue walking away.

Another block later that station wagon pulled up next to me. A passenger in back, that kid who stopped me in the hallway when I first arrived in the country, had seen me walking and pulled over. Someone inside told me to hop in, and I did so through the rear window. We returned to Conn Barracks. All of our guys made it back. Some sustained injury, a few cuts and bruises. One of the guys complained about his right hand that was hurting and already swollen. He thought he'd broken some bones.

We had all made it back by curfew. For about an hour we compared notes, battle stories, and injuries; then, went to bed. Hal was already asleep, so Jim and I decided to wait until the next morning to let him know he was avenged by our successful "military" operation.

At 0800 the next morning, our TC addressed the formation. Apparently, the Germans had made a complaint. It wasn't about Hal, but us. They found out who we were because one of their bouncers, standing on the steps at the front door of the gasthaus, watched as a few GIs who ran out the front door, crossed the street and got into the parked station wagon. He wrote down the license plate number and reported it to the German police, who eventually tracked the plate number to one of us. A quick investigation found it obvious we had planned the attack in retaliation for Hal's injuries.

The damage to the gasthaus was estimated to be valued at $3,000, not including the injuries we inflicted on the employees. Criminal charges were being considered. It was decided by the higher-ups to make a trade-off, cancelling the German's charge against us if Hal agreed to not charge them with being assaulted in the first place. The icing on the cake? The gasthaus would be placed off limits to our troop personnel.

About this time on the other side of the world, my brother arrived in Cam Rahn Bay, Vietnam for his first tour.[89]

After the gasthaus incident, things began to cool off. Hal healed well, and a few of us decided to go to Amsterdam. We had heard about the Red Light District and wanted to check it out.

With a three-day pass approved, we began our journey by train. Travel there on Friday, visit the sights on Saturday, and return back on Sunday. Because we were active military, we didn't need a passport. For crossing borders inside Western Europe, all we needed was our United States Armed Forces military ID card. Traveling by train, I took notice of its punctuality, cleanliness, roominess, and overall organization of schedules. Entering Holland, we saw huge windmills everywhere. Some were spinning, others were not. They reminded me of paintings I had seen at the Art Institute of Chicago or studied during high school, which seemed like ancient history.

As we arrived in Amsterdam, our first order of business was to find a place to stay and down a few beers. We recognized the Heineken

---

[89] About forty years later, he told me he was assigned to work with the Central Intelligence Agency and the Phoenix Program in the area of Hoi An, about 15km south of Da Nang. His missions were classified. The Phoenix program involved seeking, capturing or assassinating enemy leaders. It was a program that Ho Chi Minh personally ordered its absolute destruction. Ho Chi Minh died during September 1969.

brand, and that's what we stayed with during our time there. Once settled in, and with a slight buzz to motivate us along, we began our quest.

We collectively relied on our own instinctive resourcefulness to find the Red Light District. By sheer luck (or testosteronic tracking) we found it by late afternoon. There was no actual red light, per se. There were no street markers or placards that identified this block as being home to the world's oldest profession. But all the same, it was obvious we were in the right place. Through large pane-glass windows facing the street and canal, sat solitary woman. One or two parlors were empty, but inside the others they were reading, knitting, or doing nothing more than watching the world pass in front of them. A few wore simple dresses, but most wore short lingerie. The women were a little older than I expected. Of course, anybody older than twenty or so was "older."

We compared our impressions with each other as we walked from one window-front to another, scoping out each woman to assess their attractiveness and appeal. We didn't exchange our greenbacks for guilders. All we had was American money, and we decided that none of us would "invest" any more than twenty bucks for our pleasure. Collectively, we picked the best-looking woman. Bill volunteered to go first. Jeff and me waited along the canal side, sitting on a bench, as he crossed the street, went up the stairs and entered the house. The woman in the window left her chair and walked away out of sight.

Which one of us would go next? Should we go to another house? The two of us, outside and eager to get going, passed the time by planning where, after all of us were done here, would we go. Should we sightsee, or just find a bar? What about dinner? Maybe we could find a restaurant close to the hotel. Would the guy at the hotel desk recommend one for us? Would we have to tip him? Hey, maybe we'll find some girls at the bar. That would be better than going to a restaurant. How long has Bill been in there? Eight, ten minutes?

Before we arrived at an answer, Bill stood in the doorway, closed the front door and walked towards us. He didn't look happy.

"How'd it go?" I asked.

"Terrible" was his quick and unreserved reply.

"What happened?"

"Well, I went inside," he said. "She followed me into a side room where the bed was. The price was higher but we agreed to twenty bucks. I paid her. She helped take my clothes off. She was in a hurry, but I wanted to go slower. It's been awhile, but my Johnson wasn't cooperating. I started kissing her to get going. She's not that good looking, up close, anyway. About a couple minutes or so later she said, 'Time's up. Either get off or pay more money.' I said, 'What?' and she said, 'You used up your time.' I wasn't going to give her another twenty, so I got dressed and left. And, here I am. Let's get the hell outta here."

Twenty bucks for ten minutes? We looked at each other in agreement. We're not doin' that. No way. We left, still itchin' to get laid, but much wiser.

For years, I had been looking forward to the day. But, when it arrived, turning twenty-one years old was actually not a big deal. For all intents and purposes, it was just another day. Sure, I could vote. That's quite important, but to be honest I never really looked forward to being twenty-one for that reason. What was really important to me? Being able to purchase alcoholic beverages. But that was only in the States. Here, I could go to any gasthaus in town, even to the Rod & Gun Club next door, wearing civilian clothes and not be carded or checked for age. I could order any type of alcoholic beverage I chose and held responsible for my actions.

February 1969, arrived very quickly. Deciding to get out or re-enlist was a no-brainer. Anybody in their right mind would get out of the Army, and that's what I planned to do. My decision, which I bragged about to anyone who would listen, was met with the expected popular approval. Everyone I hung around with looked forward to his own ETS[90]. Those who wanted to re-enlist usually kept quiet to avoid ribbing from the guys about being a *lifer*. Besides, right or wrong, going back to civilian life was the thing to do. During the past three years, I didn't know of anyone who reenlisted, except, of course, the NCOs. But, I was not (technically) one of them.

We thought more about what civilian life would be like as the days to my ETS got closer. The morale was high. We told ourselves we *hated*

---

[90] Expiration of Term of Service, the date of discharge when active duty in the military ends.

the Army and all the Mickey Mouse BS that came with it. But, we did have a good time. We made the best of the circumstances we faced. We bonded. One of the lifers talked to me about the virtues of staying in, the opportunities of assignments, etc. But I decided the obvious thing to do was to get out.

The only thing I knew about civilian life was what I had before I enlisted. There were new questions I had to consider. Was I going to live at home for a while? Where would I find work? What about college? Probably not. Except for art and a few gym classes, my high school grades were nothing to be proud about. But if I went, what would I study, anyway? Visual arts?

I had broken off my engagement to Nancy months before. It hit me one day that it was stupid getting engaged to a lady I knew only three weeks at best. She didn't accept my decision too well. But, I left her just as pure as when I met her. No regrets. Barb had written to me on a regular basis. She became engaged to be married, so maybe this would be a perfect time to visit her. I needed to see for myself if I could steal her away from her fiancé. Then, too, maybe she really wasn't engaged. Maybe she was testing me to see how much I cared about her.

As I thought about my future, aircraft maintenance seemed like a logical next step. To be honest, being a helicopter mechanic was not exciting. I really didn't like it as a job. The best part of my time in the Army was being a crew chief on flight status, flying as much as possible. Maybe, just maybe, I should become a pilot.

As I was packing my stuff to ship home, I carefully folded the flight jacket left over from Vietnam. I had been wearing it the night before Tet, when we were on standby, and I had taken it off when I went to bed. During the rocket and mortar attacks, my jacket, which I left on my bunk when we got out of the building, was peppered with shrapnel holes. It was no longer serviceable. When I returned from the hospital, rather than turning it in, I kept it as a souvenir and brought it along with me to Germany.

It would have been better to leave it at home. I never wore it because of the holes, and it still had the various patches (1st Aviation Brigade, air crewman wings, U.S. Army and name tags) sewed on. During a recent barracks inspection, the TC pulled the jacket out of my wall locker and looked it over. He asked where the holes came from, and I told him.

"Are you on flight status?" he asked.

"No, Sir" I replied.

"Well," he said, "we're going to have to turn this in as a DX[91]." He removed the jacket and handed it over to one of the guys in supply who lived in the room across the hall from us.

He instructed them to take custody of the jacket and turn it in as a DX. In that I was not on flight status here, it would not be returned to me. For the two weeks before I left, we went back and forth with that jacket. Finally, I struck a deal with both supply guys for me to keep it. So, the day I packed up my stuff, the jacket was included[92].

While out-processing from the unit, one of the places I had to clear was operations. The flight records I turned in almost a year earlier were missing. The clerk looked in all the right places, but it was nowhere to be found. There was no record of where it went, if anywhere. It had been about a year and I received no orders for the additional Air Medal oak leaf clusters. That pissed me off, but I was being discharged soon, so I shrugged it off as something I had no control over. Who was I going to complain to, anyway? But, damn it, I earned every one of those oak leaves. It may not be important to other people, but it was to me.

I checked back later. The same sergeant who took custody of the form almost a year before didn't recall what, if anything, he did with my flight records. Did he throw them away? He didn't know. Maybe he did, maybe he turned them in. He wasn't sure. No matter the reason, they were gone. Vanished. No proof, no admissions, nothing. And, no one left for me to complain to.

One more reason to get out of the Army.

But, I still held out for the possibility the form was processed through channels. After all, it wasn't in operations any longer.

---

[91] Direct Exchange. A damaged piece of military gear directly exchanged for a new one.

[92] When the trunk I packed up in Germany arrived home, I opened it to find the flight jacket missing. Apparently, the trunk was de-banded in the supply room, flight jacket removed per the order of the TC, and re-banded for shipment.

Chapter 11

Discharge

Finally, on February 14, I left Germany. My first stop in the U.S. was Fort Dix, New Jersey, to process out of the Army. I took a shuttle from the airport to the base. On the way, it was absolute culture shock. I had never seen so many billboards. Traffic was going every which way, snaking past buildings and concrete overpasses. It wasn't like this in Germany. It wasn't like this in Vietnam. In Chicago, I was accustomed to it, so it wasn't obvious there. Between the airport and Fort Dix, this symphony of confusion was everywhere.

At Fort Dix, there were others in process of being discharged as well, but the room we were in wasn't too crowded. Maybe ten of us were waiting for our DD Form 214[93] to out-process. My name was called and I went up to the counter and sat. The draft form was given to me to check for errors. I would need to sign before it was signed by the officer in charge. Noticing in the awards section, "Air Medal w/ "V" (7)", reminded me of the Army bullshit I was leaving. Where were my other Air Medal oak leaf clusters? That shit-for-brains sergeant never turned it in. This entry proved it. Seven oak leaf clusters equal 175 combat flight hours. Ninety-five percent of my total flying was categorized as such. I flew much more than 175 hours since the beginning of 1967, but now had nothing to prove it. By signing this form, it became my official record of my service, and I'd never get that medal up-to-date.

I continued examining the unsigned DD Form 214. There was something else on the form, dead center in the awards section, that caught my eye. The letters "CIB" had been typed in along with the other groupings of letters for awards. It could only mean one thing, a Combat Infantry Badge. How did I get that? They don't put anything on the DD Form 214 unless there was some type of documentation in my file. I didn't ask about it, nor did I bring it to their attention. I quickly realized I cared enough to correct this obvious error just about as much as the ops sergeant in Germany cared about my missing flight records. So, I let it slide.

---

[93] The form used for an honorable discharge from active duty military service.

In my mind, it was a tradeoff. One CIB on paper in exchange for about twelve earned, yet missing, Air Medal oak leaves. Seemed fair to me. Besides, what difference did it make? I was getting discharged and more than likely, no one would ever be looking at these awards. Who cared, anyway? I was honorably discharged from active duty on February 15, 1969. That's what mattered most.

The CIB wasn't earned. I knew that. It would not be the honorable, the right thing to do by wearing that badge, ever. I have seen the infantry in action. I could not know, firsthand, the pain they went through to earn that award, combat action in the field. I could not fully appreciate living their life of combat in misery and fatigue, exposure to the elements, blood-sucking bugs, poisonous snakes and plants, carnivorous animals, or sneaky VC snipers. Most importantly, their boots were not made for my walking. I never got "jungle rot", malaria, or any other "grunt" disease. It's one thing to talk the talk, and quite another to walk the walk. And they did. I wasn't prepared to do either. I'm an aviation guy. That badge wasn't mine to wear, and I never did.

I took a short trip to Charlotte to meet Barb and her fiancé. The anticipation of seeing Barb vacillated between a willingness to connect with my old girlfriend and the faux politeness of meeting her fiancé. If not for Barb, I would not have gone to North Carolina, but I was glad I did. On my way there, I met a pretty redhead named Maureen at the airport. She and I were stuck there for the night, along with several others. Public transportation to and from the Charlotte airport stopped. We were snowed in, two inches on the ground, no flights in or out.

All employees vacated the building by late afternoon to avoid being stuck there during the night. I was among six stranded passengers, left to fend for ourselves for the night inside the abandoned terminal.

The wintry blast of wind gusts hurled snowflakes along the frozen ground and buffeting abandoned parking areas. The darkness of night, punctuated by the Van Gogh-ish spiraling image of street lights dotting the landscape, was all we could see as each of us periodically looked out the window to check the weather. The temperature inside the building was dropping with each passing hour. I was wearing my green Class A's and was actually quite comfortable. The time in Germany helped me to acclimate to low temperatures.

After completing my turn to check the weather outside, I returned to the group. We had been sharing stories among ourselves, revealing where we came from, where we were going, and stories about how the South responds to snow storms, so different from the North.

Though she did not complain, Maureen admitted to being chilled. She was a Southern girl on her way to Louisiana, and temperatures lower than 70 degrees seemed cold. Being chivalrous, I removed my jacket and draped it over her shoulders. Her thin sweater covering her pastel-colored blouse revealed an attractive young woman who was modestly dressed. I was careful not to touch her clothing or skin, even by accident.

The storm outside continued to rage. We searched for the thermostat inside, unable to locate it. The interior temperature had reached its lowest point, and by sheer reckoning I'd guess it stopped at around 65 degrees. The hours passed slowly, but we kept ourselves entertained by our conversations of various subject matters.

I felt welcome among this small group. We spoke nothing about politics, the war, the anti-war movement, draft dodgers, or protesters. We were all about the same age, and no one else had been in the military. They weren't overly curious about my previous three-year stint. It was clear that none of them were thinking about enlisting. Maureen seemed very comfortable wearing my jacket. She continued to wear it like a shawl, keeping herself warm and comfy.

My first night as a newly-minted civilian was over. Wondering what day number two would provide, I knew my destiny from that day forward was uncertain. Would I go home as planned? Yes, not because I really wanted to, but because it was expected. In that sense, I wasn't really *free*. Still under the self-perceived influence of my Dad, disappointing him was not an option. What decision could I make that would keep him happy, and, therefore, off my back?

The father-son relationship was one I struggled with for the past few years. It seemed that my choices in life so far had to pass muster as far as he was concerned. Would he be pleased? Would he probe for more information, asking questions that I couldn't anticipate, or be satisfied with my answers?

Stewing in my thoughts and trying to predict the future, Maureen smiled at me as she returned my jacket. Looking about, I noticed a few hearty employees began to arrive for work at the terminal. The outside landscape was various shades of white and light grays. We had each been awake all night except for a catnap now and then, munching on snacks from the few coin-operated vending machines inside.

"You've been so kind to allow me to borrow your coat. Thank you," she said to me in her Southern-drawl accent. "Do you think we'll be able to leave today?"

"Don't know. Let's find out."

The ticket agent expressed surprise that any passenger was left inside the terminal all night, let alone our little group. No flights in or out yet. We were still locked down due to the weather. By late morning, we were provided lodging for the night at a local national-chain motel. When the arrangements were made, and deciding if one room or two was needed for us, the ticket agent asked Maureen and I if we were together.

"No," I said. "We're not."

She booked two rooms for us, adjacent to each other, as we soon learned. Charlotte was my destination. There was really no reason for the airline to put me up for the night. The agent didn't ask and I didn't volunteer any information that would have thwarted this golden opportunity to spend a little more time with Maureen. By mid-afternoon, a shuttle arrived to take us to the motel. The other four went elsewhere.

Long story short, she didn't want to spend the night in her room alone, and I was more than happy to oblige. For a short time, everything that did not have to do with Maureen was forgotten. It was a wonderful evening. We did not have any expectation that we'd see each other again. We both knew she'd be continuing her journey to somewhere in Louisiana; and me, Chicago. Totally refreshed and well rested, we had breakfast together in the motel restaurant and talked some more about each other until it was time for the shuttle to take her back to the airport. She left, I stayed.

Barb was indeed engaged. I met her fiancé. That was that.

Once I got back home, I knew the change of lifestyle would be difficult for me. I had to look for work, but where? Cathy suggested Dad talk to his boss. Maybe I could work where he worked at Hudson Screw Machine Company. He refused, in no uncertain terms. He did not want me working there, for whatever reasons he had. He had confidence that I'd be able to find something on my own.

I bought a used 1965 green Ford Mustang 3-speed and began looking for work. Trying to adjust to civilian life was difficult. Not because anyone made it difficult for me, but because I was used to the very structured lifestyle the Army provided and found it hard to take control of my own future. All of a sudden, I was on my own—still living at home, mind you, but on my own. Maybe Dad had more confidence in me than I did for myself.

Very quickly it became obvious to me that being a veteran carried very little weight. I had received mail from the Veterans Administration, The Illinois Employment Commission, and so on, but I never felt as though anyone was actually trying to help. I was expecting something, but didn't know what it was. I missed my friends from the Army, but too proud (or arrogant) to look them up and admit failure as a civilian. I found it impossible to connect with anyone outside the Army. No one else understood what I had been through. I was a stranger in my own hometown and a stranger in my own family.

I wanted to attend college, but could I? College tuition would be paid by the GI Bill, so tuition money wasn't an issue. My grades in high school continued to be my reminder that being accepted into college would be an uphill battle. I decided to check out the University of Illinois. Why there? Going to a college closer to home might have been a better plan, but I didn't want to live at home. I took a day-trip down to the campus at Champaign-Urbana. Driving my own car felt good. I was free, but very alone.

On the way, I thought about Maureen, Barb, Nancy, the other girls I had lost contact with over the years. I really screwed up those relationships, but good. Maybe I'd have better luck with college girls.

What would college be like? Where would I live? How could I afford a room? What about money for food? I knew tuition would be taken care of, but what about the cost of books, materials, and everything else? I didn't have much money. I didn't even have a job, yet. Dad didn't have money for this. Who was I going to ask? I didn't know.

When I arrived at the campus, I parked the car and walked around a bit, but I didn't go to the registrar's office. Me, a college student? Who was I kidding?

I was not mentally prepared for civilian life, even though I thought I was. Three years in the Army caused me to look at things differently. I couldn't explain it to myself, let alone to anyone else. I got along just fine in the Army. Responsibility, scheduling, meeting obligations, and being independent as far as Army regulations would allow, became second nature. I had a few guys work for me from time to time. Yet, now as a newly minted adult civilian, Dad didn't seem to be very supportive of me making my own decisions. Maybe I couldn't, who knows?

Getting home, I told Dad that my trip down had just been exploratory. I'd think about which school to attend and what to study, then decide later. Honestly, I had no idea what I wanted to do then. In the Army, I tried to hate it just like the others around me. Too much Mickey Mouse stuff. NCOs were idiots, except for my platoon sergeants. We were smarter. (Of course, we were!) Our pilots, most about my age, acted like playboys, always getting the girls.

Now that I was out, I missed it. I missed the days of traveling to exotic places like Japan, Germany, Alabama, California and North Carolina; seeing the beautiful hills and valleys of Vietnam; taking a twenty-two-day ocean vacation on the Kula Gulf; and, most of all, flying as a crewmember in the coolest helicopter ever made.

I had to admit it to myself: The three years I spent in the Army were absolutely *satisfying*. There was no other word for it.

I took a trip to Kiwanis International, the same place I worked before joining the Army, to pay Fred and Rose in the mail room a visit. I was greeted by one of the executives who I casually knew from my time years before, who asked me curtly if I had come for my old job back. No smile. No handshake. Maybe he was having a bad day. Maybe there were no vacancies. It didn't matter. If I'd wanted to come back before, I sure didn't now.

Before I left, the executive directed me to one of the guys in the office who had been drafted and spent two years of active duty, twelve months of which were in 'Nam. His time in the military was over and he'd returned to work. I sat down in his office and we chatted for a while, as veterans do. We talked for about an hour. I left and never returned.

I had an aviation background in the Army, so I decided to try O'Hare Airport to see what I can find there in the way of work. Without an Airframe and Power Plant (A & P) license, I soon learned my Army helicopter repairman training was worthless in terms of getting a civilian job. Without a license, I wasn't allowed to even twist safety-wire. But, almost immediately, I did find work at North Central Airlines as a baggage handler. Definitely not a career, but maybe an entry-level job leading to something bigger, better.

We called ourselves *ramp-rats*. I drove one of those motorized carts with two trailers for loading and unloading baggage from the cargo hold on the plane. My shift began at 5:00 am and ended at 2:00 pm. I was netting about $80 a week.

Can you imagine how difficult it would be to be 21 years old, having to get up at 3:30 am to wash up, shave, and get ready for work; drive the 45 minutes to the airport; and clock in by 5:00 am? What about any nightlife? If I want to get a minimum of six hours of sleep, it would mean I'd have to get to bed no later than nine, nine-thirty at night. That didn't happen very often, I can tell you that. One of my co-workers at North Central was from Cuba (he pronounced it as Cū-Baa). He was about my age, single, and suggested we share an apartment close to the airport. It sounded like a good idea, but I wanted to think about it first. I wasn't sure about my future, and civilian life was not all it was cracked up to be.

About that time, the Beatles released the *White Album*. Listening to it the first time made me incensed. "Back in the U.S.S.R.," "Revolution," "Helter-Skelter," and "Happiness is a Warm Gun"—every one of those songs seemed traitorous to me. A day or so later, I listened to it again, finding it just as repulsive, maybe even more so than the first time. The group had been sliding downward, in my opinion, with their socio-political messages and drug-using innuendos since their peak popularity of the mid-sixties. This album was too much. It was counter-culture at its finest. Angrily, I broke it in half. A new album, just purchased, trashed as the piece of garbage it was. That was the final straw for me. I knew in my mind that there were forces at work making every attempt to subvert our traditional way of life, our sense of community and well-being. I never thought the Beatles would be part of that, but there they were, advocating drugs, rebellion, and a challenge to traditional thinking. I had enough. But, what was I going to do about it? Complain? Complain to who?

Every night, the six o'clock news reminded me of the growing American body count back in Vietnam. It seemed the battles and body counts of dead Americans had gotten worse since I left. It was nearly impossible to keep informed about it while stationed in Germany, but as a civilian, it was nearly impossible not to be kept informed. My guys, my brothers-in-arms, were getting creamed over there. What was I doing back in Villa Park? What was I doing at the airport, lugging bags and suitcases onto carts and ramps from one place to another? Those guys needed me. They needed every man they could get. I didn't care about politics. I didn't care about the collective national mood turning their back on us. I didn't care what happened to me, anymore. I decided to go back. I had to help those guys out.

Looking back, I wonder if the national media knew what it was doing to us soldiers. Every night, they brought the cold and harsh reality of war, combat, and fatalities into our living rooms. They brought the pain and anguish back to every combat veteran who had returned. They gave a public forum to the protesters, communist sympathizers, draft dodgers, and miscreant zealots. In the name of free speech and the First Amendment, they damn near destroyed our country by giving voice to those who engaged in criminal activity. Only they called it "civil disobedience." In the name of progressiveness, the mainstream media did incalculable damage.

The war invaded my home, every night. The constant visuals of battle scenes, soldiers shooting, bombings by B-52s and jet aircraft, atrocities, the anti-war protests, and commentaries (almost always) supporting the anti-war movement by *well-respected and trusted* TV newsmen was too much to take. That, along with the 1967 race riots in Detroit, the anti-war riots in Chicago a year later, and the assassinations of Martin Luther

King, Jr. and Robert F. Kennedy[94] had swayed the personal beliefs of many people in my neighborhood. It was because of this war that our neighborhood lost two of its own: Ted, about a year before; and, another neighbor and a high school classmate and close acquaintance, Jerry Novak. Both killed in action in 'Nam. The riots and demonstrations, so close to home, had not been experienced before in my lifetime. The high level of perceived social danger translated to a low level of social interaction. Hunker down. Wait for it to pass. People became careful of what they said to others to avoid unpleasant conflict.

No one asked me about Vietnam. In fact, the subject was avoided. To admit I was a combat vet to anyone was asking for alienation and mean-spirited discourse, which I quickly learned to avoid. I was lost already in this world of civilian life. There was no need to make it worse.

For three years, I lived in somewhat of a protected bubble. The military had a certain structure of formality, a sharing of respect that I found lacking in civilian society. The remembrance of it protected me from the confusion I found at home. I clung to the pomp and circumstance of the military. I understood it and never found it annoying. I liked the spit-and-polish of military life.

For me, being in the Army translated to safety and security. It required attention to detail, like maintaining a Huey to make certain it worked as designed provided me the safety and security of flying. Cleaning my weapons, paying attention to the details involved, made sure it worked properly. Lives depended on it. There was a certain pride in doing things right, and being recognized for doing a good job. No room for mistakes. No room for fuck-ups. Do what you're told. Do your best. Don't complain. There was no rebellion in the Army. It wasn't permitted.

The rewards in the Army were, many times, intangible. You couldn't touch it, feel it, or eat it. But it was real nonetheless. It was really simple: Permission granted, permission denied. Reward the positive, punish the negative. Effective strategies to manage and transform adolescent boys into young men. We abided by the military Code of Conduct (paraphrased):

---

[94] The brother of John F. Kennedy, President of the United States. RFK was a U.S. Senator from Massachusetts who was assassinated on June 6, 1968 while campaigning for the U.S. Presidency.

I'll give my life in the defense of my country and our way of life.

I'll never surrender and will resist capture.

If captured, I will resist by all means necessary.

If a prisoner of war, I will not provide information or assistance to the enemy. If I am senior, will take command; if not, I will obey orders of that command.

I'll provide only name, rank and serial number to the enemy. I will make no oral or written statement harmful to my country or its allies.

I am an American, fighting for freedom, responsible for my actions. I will maintain my trust in God and country.

I came home to a different world. What happened to the one I left? In 1966, people I knew were polite, supportive, and patriotic. Three years later, the people had turned against the government, politicians, the military, and the war. Race relations went sour and the invisible fence went up between certain communities. Many areas became too dangerous to go, for whatever the reason to visit. Cops were battling war protesters and race rioters. State National Guards were called to back up the cops. Chaos was rampant. Events were becoming dangerous and uncertain. The body count in Vietnam was growing. I didn't belong here as a civilian.

Dad and Cathy were careful not to discuss the war, or protesters, in my presence. I think Dad felt he needed to respect my time in the service and in Vietnam, so he didn't talk about what was going on here. He didn't say much about the counter-culture taking place, except subtle negative comments when the opportunity arose. So, neither one of us discussed what was going on. He was still a very patriotic man, a war veteran himself. After all, I was named after the man who saved his life during WWII. I believe he was conflicted about what, and how, to think of the social changes taking place.

Scott was busy with high school and spent much of his time in sports with his buddies. Janie was four. Cathy was still homebound unless Dad or Scott drove. Dad, Cathy, Scott and Janie became a very tight family. Dad thought he was calling the shots at home like he always did, but I noticed

Cathy was very involved in raising Janie the way she wanted. Dad had his "little girl" at home. Did he forget his other "little girl" in Michigan? Still, the enmity between him and Mom was always present. To keep Dad from going on a rant, Scott and I found it better not to mention Mom, Steve, or Sue at all. I missed them but couldn't admit it, even to myself at the time. The loss was too emotionally painful. Outta sight, outta mind. I hated myself for that.

Keeping an emotional distance from Dad's underlying paternal hatred for the "other side" of our family worked very well for me. By avoiding the triggers that set him off, I learned life was relatively peaceful. Even though adjusting to civilian life was difficult, I could always drive around in the Mustang, listening to WLS on 890 AM. Dick Biondi was still broadcasting the top tunes at 10 pm. Dad and Cathy probably figured I was a social butterfly, being gone so much at night. But really, I was lonely, wasting a lot of gas just driving around.

I came to realize the hard truth: I was no longer the son they knew just a few years before. I did not feel comfortable at home nor a part of the family picture. Was it me, or was it them? It was impossible for me to pick up where I left off.

After work one day, I decided to visit the Army recruiter in Elmhurst on my way home. For weeks, I had been toying with the idea of going back. I began to give it serious thought, doing the pros and cons of going or not. If I reenlisted, I would be eligible for a VRB[95], but only if I kept my MOS. The dollar amount (up to about $7,000) of the VRB would depend on how many years I signed up for. It would not be available if I signed up for training in a different MOS as a condition of re-enlistment. Also, there was a time limitation for me to make my decision. To keep my paygrade, I would need to take the oath of re-enlistment within ninety-days from when I had been discharged in February. Time was running out.

If ninety days passed, or if I chose another branch of service (like the Air Force) I would drop down one paygrade. Being an E-4 was not an incentive. I saw no pleasure in pulling details again. If I did reenlist, I had to keep my E-5 paygrade. And, the money maxed out if I signed up for six

---

[95] Variable Reenlistment Bonus

years. If I went back to Vietnam and received the money there, it would be tax-free.

Going to flight school or officer candidate school required high scores in a number of different aptitudes, especially the GT (General Technical) score. This was *the* most important score. To be accepted into training as an officer (i.e. pilot) it had to be at least 115. Mine was 103. Reenlisting in my own MOS (67N20) was the only option left. It also meant a good chunk of change for me if I signed up for six years.

Since I left Vietnam, I had written back and forth with DB. He had returned to California; Long Beach I believe. He avoided any reference to his adjusting to civilian life. His choice in music changed. He was "into" Canned Heat, a group I never heard of before.

Going to California was out. College was out. North Central Airlines was out. Sharing the apartment was out. Living at home was out. Staying in Villa Park was out. Even remaining in the greater Chicagoland area was out. Going to Michigan was out. I was running out of other options. I actually had a good time in the Army. Why not go back?

I wasn't sure what my actual job would be going back, but my job during my last tour in 'Nam was not the most dangerous. Maybe I'd be flying again. Of all the U.S. Army occupations in 'Nam, from my experience and word from others, the most dangerous jobs in the Army were: tunnel-rats[96]: EOD[97]: Special Forces, Rangers and LRRPs; medics; Dust-Off crews; infantry, especially when engaged with the enemy; and then helicopter crews. Slicks were most vulnerable during the approach to, loading or off-loading within, and departure from a dangerous LZ. Gunships were most vulnerable from the time they arrived at the AO until they left, which was a majority of missions. But even though we were a higher value target, we were always moving, harder to hit. The slicks were sitting ducks.

During a dinner table discussion one evening, I shared my thoughts about reenlisting. Dad was quiet and didn't attempt to dissuade me. Beyond this, there was no discussion. I made up my mind. My VRB would be approximately $7,000. Besides, I told myself, if society went to hell in

---

[96] A small stature infantryman who would crawl into the enemy's tunnel and bunker complexes to engage the enemy. He would be equipped with a .45 caliber semi-automatic handgun, flashlight, and maybe hand grenades.
[97] Explosive Ordnance Disposal specialists to render explosives non-dangerous.

a handbasket, as I was certain it would, I knew where I wanted to be: somewhere else with an M-60 on my lap, locked and loaded, ready to go. I told Dad I reenlisted for the same job I had and would be going back to Vietnam. Cathy would tell me the next day that he cried that night[98]. A few days later, I left. After two months and 28 days of trying to adjust to civilian life and failing, on May 14, 1969, I reenlisted for six years and my request to return to Vietnam was approved.

I had places to go, people to see, and things to do.

---

[98] I know the feeling all too well. I cried each time when my son, Brian, went to Afghanistan [2008 and 2012] and when my other son, Daniel, went to Iraq [2011 and 2015]. I'm so pleased that my other son, Aric, holds a regional executive position with a corporate chain of hospitals and resides nearby.

Pvt. E-2 Alexander, Ft. Bragg, 1966

Babe (in shades) and Tom aboard Kula Gulf

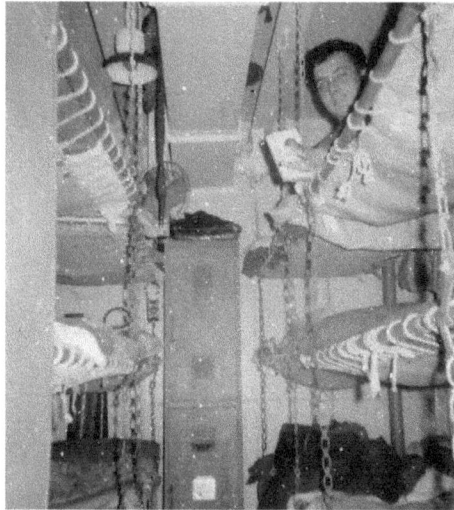

Tom in upper bunk, mine next one below

1. DON 2. ME 3. TOM 4. BABE

En route to Vietnam aboard Kula Gulf

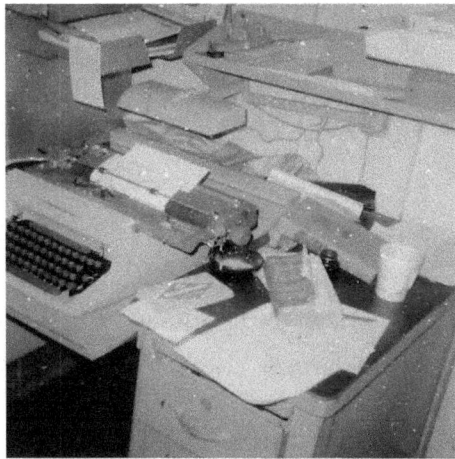

Broom-closet office aboard the Kula Gulf, en-route to Vietnam

City street scene, Vung Tau, Vietnam

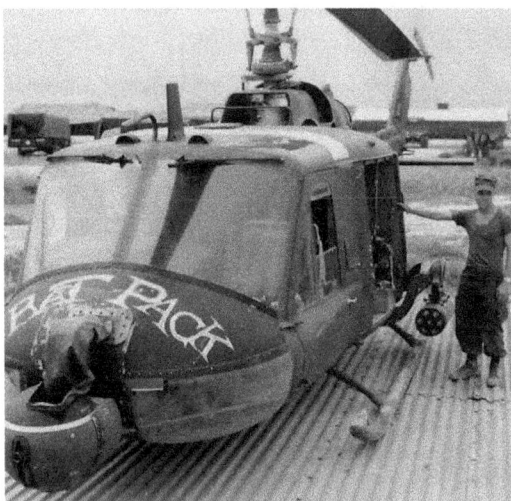

UH-1C gunship, 40mm turret and left 2.75in rocket pod

Tay Ninh, Vietnam, 187th Aslt Hel Co., Rat Pack

Maintenance area of 187th Aslt Hel Co at Tay Ninh, early 1967

Rained buckets the day of this photograph

Refuel and re-arming Rat Pack gunship, 1967

No protective revetments had been constructed yet.

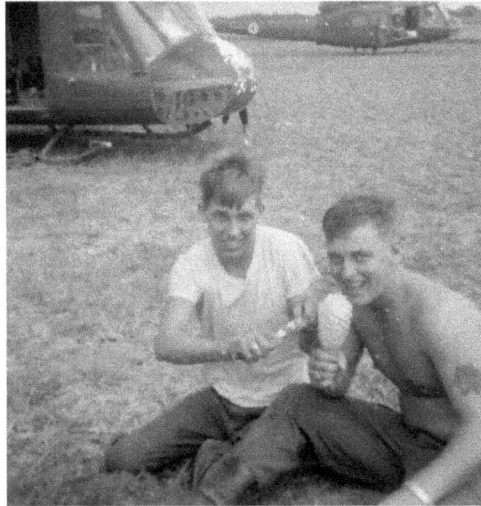

SP/4 Dick Brauher, my gunner with 187th Aslt Hel Co "Rat Pack",
Holding pineapple during break in combat assault mission.
Location: middle-of-no-where.

Our aircraft commander preparing for up-close-and-personal air support. Early 1968 in Vietnam, somewhere. Note the lowered rocket aiming device.

Aerial drop of supplies at Khe Sanh from Air Force C-130; October 1967. Our two gunships are in the foreground.

The Catholic Cathedral in Huế, Vietnam

October 1967

SP/5 M. Alexander, crew chief/door gunner, late 1967

Travelling north along Highway 1 near Phu Bai, Vietnam, 1967

SP/4 Douglas B. "DB" Meckling, door gunner, 190th Assault Helicopter Company,
Gladiators.

DB and I had this photograph taken on January 30, 1968.

Bien Hoa, Vietnam

A mile or two south of Duc Pho, Vietnam. The cleared area, with Highway 1 running through it, was known as "Ambush Alley", 1969. Mt. Montezuma is the hill in background.

Shark UH-1C gunship, 174th Assault Helicopter Company, Duc Pho, Vietnam, 1969.

SP/5 Jim Kildall in front of junior NCO hootch, 174th Assault Helicopter Company area.

Operations is left side of photo, Sr. NCO hootch right side. 1969-70, Duc Pho.

Hot refueling of Shark gunship on tarmac. 1970. Unconfirmed reports indicate this UH-1C was later captured by the VC (or NVA) and put on display in a museum at the end of the war.

Proof of a mistake every gunship crewman dreads: failure to remove the metal safety-rod from the minigun before taking off on a mission.

L-R: me, Welch and Cowling. 174th Assault Helicopter Company, Shark Platoon,

Duc Pho, Vietnam, 1970.

Kiém Liên

I interrupted Jim Kildall while he was pulling a scheduled
inspection on his ship.
174th Aslt Hel Co. "Sharks"

Jim, seated in his ship, with me.

SFC Joseph P. Barnett, III (Shark platoon sergeant) closest to jeep. I am at his right. 1969.

My 1970 Triumph GT-6, Colorado Springs, CO, 1970.

The same 1970 Triumph GT-6, then owned by the insurance company, 1970.

Jim Kildall, my friend and brother-in-arms.

Colorado Springs, CO

1970

Chapter 12

Back to da 'Nam

The flight from Chicago to Tacoma, Washington was spacious, like all other plane rides I'd been on. There was plenty of time to think of what I had just done. Once airborne, I took out my Zippo, lit my cigarette, and inhaled deeply. Surprisingly, there was no regret as I thought about the next six-year phase of my life. Comradery among soldiers is addictive, and being tested in battle is more so. That addiction was intense and I needed, more than anything, to satisfy the craving.

In a way, it was as if I was on the varsity team, winning and scoring points with almost every move against the opponent. The other team had scored big with Khe Sanh, Tet, and Hué, but we were coming back. It was no time to sit on the sidelines cheering my team onto victory. I had no choice, really, but to get back in the game.

The small armrest ashtray was full by the time we landed. I suppose I smoked about six or seven cigarettes on the plane. After landing I took a taxi to Fort Lewis. Feeling generous, I tipped the driver ten bucks. Why so much? Maybe because I was going to war and wasn't too sure I'd be coming back. Besides, who cared? It was too late to go back and undo the reenlistment thing. I was locked in from the moment I took the oath and signed on the dotted line.

Arriving at Fort Lewis in civilian clothes, I was told that there was no sense in issuing me military gear and clothing, only to have it all exchanged for jungle fatigues and so on when I arrived in Vietnam. So, I wore civilian clothes to Vietnam, while almost everyone else was in fatigues. Did I feel out of place? Absolutely. But I was happy.

We flew to Nome, Alaska; then to Tokyo, Japan; and, finally, arrived in Da Nang, Vietnam. Walking out of the air-conditioned passenger compartment of the plane to exit was a sensation I'll not forget. As I stepped through the opened fuselage door onto the mobile stairway, the air blast from outside was so hot it felt like an oven door opening in front of me at 400°F. As I walked down the mobile staircase, I noticed a couple ramp-rats in carts hauling many trailers loaded with dark colored caskets, waiting off to the side, to be loaded on this plane for the return trip back to the States. *Oh, boy*.

I was assigned to the 23rd Infantry (Americal) Division. The patch was blue with four stars, the "Southern Cross." New jungle fatigues, boots and gear were issued to me. Most everything was out-of-the-package green, very easy for anyone to see me as an FNG. Not a bit of faded clothes, not an inch of tanned skin on my Chicago-winter skin. The clothes make the man, and that man, me, was the FNG.

Division's standard policy was for everyone arriving in-country to go through a five-day infantry refresher course. It didn't matter if this was your first or fourth tour, or if your job was desk or field, you went through the training. In my group, we were all E-5s and below. Maybe E-6s and above were exempt.

I made a new friend with one of the other new guys, (Buck) Sergeant (E-5) Sandy Combs. He was infantry and was familiar with the things they were teaching us. Among the many relevant topics in this practical training course, we were specifically introduced to punji-sticks, trip holes and wires, anti-personnel mines, tracking techniques, camouflage, snakes and poisonous vegetation, emergency first aid and amputations, PRC-25 radio usage, and more. Just an overview of these many subjects with hands-on training. He became my mentor that week.

This was Combs' second tour, too. He was wearing his CIB on his not-quite-new jungle fatigues. I asked him about that badge because I never really spoke to an infantryman in Vietnam before, except the one with a string of ears on his backpack. Sandy explained that to qualify for one, you needed to have an infantry MOS, assigned to an infantry unit for a minimum of 24-hours in a combat zone, and come under enemy fire.

Sandy was going to Chu Lai (pronounced: *chew lye*). I was going to Duc Pho (pronounced: *duck foe*), a/k/a "Rocket City" and assigned to the 174th Assault Helicopter Company. Duc Pho is located in Quang Ngai (pronounced: *quang nye*) Province and close to the eastern shoreline. There was heavy VC activity there.

The 11th Light-Infantry Brigade was headquartered at the Fire Support Base (FSB) at Duc Pho, also known as LZ Bronco. A huge hill (almost a mountain, elevation maybe 750 feet) inside the base perimeter was named Mt. Montezuma. An American military signal "MARS" station was positioned on top. We had an artillery unit at the north side of the base with 175mm howitzers. The main north-south highway in Vietnam, Highway 1, ran through the village of Duc Pho just to our west. To keep the road open, many search-and-destroy operations were sent to find, kill, or take Viet Cong and NVA prisoners. People were saying Duc Pho was the most dangerous district in this province, and the province was at least one of the three most dangerous ones in country.

I finally arrived to my new unit on May 28, 1969. The 174th AHC had been there since 1967, part of the 14th Combat Aviation Battalion. I was told the enemy presence was felt here, as well as in most parts of that province, quite often. Charlie was everywhere, even in the small village next to us. For that reason, it was off limits.[99]

The company area was like an array of bunkers. Each hootch[100] and the operations building were made up of single level, wood-frame buildings surrounded by sandbags stacked 24-inches wide, eight to ten feet high. The flat frame roofs were reinforced with corrugated steel and sandbags two-deep. The gable roofs were covered in another layer of corrugated steel to deflect the sun and rain—and hopefully incoming rounds. The mess hall had sandbags only as high as four feet along the exterior walls.

The source of electricity for the company area was from two large 100KW generators near the north end of the company area. Each building was used exclusively for the Enlisted Men's (EM) Club, a smaller one for the NCO Club, a larger one for the Officer's Club, the senior NCO hootch (nearing construction completion), the (new) junior NCO hootch, the orderly and supply rooms, operations, dispensary, motor pool, and, a separate hootch for members (officer or enlisted) of each platoon. A large open Quonset hut-style tent was used to show movies at night, and another for the Vietnamese workers to launder our clothes during the day.

Our ships were parked just west of the company area not a hundred feet away. The flight line (air-strip) was just on the other side of our aircraft.

---

[99] Years later I learned that the 190th AHC slicks, with all crews, had trained in Duc Pho during the late fall of 1967.
[100] Hootches, used for living quarters, housed as many as sixteen men.

Handing in my records to the clerk in the orderly room and signing in, I was introduced to Sergeant First Class (SFC, E-7) Joseph P. Barnett, III. A career soldier on his first tour in Vietnam, he was to be my platoon sergeant. His brown skin, darker at the forearms, neck and face revealed he was an outside guy, exposed day-after-day to the blazing sun. His black hair was short as one might expect for a career non-commissioned officer. Clean shaven, standing tall, and exuding confidence and purpose, I was immediately impressed with him. I could tell he was well respected, by everyone I saw this first day, because of the way others greeted him as we left the orderly room.

He and I walked over to the NCO Club to get acquainted over a cup of coffee. The company call sign was "Dolphin". I learned he was the platoon sergeant for the gunships, call sign "Sharks"[101]. As with other assault helicopter companies, the 174th had eight gunships. Here, the Shark nose art depicted a large red mouth and white teeth. The design extended onto the ship's pilot doors and was very distinctive.

SFC Barnett and I spoke about my previous tour with the 1st Aviation Brigade and my experience crewing both types of gunships: miniguns and 40mm grenade launcher. I was very familiar with the C-model Huey, 540-rotor-head system, and hydraulic systems. He read my awards from reviewing my 201-file[102] in the orderly room. I was surprised he did that. We talked about that for a bit. He was curious as to why I had reenlisted. The generic answer I gave him was about the money from the VRB. My motives were not heroic.

Almost as a footnote, he mentioned that the guys here were a little jumpy. A little more than a year before, his platoon was involved in a combat operation at My Lai, a small village north of Duc Pho. Those pilots and crewmen had DEROSed already. The CID[103] recently investigated charges of a massacre of civilians there. The pilots and crewmen involved were interviewed, and no one in the company faced any charges yet (as far as he knew). But, the word was out that the investigation was continuing.

---

[101] Our unit had the written approval of General Claire Chennault's Flying Tigers (of WWII fame) to use the Shark logo (shark mouth) for the 3rd Platoon gunships.
[102] A listing of active duty assignments, schooling, proficiency test scores, awards, dates of rank, etc.
[103] U.S. Army Criminal Investigation Division.

"Do you have anything to do with that investigation?" he asked me directly.

"No," I said, puzzled.

With that, he welcomed me to *Rocket City*[104] and briefed me about the company area, why the buildings were bunkered as they were, the recent fatalities and loss of aircraft. The timing of my arrival was just right, as they had recently lost two gunships and three crewmen from the Shark platoon. I would be one of the replacements. Also, a rocket attack targeted the company area recently. It had killed the company commander and another officer by a direct hit on their hootch.

More recently, almost three weeks prior to my arrival, there was a CA just south of Quang Ngai. The Shark gunship crew chief, SP/5 Dennis Schmidt, spotted an NVA flag attached to a pole on a tree limb. The pilots descended low enough for the crew chief to grab the flag. It was booby-trapped. The explosive device (later determined to be a 500-pound bomb) on the ground was connected to the flag and exploded. Severely burned, he was flown to a stateside burn center where he died. Since, the remaining crew chiefs have been jockeyed around to meet the requirement that one of them accompany each gunship on a mission. I was the replacement they'd been expecting.

Enemy activity in this area had been massive. He told me that outside the gates of this FSB it was really quite dangerous, especially at night. As if to highlight his comments about VC activity, he informed me about a middle-aged Vietnamese man who worked near the latrines. The base had been receiving a lot of incoming fire from mortar, rocket and artillery rounds over a period of months. Many hits were deadly accurate, like the one that hit the company commander's hootch recently. By accident one day, one of the guys on the flight line had been standing on top of his helicopter doing maintenance work. He noticed a flash of light coming from the company area. Not knowing the source, or cause, he ignored it until he noticed another two quick flashes a few moments later. This time he left the tarmac and walked over to the latrine area, casually so as not to draw attention, to investigate.

---

[104] I later learned any base that received incoming rocket barrages from the VC earned the nickname *Rocket City* by those assigned there. Maybe it was for bragging rights, to show others that 'we went through some shit, man", as opposed to places that rarely, if ever, got hit such as Long Binh (except for Tet '68).

What he found astounded him. The old Vietnamese man, who had been working quietly in their company area as a shit-burner, appeared to be surreptitiously aiming the sun's reflection with a small mirror to a target-point westward in the surrounding mountain range. This guy was signally the exact location of our company area to his comrades in the hills. He was immediately apprehended and taken prisoner, never to be seen in our company area again.

What had I gotten myself into? Only a couple weeks before I was at O'Hare Airport working as a ramp-rat. My biggest worry then was getting to work on time, getting the baggage to the right place and on time, with no room for error. Arriving here, my biggest worry became staying alive. But, I still didn't regret my reenlistment, not yet anyway.

It was mid-day when SFC Barnett and I finished talking. He escorted me over to the Shark hootch and introduced me to some of the guys who weren't then flying. This hootch, much like all the others, was mostly constructed of wood planks leftover from a great number of emptied ammo boxes over the years, five rooms on each side of the hallway. There was no door to close at either end of the hootch, nor did any of the rooms have a door, per se, just an opening.

Some room entry-openings were draped with cloth material to provide a sense of privacy. One room had a series of vertically strung beads. A couple rooms housed three guys; the others had two. My room was the first one on the right as you entered. The top bunk would be mine. The bottom belonged to Bud Vann, my gunner. There wasn't much space inside, a steel-frame bunk bed (standard Army issue) separated from two narrow wall lockers by an isle no wider than thirty inches. This room, paneled in vintage ammo-box lumber, was no larger than sixty-four square feet.

From a room in the back, the faint sound of "Babe I'm Gonna Leave You" by Led Zeppelin permeated the hootch. Barnett left, allowing me time to get settled and acquainted with the guys. During that first afternoon, there wasn't much to do, apparently, as five or six guys were in the hootch shooting the breeze. A couple of them were talking about a recent battle up north that was typical of the way things were becoming.

It was the first I had heard about Hamburger Hill (Hill 937) and the encounter between the NVA, a few American Army and Marine units, and the ARVNs. Our company wasn't involved in it, but word spread quickly. Hamburger Hill (officially Ap Bia Mountain) was located at the western side of A Shau Valley. The battle had begun just a few weeks before (May 10, 1969) for control of a hilltop. The Americans fought their way up the steeply-sloped hill where the NVA were well entrenched. Ten days and a huge number of casualties[105] later, the hill was captured, only to be abandoned almost immediately afterwards. The main topic of their conversation was searching for the purpose of that abandonment.

"Fuck that," said one voice angrily, interrupting the serenity of the preceding moments. "That's bullshit." Then, the conversation returned to the quiet, symphonic cadence of men talking about war.

Some would later say this battle was instrumental in our evolving *political-military*[106] strategic thinking. Also, the Vietnamization program placed more responsibility for prosecuting the war onto the Vietnamese, while American soldiers were being withdrawn[107] in greater numbers. Word of this "strategically negligent" battle spread quickly in the American press and the guys were reading about it more in letters from home than the *Stars & Stripes* newspaper. The resulting adverse public opinion apparently influenced President Nixon to end major tactical operations on the ground in Vietnam. The procedures we followed in combat, under General Abrams, were much different from what it was (aggressively pursuing a winning strategy) under General Westmoreland. For me, that was fourteen months ago, a time when the troops intended to win the war.

Some "Monday morning quarterbacks" in the hootch questioned why we were in Vietnam at all. Based on that and recent mission protocols, they spoke about the lack of aggressively seeking out the enemy.

"Why should *we* put our lives at risk? For what, so some asshole in Saigon can get his jollies off?" another voice asked.

My "briefing" from the guys was clear. Do what you have to do here, but don't be John Wayne. It's not worth it.

---

[105] U.S. losses were 72 KIA and 372 WIA. The NVA lost an estimated 630 KIA. Their WIA was unknown.
[106] Political-military decision making by President Nixon seemed to be a little too concerned about public opinion from the anti-war crowd when deciding not to act on the advice of his Secretary of Defense and generals.
[107] Mostly through attrition.

Did I mention how rustic the company area was? We all shared a double piss-tube surrounded by steel roofing material placed sideways for privacy. We had three crapper huts, one each for the officers, senior NCOs, and enlisted men. Inside each there were bench seating for two to five at a time. Modesty was never one of the Army's strong points. Every man's "dump" would drop into a cut-down-in-half 55-gallon barrel. This in turn would be removed from time to time by a daytime older male Vietnamese worker—papa-san[108]—who would add diesel fuel and burn the contents. The barrels were removed from the crappers at random. It didn't matter if you were done or not. Surprise!

Not only that, any one of the older mama-sans would walk in, unannounced, to sweep the floor, replace the toilet paper if necessary, and remove any newspaper or the like as part of their daily clean-up detail. They didn't seem to care if we were using the facilities. There was not much we could do, under the circumstances, except to yell at them (in a language they most likely did not understand) to get the hell out.

And to think, I had about three hundred and fifty days to go.

We had our company formation the following morning. Our platoon was missing four guys who were on a mission and had left earlier. I hadn't had a chance to sew my crewmen wings onto my shirts yet. And, just by looking at me there was no way anyone could know I had been in Vietnam before, as the 1st Aviation Brigade patch on the upper right arm of my new jungle fatigue shirts was not sewn on, either. I was the typical image of the FNG: no tan or sunburn, out-of-the-box green uniform, and patchless.

Immediately after formation we lined up for police call. This routine Army detail involves everyone Spec Five and below to line up, almost shoulder to shoulder, and walk through the company area to pick up debris from the ground. The type of debris, as always, consisted of cigarette butts, paper and cigarette packs, and anything else that didn't grow, could not be painted, or had no purpose of being there. Some of the guys moved ahead while others lagged behind the line.

---

[108] Vietnamese older men were referred to as *papa-san*, older women as *mama-san*, and children as *baby-san*.

I damn near tripped over a small, clear plastic bag on the ground. Looking closer, I saw it containing about eight roll-your-own cigarettes. Why hadn't the guys ahead of me seen this? Why didn't one of them pick it up? Why leave it for me to dispose of? As I looked carefully at that package on the ground at my feet, my guess was that the "cigarettes" were actually marijuana. It was the responsible thing for me to pick it up. But, then again, was I being watched to see what I'd do with the package?

Immediately I realized I had four options: ignore it and walk past; pick it up and hand it over to the NCO supervising our section of the police call; pick it up and discretely put it in my pocket; or, pick it up and toss it away in one of the well-worn empty 55-gallon garbage cans placed throughout the company area. I didn't appreciate what I first thought to be a test. Anybody could have dropped that package there intentionally. Then again, maybe it was a "welcome to the 174th" gift from one of the guys. Who knew? Well, I wasn't going to go to jail for this[109]. I took care of it.

My gunner, Bud Vann, was as good a gunner as anyone could ever expect. We got along immediately. Our gunship had a caricature of the Pink Panther painted just outside the A/C's side window. Our ship was not unlike other UH-1C gunships with mini-guns, rocket launchers, etc. Vann took good care of the armament. The ship was in good shape. Vann was a straight arrow, meaning he didn't get drunk, smoke dope, or engage in any type of self-destructive behavior. I could, and did, trust him with my life.

From bits and pieces of conversation I learned over time, my arrival in this unit was met with suspicion from day one. I did not keep my first tour a secret. I readily told anyone who asked that I spent a year crewing a gunship. But, some had their doubts. It could be a cover story.

First, some thought I was a 'shake-and-bake' E-5. These were guys selected to go through special training and instruction, lasting about six months after basic training, that allowed them to be quickly promoted to Spec Five when they graduated. I looked young enough to be considered a candidate for that idea.

---

[109] It was a well-known fact that possession of marijuana, or a seed or stem, was illegal. During this period of the U.S. military, possession of marijuana seeds and/or stems of the plant was just as illegal as a joint. Conviction could mean a sentence of six months at the jail in Long Binh, and a permanent blemish on your military record affecting future promotions, assignments, security clearances, etc. One small seed equal six months in jail.

Others suspected I was a special agent with the CID, sent under-cover to find what I could about the My Lai incident a year before, or to investigate the suspected rampant use of drugs in this company. Being as-signed to the gun platoon as a crew chief was a position coveted by guys in other platoons. A few had made their intent to transfer-in official by putting their name on a waiting list. So, when I arrived and was assigned to the Sharks immediately from day one, they assumed something was not right about my jumping ahead of the line.

Over the next couple months, Vann and I flew a lot of missions. I wasn't out to prove anything, but my experience in gunships became ob-vious. I was not a rookie. In addition to the usual missions, we flew close air support for LRRPs and Special Forces in the area much more so than in I Corps. The area around Duc Pho has many mountain ranges, valleys, etc. There were very few rice patties nearby. Highway 1 ran right through the village. Along the highway about a mile south was an area between two hills we called Ambush Alley. The VC used these hills to ambush motor convoys passing through, or aircraft on final approach or lifting off from our airfield. The hills had each been bulldozed free of trees and vegetation months before. Even though the sniping had diminished, the name, Am-bush Alley, stuck.

Mail call was usually at 1700 hours. I'd get letters from Dad every two or three weeks. One of them informed me that Barb had called the house to speak with me. Dad told her I was back in Vietnam and gave her my mailing address. Soon enough, I received a letter from Barb. She didn't mince words. She was shocked that I had reenlisted in the Army and gone back to Vietnam.

"Are you crazy, or something?" she wrote. "Why did you do that?" She wrote that she loved me, not as a boyfriend but more as a brother. She always ended her letters with "Love, Barb" but this was the first time she ever expressed that in a letter. I always wanted to hear her say that, though in person would have been better. But I never said it to her, either.

If I wasn't crushed when she told me she was engaged, and if I didn't get the message when I went to visit her in North Carolina, I got the message crystal clear with that letter. She signed off with her name only, omitting the "love-comma." I also noticed in the return address corner of the envelope her new last name. She married the guy.

224

I made many failed attempts to compose a letter back to her. The words I wrote always seemed contrite. I had not learned how to respond as a friend, to wish her well and happiness. Instead, I considered her correspondence to be a *Dear John* letter. I felt I had no business in writing back and forth with a married woman, so I stopped trying.

The combat maneuvers of the gunships were *different* here from what I experienced down south a year before. The Shark pilots were not too inclined to remain at treetop level during missions. Many times, during a gun run, the A/C would fire the rockets at targets on the ground from an altitude of a thousand feet over the target. Fire teams still consisted of two gunships and we still used one team for standby each night. We had no "stand-by hootch," per se. The crews remained in their own until "scrambled" by a man who ran from operations to the doorway of each hootch to wake the guys up.

Our province was well known to battalion S-2 as a haven for VC. You wouldn't have to go too far away to find them. Teams of five to ten VC each had infiltrated the province and made their base of operations the general area of Duc Pho, exercising coercive influence over the villagers. Being at the southern tip of I Corps, they weren't a threat to the grand scheme of things, but the locals were afraid. Within five miles from LZ Bronco, they had ample manpower and weaponry to provide constant harassment to our base. We were too large for them to launch a frontal attack against us. We were too small to be the shining beacon of freedom in the province.

My ship was on standby one day. Our work at the flight line had been completed earlier, so we went back to our hootch to kill time. The man from ops, running towards our hootch, was yelling.

"Fire Team, yer up. Scramble. Go. Go. Go."

Vann and I dropped everything. Within minutes both ships were in the air.

On the way, radio transmissions indicated a small patrol was in trouble. Their mission compromised. They had engaged with an aggressive and numerically superior force of VC. Back and forth radio transmissions ensued. From the gist of things, someone in authority decided to have them extracted rather than send in reinforcements.

Soon, we arrived at our destination. The triple-canopy of jungle was too thick for a slick to land except for a clearing some distance away. To the best of their knowledge, the patrol had been seen but Charlie was still a hundred meters away, positioned and well-hidden at the top of an adjoining ridge, taking potshots. There were at least twenty or more of them. We orbited the area to engage. The heavy triple canopy made it difficult for us to see through.

The patrol leader radioed coordinates and we laid suppressive fire. A few rockets were launched as we began our gun run, punctuated by mini-guns spraying the surrounding foliage. The problem was the upper sections of trees and such would cause a premature detonation of our rockets. I thought artillery or maybe an F-4 Phantom jet would have been better suited, but it wasn't up to me.

Someone popped a smoke grenade. The yellow haze waffled up through the trees and the immediate area became a blend of heavy and faint yellow fog. That had a dual result. One, the smoke pinpointed their location. Now, everyone in the area knew where they were. For us it was good because we would avoid shooting in that area. And for Charlie, they, too, became aware exactly where the Americans were and could concentrate their fire into that area. Two, the grunts could hide within the thick portions of the smoke, using it as concealment. Or they could use the smoke as a decoy and avoid that area.

On the way, I had reached overhead to turn off my ADF to focus my attention on the whispered instructions from the man speaking into his PRC-25. Though we were in a mountainous region, it was necessary to lower our altitude a few hundred feet. A slick had been dispatched for the patrol's extraction.

Men's lives were at stake, as were the lives of my crew. Knowing that an RPG could be launched at us at any time, we were all at risk. Be alert. Observe everything as much as possible. Concentrate. Listen. Watch.

Meanwhile, as we were busy engaging with the VC, the slick arrived and positioned itself to hoist the men up. They hovered as close to the canopy as possible and dropped the line near the yellow smoke to the men below. The first of the ground team was lifted into the ship as we continued to suppress the ridge and surrounding area. If we couldn't kill Charlie outright, then at least we could keep their heads down. It was tight quarters, very tight. Neither I or Vann fired our M-60s as the target was, for the most part, always directly in front of us. Our job was to keep an eye of the other ships and continue our visual ground search the best we could for signs of enemy activity.

The second guy was being lifted up, fully exposed while attached to the hoist-line. The slick began to take fire. A sniper, maybe? The man on the line fired back into the jungle as did one of the ship's door gunners. Nevertheless, it remained hovering just above tree-top level. Being exposed to enemy fire, that close, and being a relatively stationary target, I admired the A/C's nerves of steel.

We focused on that area as well, learning that Charlie was in various locations surrounding the extraction point. Due to the tight quarters, our M-60s were better suited for this engagement. Gunships do not hover while firing their weapons. But, sometimes, we'd fly slower than usual when engaging the enemy. This was one of those times. Our speed was cut in half as we skimmed the canopy, trying to draw out their fire so we could pinpoint their location. Red smoke at the ready, dangling by the pin's metal ring attached to the carry handle of my M-60. Yank and throw, that's all I had to do before firing.

Where are they? I asked myself. Every now and then, the ground was visible. But not Charlie. Vann searched his side; I searched mine. Looking to my right, to the ship's eleven o'clock, I saw nothing but treetops. Same thing looking to my left, back to the seven o'clock. I had to focus my attention to our nine o'clock, a little to the right, a little to the left, and below us. Blurs of green with occasional browns. Every now and then, I'd catch sight of our other gunship, also skimming, trying to draw out Charlie from his hiding places. Up to the ridge, back down again, nothing. The slick was hovering some distance away as we continued to keep it centered to our search patterns.

After the last man was aboard, the slick took off. We followed. No RPGs were launched at us. None of us got wounded, but the second grunt lifted up took a grazing round to his arm, not serious.

Back at LZ Bronco, we learned that the slick had taken a few rounds. The damage was just a few holes, nothing that the sheet metal shop couldn't fix. For now, they would use 90-mile-an-hour tape[110] to patch the holes until maintenance could schedule them in for repair. Nothing internally on the ship had been damaged. Still, if we hadn't done our jobs, that slick could have gone down, and all the grunts with it. Like riding a bicycle, my war skills returned easily.

The crew chief of the other gunship was a former Army truck driver. He had reenlisted, gone to helicopter repair school, and been assigned to this, his first tour in Vietnam, a few months back. I became good friends with him, Emil James "Jim" Kildall[111]. Jim was a quiet man. Tall, lanky, and maybe a little too withdrawn from the others, he was from Flint, Michigan. He was about four years older than me. He and I, as newly minted lifers, bonded quite easily. I began to notice Jim didn't speak much about his family back home. He wasn't married, that much I did know. But, he never spoke about a girl waiting for him, his parents, or any other loved ones.

We used to talk about making a movie about an aviation unit in Vietnam. We toyed with different titles and decided upon *A Day in the Life*. The film was going to follow a gunship crew chief from 2100 hours one day all the way through 2100 hours the next day. The bulk of the film would document the intensity of shooting at an enemy rarely seen, well hidden in the bush. There would also be cameos of Vietnamese actors portraying the VC in their tunnel complex, regrouping and planning their counter assault. The movie would end with the gunship fire team flying off into the sunset, en route to lend air support for other Americans engaged in a ground firefight somewhere else in the mountains. The sky would have brilliantly colored clouds outlined in reddish orange from the setting sun. With the sunset still in vivid colors, the credits would roll. The plot? The storyline? We were still working on that.

Jim, that dream lives on, brother.

---

[110] Years later called Duct Tape.

[111] During the mid 1980's I visited him at his home in Flint, MI. He was working as a truck driver for Coca-Cola. He didn't seem to be content as a civilian, collecting as much Vietnam memorabilia as possible, possibly to remind him of his days of glory during 1969. He died, alone, on November 24, 2009, Flint, MI; RIP my friend.

Without much access to a radio, all of our news from the outside world was delayed by a day. Even the biggest stories, like the Apollo 11 moon landing in July 1969, we heard about after the fact. For me, though, three astronauts going to the moon was more of a curiosity than a historic event. I didn't feel connected to what was happening. It seemed so distant. The build-up, anticipation, and success of that mission were lost on us. No one in my circle of friends spoke much about that. The United States might just as well have landed a spacecraft in Texas.

The *Stars & Stripes* paper was not available much at LZ Bronco. It wasn't as if the paper arrived every day where we could sit down and read it over a cup of coffee during breakfast. That seemed like something the Air Force[112] might do, but not us, not there. Many of us enviously thought of the Air Force as the 'country club' branch of the military. I'm sure some Army grunts thought about us exactly the same way: guys with clean and dry uniforms, clean and dry bed every night, hot chow in the mess hall, flying as our primary means of transportation, and safe from jungle threats.

Every four or five days, Vann and I were on standby again. On one particular occasion, our turn came up at on a particularly bad night. If we got scrambled that night, we'd have to rearm and refuel the ship before a scheduled mission the following morning and fix anything that broke or got shot up, not to mention the sleep we'd miss. But we'd done it before. We could do it again, but hopefully not. Fully dressed, boots on, and ready to go at a moment's notice. We rested on our bunks. As the night got later, the sounds inside the hootch became quieter.

A few of the guys, visiting others elsewhere, returned to the hootch. Their conversations were just loud enough to be heard, but not understood. Perfect for a tired crew chief trying to get some sleep. As an aside, I still passed the flight physical, but my hearing just hadn't been the same since Tet of '68. I had noticed a constant rushing sound, as if I could hear the blood rushing through my veins.

---

[112] I have great admiration of the United States Air Force. Inter-service ribbing is natural, and sometimes expected.

Eventually, all outside noise was quiet except for the constant, comforting drone from one of the dual generators at the far north end of our company area, just past the mess hall. I could hear Vann below, his rhythmic breathing and occasional snore told me he was fast asleep. Somebody's music was on. The volume was low and barely audible. Soon, that sound faded as did the generator's. As I drifted off to sleep my thoughts about the last few weeks, the changes, and my decisions faded as well.

I was abruptly woken up by the guy from operations, standing just inside our doorway and not four feet from our room, yelling, "SCRAM-BLE, SCRAMBLE." His voice was loud and purposeful. I'm sure he didn't know which room we were in at the time. He ran off. Rolling out from the top bunk, I swung my legs a bit to avoid knocking Vann over. My feet hit the floor. I quickly glanced at my watch. It was 0345 hours. We bolted out and ran across the company area, passing operations, and towards the tarmac.

As we approached our ship, Vann veered off to the right, me to the left. At the end of the tail boom, I unlatched the tie-down bar from the end of the aft rotor blade, rolled the strap around it, and stowed it behind the ammo trays. The peter-pilot was in his seat by then, strapped in, but his door was still open. He started the engine. The Lycoming L-11 jet turbine engine roared to life and the rotor blades were quickly spinning at full speed. Using the red glow of the navigation light above my door and the instrument lights for illumination, I checked his harness and pulled his side-plate forward, making certain it was latched. I sat in my seat, inserted the barrel into my M-60, which was dangling from its bungee cord with the end of a belt of ammo already inserted. We waited for the A/C to arrive.

The A/C ran from operations and got in. The red rotating beacon reflected off of Vann's navigation-green-light-tinted flight helmet as he stood outside the A/C's door, sliding the side-plate forward. When he closed the A/C's door, and jumped in himself, we were ready to go at 0350 hours. Five minutes flat.

It was still dark when we took off. Our heading was 265 degrees. We were going towards the mountains, still unseen before dawn. Leaving LZ Bronco, the only light came from the moon. I listened in on the FM channel. As lead ship, our A/C was in contact with the OIC[113] on the ground. Charlie had unsuccessfully attempted to penetrate the perimeter of their outpost. He reported one Whiskey-India-Alpha[114] and requested a Dust-Off to take his wounded man. I could hear the anxiety in the man's voice.

"What's your Echo-Tango-Alpha[115]?" he asked.

"Fifteen Mikes," our A/C calmly replied, "Dust-Off's on its way." I angled my watch, using the red light above, to check the time. Fifteen minutes, we should be getting there by 0405 hours. Continued dialogue between our A/C and the OIC on the ground described their situation, Charlie's approximate position by grid coordinates, and the layout of the AO.

When we arrived, the sky behind us had that faint glimmer of amber light, the sun pushing its way up from the horizon to usher in the new day. The mountains were a silhouette, still dark, a deep greenish black. We descended a bit from the 3,000-foot altitude we took to arrive, seeing areas lit by flares. The ground OIC provided a sit-rep[116] to our A/C, and their coordinates. They had been receiving mortar and small arms fire from the north. Charlie's exact position was difficult to pinpoint, but estimated to be at the far side of a small oblong clearing. Searching in the twilight of dawn, Vann spotted the only area without trees and underbrush and let us know. It had to be the same clearing.

With the aid of a red-lensed flashlight, the map coordinates of the suspected VC area were checked by our A/C. Only he had the topographic map, covered in well-used, not-real-clear plastic. It lay on his lap as he used his grease pencil to write the set of coordinate numbers and radio frequencies on the upper right of his forward windshield.

Our peter-pilot, meanwhile, had taken control of the ship and we began flying in a clock-wise orbital pattern some distance away, circling the target area. He was in communication with the Dust-Off. They were about five minutes out. The outpost was difficult to detect from the air due

---

[113] Officer in Charge
[114] WIA, wounded in action
[115] ETA, Estimated Time of Arrival
[116] Situation Report describing the layout of the outpost's current location and status of their tactical situation.

to the semi-darkness, foliage and canopy of the trees. The light of the flares was yielding to the emerging light of the sun. Day broke.

Soon, a plume of faint yellow smoke, wafting upward, billowed just above the treetops and marked the spot for the Dust-Off to land. It stayed there, hanging in the early morning air like a small cloud with no place to go. The sun was just coming up, and images on the ground were becoming clearly visible. A slight fog blanketed the area, wisps of light gray laying low among the foliage.

Our orbital pattern ended as we took a position east of the target to initiate our gun run. We went first. **WOOSH! WOOSH!** The first two HE[117] rockets were fired, one from each side of the ship. I watched as the exhaust flames trailed the trajectory of each, flying parallel to each other, one slightly higher than the other. Almost immediately after they impacted the ground, the right mini-gun roared as 750 rounds sped towards the ground with each 15-second burst. The left mini-gun remained silent.

"Alex," the peter-pilot called me on the intercom, "the left gun's not working. See if you can find the problem."

We banked left. I quickly scanned the aluminum feed belt winding its way out to the mini-gun from just below my feet. No kinks there. Then, I saw it. The safety rod[118] was still inserted in the housing, preventing the barrels from rotating. *Crap*, I thought to myself. I keyed the mic.

"Uh, Sir," I transmitted rather sheepishly, facing the back of his helmet. "I found the problem. There's an obstruction with the gun. I can't reach it to fix."

The peter-pilot couldn't turn around to see, but the A/C did. I watched him as he looked over his left shoulder. Blocking the rising sun, his tinted face shield was down, hiding his eyes from my view. The helmet mic and mic-boom hid his mouth. He said nothing as his head turned back to the front.

---

[117] High Explosive

[118] A thin metal rod, about 18 inches long, that was inserted downward through a hole in the support bracket and through the middle of the six barrels. This prevented the barrels from rotating and discharging a round. Quite often, especially when on stand-by, the mini-guns were armed, one round chambered, and ready to fire. Without the rod inserted, any rotation of the barrels would cause a round to be discharged. Not removing it before take-off was such a rookie mistake. They knew as well as I that it was a screw-up. There were no repercussions, thankfully.

232

Following the same suppressive fire by our wing-man, the un-armed Dust-Off arrived. We made another gun run, two more rockets let loose, and another burst from the right mini-gun. Vann added a few bursts from his M-60 as we passed. I hadn't heard much over the radio as they approached. But I watched as that Huey, with the subdued cross on the nose and each side, hovered at the south end of the yellow smoke, close to the outpost. The bed of long grass, flattened by the downwash of the rotor blades, spread equally in all directions, as did the remaining fog and smoke swirling upwards in curly-cues.

The Dust-Off remained stationary, about a foot off the ground. Two grunts carried a third between them as they walked quickly to the ship. The wounded guy, in the middle, had his shirt off and bloodied bandages wrapped around his torso. He was walking, so maybe his wounds were not too serious. The Dust-Off dipped slightly as the wound-ed man was brought on board. As the two other grunts turned to return to their encampment, the ship pulled pitch and lifted off, making a quick roll to the left as they headed southward.

The A/C of the Dust-Off radioed, "We're taking fire." The nose lowered and they sped forward, skimming treetops with the skids as they increased altitude and left.

"Three Charlies spotted, south end of a small clearing, ten meters east of ravine." Our A/C and peter-pilot both spotted that area as well as two of the three enemy soldiers. They were wearing tan uniforms, pith helmets, and each carried an AK-47. These were not VC, but NVA.

The OIC on the ground was informed of their location via FM ra-dio. "We've got those bastards sighted," he said. Almost immediately, dust kicked up and small plumes of light gray smoke emanated from the NVA location. Tree limbs broke off and fell. The grunts had immediately fired in that direction with everything they had. Minutes passed. We and our wingman had gained altitude to keep out of the way, orbiting the area from a distance close enough to monitor the events, but out of rifle range.

Maybe an hour past daybreak, the engagement ended and we were released by the ground commander. We flew back to LZ Bronco, refueled and rearmed the ship, and returned to our revetment on the tarmac to wait. The scheduled mission was still a go.

There was no time for breakfast. We were the second of two gun-ship teams scheduled for this mission. SFC Barnett was busy at another ship that was having a minor mechanical problem, so he wasn't able to deliver any C-Rations to us. Neither Vann nor I could leave to go to his jeep to fetch a case of Cs. The flight was ready to go. Slicks were getting into position.

Our A/C informed us that this mission should last no more than a couple of hours. For certain we'd be back by lunch. He also informed us about the Dust-Off. They had taken one round from beneath, through the cabin floor and out through the roof. No control rods, electrical cables, etc. had been damaged. For the ship, it was a "through-and-through." The sheet metal guys would be busy making repairs well into the night.

It was 0718 hours when, at the LZ, a platoon of grunts was inserted into an area of suspected NVA activity. The AO was thick with trees and other high vegetation at the far edges, providing numerous places to hide. As the slicks landed, one of them received heavy automatic enemy fire. That A/C transmitted a message to the flight leader that his controls were stiff and limited. Neither the crew nor grunts aboard were injured. The slick lifted quickly without further incident. Due to enemy activity, we remained to help the grunts flush out, or destroy, the NVA positions. They did all the work while we orbited the AO.

My stomach growled. Focusing my attention to the radio transmissions and the AO in general, I tried my best to forget about food. As a matter of SOP, we door gunners did not shoot unless instructed to do so by one of the pilots. So, if we did engage, maybe that would help me forget about being hungry. My hopes for a little action were in vain. I stole a few seconds to search the interior cubbyholes of our side of the ship's cargo area for any leftover C-Rations, finding none. The fuel level began to get low. All I could think about was getting some food when we got back.

We arrived to rearm and refuel. No time for food. We were going back to the AO. Then, as it turned out, a couple more return trips to shoot, go back, rearm and refuel, and go back again. It was late afternoon. On the way to LZ Bronco, we heard over the radio that additional troops would be sent out. That mission was scheduled to start at 1700 hours. We were a part of that mission, so time was of the essence to rearm and refuel, to check the ship for any holes that shouldn't be there, and try to get some food. It was about 1600 hours when we arrived back at base. The A/C told us to be ready to go at 1700 hours. He would inform the mess hall sergeant that there were crews that needed food before chow was served.

The ship ready to go, Vann and I went into the mess hall. We were in a hurry. It was about twenty minutes before five. I asked the cook at the front grill to give us some food before we shipped back out.

"No. Come back at five."

"We're not gonna be here then," I told him. "We have to leave at five, and we haven't eaten all day. Come on, help us out."

As he stacked the cooked hamburger patties neatly into a corner of the grill (within my arm's reach), he told us, "The mess hall opens at five. Until then, no food. Period."

He was a Spec Four, so I thought quickly about pulling rank on him, but didn't. Not enough time to argue the finer point of me outranking him. It quickly became a macho battle of REMF vs. combat soldier and, so far, he was winning.

I quickly assessed the situation. I was hungry, so was Vann. The hamburgers were well within my reach. If this cook was not going to give us any, we'd have to do something quick. The stack of hamburgers was in front of me. As I drew my survival knife from its sheath and held it in my right hand, I told Vann, "Cover me at the pass." I quickly eyeballed the stack of meat and made an instantaneous mathematical calculation of timing, distance, and angle.

The cook had other plans. He held his steel spatula in his right hand as if to strike. Holding my knife up in a defensive position to parry any blows from the cook, I reached in with my left. In so doing, I looked away, oh so briefly, to coordinate the hand to the meat. I looked back just in time to witness the large, shiny, sharp steel spatula swing in a wide arc toward my right hand. It struck my middle finger. The cut was deep. The flesh was flayed open. The white fat cells were protruding out. Blood was slowly coming to the surface.

The cut was down to the bone. *Damn, that hurts*, I thought to myself. I forgot about the food. The bleeding wouldn't stop. I couldn't go on the mission like this. While I walked quickly to the dispensary, Vann was at my side and said he'd let Barnett know I might be late due to going to the dispensary. He left.

The medic cleaned the cut and told me one or two sutures would be needed. Placing my hand on his table as he cleaned it, I watched intently. It may have been the odor of disinfectant, or the sight of the needle approaching the proximal phalange of the middle finger on my right hand when the room got blurry, closed in and rotated slightly. In a second, the various subdued hues and shades of color in the room vanished. I fainted.

When I came to, the medic was kneeling over me, holding a capsule of smelling salts near my nose. Getting back up and sitting down again, I looked away as he closed the cut with one stitch, and covered it with a Band-Aid. One stitch? That's all? I thought it was a lot worse than that. (For those who may wonder, no; a Purple Heart is not awarded for stupid things like this.)

I walked out, heading back to the flight line. Glancing over to the revetment, my ship was gone. The flight had taken off. I was still hungry but not in a mood to go through the chow line and have a face-to-face encounter with that cook again, who was very likely still working the line.

Later that evening I spoke with Barnett and explained what happened. With no time to spare, he had taken my place as crew chief and the flight took off as scheduled. The mess sergeant was informed as well by the cook. No charges would be filed either way. Just forget about it, and don't let that happen again.

In September 1969, I received a letter from my brother, Steve. He responded to one I mailed to him a week earlier, asking if he'd like to meet up somewhere near Da Nang before he left country. He gave serious thought about taking advantage of the "extend six months for an earlier ETS date" plan and had submitted his extension request. It had been approved. But within days afterwards, there were some very odd goings-on at his compound. He wrote that things just felt weird to him:

> "[The] Hand of God literally and figuratively came down and smacked me upside the head. This is how that 'message' made me feel: 'Dude, you need to GET OUT of this God-forsaken place ASAP, post haste, if not sooner.'"

So, he spoke with his Commander and submitted a request to rescind his 6-month extension approval. Meanwhile, as that waiver was being processed, some VC/NVA documents were captured. Among the papers was a hit list. His name was listed along with a few others. In two weeks, his waiver had been approved. On September 23, 1969, my brother DEROSed back to the world. I didn't get a chance to see him in Vietnam. I wouldn't see him again until 1976.

When Steve arrived in California to fly back to Michigan, he later told me, he encountered a small group of hippies at the airport. They confronted him and spat upon him. Until his flight to Detroit was scheduled to board, he and a couple other GIs sat in the USO lounge for "safety" (I'm not sure if it was for his safety, or the hippies). For 365 days in Vietnam, one second at a time, he dreamt of going home, of going back to the world he left behind. Only then had it changed. He answered his country's call, risking life and limb, when so many others did not. What had he done to deserve such vitriol?

I always wondered what, exactly, he did in 'Nam. The most I could glean from him was that his MOS was in military intelligence. He worked with the CIA and Special Forces, going on patrols. He took an oath not to discuss his assignments, even to me. For 47 years, he has kept his word.

Chapter 13

Hunting for Sport

Toward the end of summer 1969, I submitted paperwork to go on R & R, and finally the day arrived that September. There were many places to visit, but I figured the opportunity to visit Sydney, Australia would never come again. And, most importantly, rumor had it that girls were plentiful and good looking. It was as close to going Stateside as I'd get.

The first leg of my journey had been an exercise in logistics and timing: catch a flight to Chu Lai, then hop another flight to Da Nang. So, I informed our operations where I needed to go. I was directed to a wooden shack on the opposite side of the airstrip. It was like a passenger waiting area and constructed just for that purpose. Wearing civilian clothes and carrying a small AWOL bag, I walked across our tarmac and the airstrip to the shack.

As I approached the shack and looked inside, I noticed the faint image of a guy sitting on the bench in the shadows, away from the open doorframe. Stepping inside, I saw he was wearing civilian clothing, but it took a few seconds for my eyes to adjust in order to recognize his face. He was one of our cooks. In fact, the very one I encountered under less than favorable conditions: the assaulter of my middle finger. I so much wanted him to see it, in all its glory, pointing upwards. But I stopped myself. This was the man who protected his hamburgers, and stuck to the established schedule, above and beyond the call of duty. His eyes told me he recognized me, too, as I stepped in.

It had been a few weeks, and we hadn't expressed any overt anger towards each other, just wordlessly eyeballing each other in the chow line. Seeing him in civilian clothes suggested he, too, was going on R & R. My mind raced as I thought of what to do. No one else was around. I could have cold-cocked him. Or he could have decked me out. Maybe that would have been enough. But he didn't seem like a fighter to me; just a short, fat ass cook.

I don't know what got into me, but I engaged him in small talk. He, too, was going to Sydney. I figured it was best to confront the incident now, lest we run into each other out in the real world.

"Listen," I said, "why don't we just bury the hatchet and forget about it." I said that? I couldn't believe those words came out of my mouth.

Inside that dark shack, lit only by reflective sunlight through the north door, he smiled and we shook hands in agreement. Nothing more was ever said between us about that event. At least we would travel together on good terms.

When we arrived in Sydney, a few permanent party guys directed us to a room where we sat and waited. There must have been a hundred of us from 'Nam. They briefed us about the customs, habits, places to go and not go, and so on. We had five days until we were to return to that very building, no later than the time and date indicated. The NCOIC[119] was very specific when he also told us not to go to the King's Cross District. There had been far too many problems there. We all poured out of that room, anxious to find taxis and begin our week of rest and relaxation.

We weren't able to get drunk much back at base because of our mission. So, I wanted to find a bar and buy a few beers, just to get the week started on the right foot.

The first place a few of us went to after the briefing was King's Cross, naturally. At random, I selected one of the many saloons, and entered into a darkened room. Sitting there at the bar, by himself, was a very familiar face. It was my buddy, Jim Kildall. I knew he was on R&R, but forgot where he had gone. This was his last day on R & R. We had a couple beers together, talked about what places to go and sights to see. He also told me the ratio of women to men was six to one. I still had to get a place to stay, so we said so long to each other.

I didn't go back to King's Cross after that but focused my attention on enjoying my R & R the best I could. Walking around one afternoon I came across the theater where the play *Hair* was performing. No reservation was required. Buying a ticket, I went inside, glanced around the auditorium and made a quick headcount. There were forty-two people inside. Maybe this was the matinee. I supposed that most everyone else was at work that afternoon. I sat through the entire performance. My thoughts were not focused on the play, but wondered back to 'Nam and my decision

---

[119] Non-commissioned officer in charge.

to go back. To this day, I could not tell you what the plot of the play was. The orchestra played "Age of Aquarius," a song I became familiar with as sung by The Fifth Dimension. As the performance ended, what I most remembered was the final line-up of the cast on stage. Men and women, all buck naked and standing tall and proud, facing the audience. There must have been thirty or so standing elbow to elbow. I had never seen anything like that before or since. Crazy shit, for sure.

I met a young woman and we spent some time together towards the end of the week. We took a boat tour of the Sydney coastal area where I noticed a huge concrete structure under construction. Its design was very unique. She told me it was going to be the Sydney Opera House at Bennelong Point. We had dinner at a nice restaurant later on. We traded more stories about the customs and other differences, and similarities, between the USA and Australia. Our two cultures were quite similar.

The more I learned about her as a person, about her hopes and aspirations and relishing her humor and wit, the more my thoughts were reinforced that people all over the world are the same. Basic human nature, I supposed. For those few days, we enjoyed each other's company, not as an Australian and American, but as two people. Life in Sydney was not much different than life back home.

When I got back to 'Nam, I became SFC Barnett's assistant. There is no slot for an *assistant* platoon sergeant, per se, so I kept my regular job as crew chief. We were shorthanded, and he needed someone he trusted to take his place when he DEROSed in a few months. He had taken me under his wing and began showing me the ropes regarding his job. We talked with each other quite a bit. He didn't feel Jim, who had more time in grade than I, was up to the job as his assistant. There was an opening for promotion to staff sergeant, E-6, and he asked me if I was interested. I said I was. I didn't think twice about my answer, though his question came as a surprise. Protocol dictated that the promotion be offered first to the Spec Five in our platoon having an older date of rank than me. I understood that.

Barnett gathered the Spec Fives together after formation one day. Although he already knew the answer, he asked them a question. "Who, among you have a date of rank earlier than 1967?"

Only one, my buddy Jim, raised his hand to respond to the question.

"We have an E-6 slot open," Barnett continued, "are you interested in that?"

Jim outranked me by two years. We had previously talked about our jobs as crew chiefs and I knew he liked the job. Jim asked, "Would the promotion require me to stop flying, stop being a crew chief?"

"Yes," replied Barnett.

"Well, no thanks. I want to keep flying," Jim said. That left me as the next senior Spec Five in the platoon and the prime candidate for promotion.

Barnett and I worked very well together. In selecting me, my Spec Five rank was officially (per written unit order) converted to buck sergeant (E-5). Same pay grade, more responsibility. My additional duties, beyond being a crew chief still, were to: monitor the flight hours and scheduled maintenance for our ships; assign ships and crews for the next day's missions and those on stand-by; check in with operations every night to learn how many gunships would be needed for the next day's mission(s), and return later to tell them which ones were scheduled; supervise the fencing of the ammo dump at the north end of the flight line; and, anything else he could dream up for me to do.

Barnett was set to DEROS in late November, and I suppose I was being groomed to take his place. All the while, I was still flying and scheduled myself. Along with my additional job privileges, I had access to the Shark jeep. I signed it out from the motor pool every chance I had, but I had to share it with Barnett. I loved driving that thing. The motor pool sergeant seemed belligerent, so I kept out of his way as much as possible.

With my new status as an NCO, I was required to leave the enlisted Shark hootch and move into the junior NCO hootch, built in the traditional manner, vacated by the E-7s and 8s who had recently completed construction of a new and much nicer hootch next door. Their building was not made of leftover wood planks from ammo boxes. They used what appeared to be 2 x 4 framing, plywood that was scorched with a kerosene blowtorch to bring out the grain, and then varnished. Each room of theirs had a small air-conditioning window unit, ceiling lights, light switches, electrical wall-sockets, etc. I recognized the result of what must have been many trades and deals to get the materials and construction completed.

My new living quarters weren't too bad. Here, too, there was no door at either end of the building, just doorframes. On the west end was an enclosed screened-in porch with a minimal view of our flight line and the western horizon. Stacked sandbags blocked-off most of the scenery. Walking in from the porch, the long and narrow hallway greeted me. The ceiling, walls and floor were all leftover ammo-box wood.

My room was the second on the left. Inside was one steel frame bed, a small ammo-box wood table, a wall locker, and closer to the door an area set apart with shelving. Cozy. I had one of eight rooms. Next to me on one side was the new assistant platoon sergeant of one of the slick platoon, Charles "Chuck" Gholson. He was also a crew chief whose Spec Five rank had been converted to buck sergeant. We had two hootch-maids who washed our clothes, polished our boots, and kept the hootch clean. It cost each one of us ten MPC dollars a month to pay for their services. One was about thirtyish and spoke some English. Though her name was Hoa, we called her Mama-san. The younger one, about fifteen or so, spoke no English whatsoever. Her name was Kiém Liên.

Just off from the front porch we had a wooden shower stall. One 4' x 4' area was to place your toiletries, hang your clothing and towel on a nail, etc. Adjacent to that was another 4' x 4' space that was the actual shower stall. Above the wood framework was an immersion heater (the same type I once used during KP at Tay Ninh). It was a gymnastic chore to climb up the framework to get the thing lit, but we managed. We took turns each night. I guess we could have constructed a ladder of some type to make it easier[120], but the framework was sufficient.

Taking a shower in our stall required some forethought. We wanted to make sure the potable water truck came by earlier to fill up the aluminum water container that was originally designed as an external fuel tank on an F-4 Phantom jet. The water often needed to be heated, especially during the monsoon season. If it was raining, lighting the fire in the immersion heater became too difficult. Taking a shower with cold water in

---

[120] Nails and hammers were scarce.

cold weather meant washing where necessary, and very quickly. During the hot season, the cool water felt refreshing.

Recognizing the skills needed to supervise others (more than just my gunner), and not really knowing the best way to be that leader, I purchased a college-level management textbook by mail order. Of course, I let Barnett know. I wanted to learn, but also to show off, actually. It worked. But now I had to put into play the methods I read. I quickly learned that in practice one could be a nice guy at one end of the spectrum, encounter resistance to getting the job done, and swiftly become a hard-nosed prick. Somewhere in between is where I was hoping to be.

I still hung around with Jim. But, as I was 'moving up' I was 'encouraged' to learn the traditional Army system of not fraternizing with those who were not NCOs. Well, Jim was still my friend. I wouldn't be able to show favoritism, but I couldn't treat him like the others, either. Over time, we learned to be professional during the work day, but shared a couple cold ones at the NCO Club at night. I sensed no ill will from him. He was quite happy with his job as a gunship crew chief.

As part of the transition from enlisted to NCO, my M-16 was turned in, exchanged for a Colt .45 caliber semi-automatic pistol. No training. No qualification. Just the gun, two magazines, leather holster left over from World War II, and a box of bullets. Chuck and I did take a ride in the Shark jeep to go to the range on the other side of Mt. Montezuma, once, to practice firing a few rounds. But, once again, I had been issued a weapon while in Vietnam without proper training or qualification.

It was standard practice for our company personnel to stay close to their weapon, steel pot, flak jacket, and ammo. It was not required wearing if you stayed within the company area. But you better damn sure have these with you if you ventured away. Common sense would dictate the necessity of having these when working on the flight line.

The afternoon heat could be brutal. The temperature gauge in the ship's windshield had read 50 degrees Celsius quite often. Most days, cloud cover was minimal. The sun, brutally hot, beat on us day after day. The Navy Sea-Bees had constructed our tarmac flight line and applied a tar-like substance, a thickness of two and a half inches or so, over the packed-down sand. On most days, it was sufficient and durable. But, when it got really hot, walking on the hot tarmac caused the tar to be lifted onto the soles of our boots. It would not be unusual to have, what felt like a pound of, melted tar on each boot if you walked more than twenty feet. The footstep pattern of naked, tar-less sand left behind was often a visual clue as to how hot it was.

For most of the day, our hootch-maids had the run of our building. Usually I was working and wouldn't get back until sometime after 1630 hours or so. But, once in a while I'd go back during the afternoon to get something and find Kiém Liên napping on my bed. It became her habit to use my room during when I wasn't there. Maybe it was the same thing when the senior NCOs lived here. I trusted her, but kept my gear in my wall-locker, locked. I always wore my .45 on my hip whenever I left my room.

We received word, again, that our perimeter was being probed by Charlie. One night a couple sappers were shot dead as they tried to crawl through the wide area between the outermost coil of barbed wire and the line of perimeter bunkers. In between, there were rows of coiled razor-wire strung parallel to our perimeter. We called that inside area "no man's land." Sappers, striped to the skinny except for a loin covering, were very skillful negotiating their way through each row—crawling, slithering, using every move of a contortionist while attempting to remain undetected. One would get through, occasionally, with a satchel of explosives. Other times, they would just get close and drop off the satchel, and try to make it back out, undetected.

Most of the time, our sometimes-trigger-happy perimeter guards fired off a flare at the slightest provocation, and sometimes for no reason at all just to keep everybody on their toes.

At daylight, the perimeter guards located a satchel charge of explosives left by a sapper. Unbeknownst to me at the time, this wasn't the first. We had the 11th Light Infantry to our south and a howitzer battery to the north. Their guards had stopped Charlie a few times before, some getting as far in as the airstrip. From that point on, not only did I keep my .45 loaded, I also began to keep a large fixed-blade knife, in a leather sheath, within easy reach when I went to bed, just in case. Only I knew that it was kept tucked underneath my mattress between the metal wires of the mattress spring. The door to my room was the last barrier between me and Charlie, should they make it in that far.

Water buffalo are common in Vietnam. These beasts of burden were used for plowing fields and transporting heavy material. The VC and NVA were known to use them extensively along the Ho Chi Minh Trail to haul food, ammo, weapons and other battle materials into South Vietnam, via Laos. On a routine reconnaissance one day, the pilot of a bird dog[121] had spotted a small herd of water buffalo about twenty kilometers west of us. He radioed in the coordinates to our ops people. They in turn initiated a mission for one fire team to respond to the sighting of NVA transportation vehicles. My ship was on standby, so off we went.

The herd had moved by the time we arrived at the designated location. But the bird dog was on their tail and guided us in. My A/C, who also happened to be the team leader, communicated with ops to discuss the possibility of us taking one KIA back to base for dinner. They agreed and dispatched a slick to hoist it out. While we waited for the slick to arrive, the bird dog was released to continue its mission while we continued to orbit the four-legged *transport vehicles*. The pilots selected the largest and fattest one of the herd. I had the honor of shooting it first with my M-60. During the first pass, I shot off a few rounds. I was pretty sure the bullets found their mark, but the animal didn't fall or stumble. The pilot asked me if I thought it might take more than a few rounds to bag this animal. That's going to be some tough steaks.

Our second ship tried next, and finally it fell. We continued to orbit until the slick arrived. During the hoisting operation, which required the crew chief or gunner to get out and attach a cable around both horns, we flew cover. Once completed, they airlifted that half-ton NVA animal, KIA, back to base. We followed a short distance away. That evening it was butchered and grilled, and every man in the company ate their fill. A great morale booster—one we needed very badly.

In our company area, the odor of pot was lost among many other noxious fragrances. The wide varieties stemmed from the shit burning in barrels, diesel fuel exhaust from trucks, jet engine exhaust from aircraft, food cooking (or burning) in the mess hall, the urinal tubes and crap-shacks, the countryside, soaked sandbags, laundry, tar from the tarmac,

---

[121] A Cessna O-1 single engine airplane flown by the U.S. Air Force in Vietnam for reconnaissance and observation of enemy activity.

incense, and whatever else contributed to the overall stink. Oh, did I mention the odor of burnt shit? Stay upwind, my friend, stay upwind.

During the evenings when most of the guys had finished work, ate, and retired to their hootch, the NCOs gathered together around 2000 hours to search the company area for stashes of marijuana, hashish, or heroin. The hiding places most used by the men were under sandbags at locations known only to the potheads. Our search technique was to split up in groups of two or three, walk around a hootch to spot a corner sandbag that appeared to have been moved, or had a bulge. We were looking primarily for plastic bags with homemade roll-your-own joints inside. They were not likely to create a bulge that could be observed, especially at night, so lifting sandbags at random was the general routine. Our second objective was to catch anyone smoking them.

As a new NCO, I was expected to participate. The plan to search was kept quiet, as was the actual search itself, so as not to alert the troops. Barnett warned me to be careful. In one of the recent previous searches he found a hand grenade hidden beneath a sandbag. An attached note warned the finder to stop searching, or else. The pin was still in. The next time, maybe not. Night after night, we conducted our search, ever so carefully.

One night, during a search, one of the NCOs from the other side of the company area ran over to us, where the first sergeant was. One of them spotted a noticeable bulge and carefully lifted the top sandbag. He found a hand grenade with the pin out, lying beside it. The handle was taped closed. No note. As we returned to our rally point, we learned the pin had been re-inserted, rendering it safe. That was enough for me. I stopped participating in these searches. Chicken? You bet. I didn't tell Barnett the 'why' of my decision. I just made sure I was never available when these searches took place. There was always something else to do, scheduling aircraft and crews, supervising repairs and inspections of our ships on the flight line, etc.

The use of drugs was not limited to our company area. It was common knowledge that occasionally, some of the guys guarding our section of the base perimeter smoked weed. It was difficult to prove, except for their glassy eyes, that they were high on something. We had no means to test for illicit drugs. Whether the guys used illegal substances during their off hours, or got drunk the night before, they still had a job to do. I knew of only one example that anybody in the company was ever drunk or stoned while doing his job. That's not to say that sometimes a few guys weren't hung over from the night before. But, that one time involved the two guys at the ammo dump. For most of the day they were left alone to unpack, assemble, and stack 2.75-inch rockets, smoke and hand grenades, and hundreds of boxes of 7.62mm and 5.56mm ammo from shipping crates. Mostly unsupervised, and some days with very little to do, everybody knew they got stoned.

The most common drug of choice was marijuana, but occasionally some smoked hashish or used heroin one way or another. Drug use was an open secret. People using were usually extremely careful about the threat of being caught. It was a known fact that evidence as small as a marijuana seed was enough for criminal prosecution, and six months in prison if convicted. How high (no pun intended) in our command structure used drugs on a regular basis? Of course, we didn't know, but there was an unconfirmed suspicion that some pilots and maybe one or two platoon leaders had used some type of drug. But it was just rumor.

Where did the illegal drugs come from? Town was off limits. How did that stuff get inside the base? The hootch-maids? As an NCO, I tried several times to ferret out the source, but with no success. In retrospect, I believe marijuana, hashish, and heroin were made available to American GIs as a form of warfare, in and of itself. Whether or not they sought out a source of drug supply (to continue a drug habit from civilian life) or were initially introduced to illegal substances in country, some guys needed drugs. And, some Vietnamese were very willing to meet the American demand.

Maybe supplying mind-altering substances to Americans was, indeed, a method of warfare both there and in the States. I could easily imagine a VC or NVA high commander designing a strategy around using drugs to defeat us culturally, politically, and mentally. Make drugs available by whatever means possible. If constant use can be developed, the will of the soldier could be expected to be compromised. Turn us against this war. Poison our minds. Weaken our resolve.

Let's face it. Some guys didn't want to fight, no matter the cause. To them, there was no fight worth dying for, there or anywhere else. Of those who didn't want to be there, a lot were quite vocal about it. They didn't even want to be in the military. For some, any escape from reality was worth the consequences.

On one blustery and cloudy day, we were returning from an AO where we had been scrambled during the day to help the LRRPs in the area. They had spotted some NVA. They needed to remain there to continue the mission, but the NVA had to be taken out first for them to proceed. We were the answer to their problem. As usual in these type of circumstances, we were 'steered' to the location of the NVA's position by whispered instructions over the LRRP's PRC-25. Our two ships took position. The lead went into a gun run, let loose a few rockets, and banked away followed by us. We also let a few rockets loose to find their mark. Neither ship fired mini-guns, and none of our M-60s were fired on this mission, but we were ready. The rockets had taken care of the problem and we were released.

Going back, we were flying low level on the deck, sometimes referred to as *nap-of-the-earth*[122] flying. This type of flying is absolutely joyful. Just about every air crewman I knew enjoyed flying like this. We'd follow the curvature of the earth, skimming over tree tops, going into valleys, banking gently to the left or right, never gaining altitude over a hundred feet. Fast and low. Armed to the teeth. I loved it.

My A/C observed a Vietnamese man standing alone at the top of a knoll next to a single tree ahead of us, a few hundred meters ahead.

He asked me via the intercom, "You see that gook ahead? There, on the knoll."

I looked ahead and noticed the man, and told the A/C, "Yeah."

He asked, "How good's your aim?"

I told him, "Fairly accurate."

He responded, "Well, let's see how good you really are." The inference to kill him was obvious, but I didn't see the need. Our mission had ended. We were going back to base. Both pilots were young, maybe twenty, twenty-one. Killing that man would be nothing but sport for them.

---

[122] Very low-altitude flight path to avoid detection and attack by the enemy.

We were bearing down on him, fast. I had to make a decision. Killing VC or NVA in the field was not new to me. I had done that many times, but this was different. Was he one of *them*? Or, a farmer? Or, a lookout? One part of me had become numb to killing. Ever since my last tour, it no longer meant anything to me if I shot an enemy soldier or if that person lived or died. I had crossed *that line*. Killing became an easy thing to do. I never allowed myself to think about it.

There were no consequences here, as long as I was acting under orders. But was it right? Was it moral? What about God's commandment? Yes, this was war, but was killing an unarmed man the same as killing an armed enemy soldier? Maybe, maybe not. The difference between the two faded every day.

I didn't know what it was called, but my "posture" for killing required me to be seated inside the cargo door of a Huey, wearing my flight helmet and flak jacket, being strapped in with an M-60 on my lap and a full box of ammo at my feet. With this set of equipment, I could shoot just about anything as long as I didn't allow myself to question the intent and justification. But this was different.

As we were bearing down, I thought quickly about that guy in red shorts—*stop him, stop him*—during my first tour, about the trouble at My Lai, investigations, cover ups, and jail.

Was I going to obey orders or not? If I did, so what? Just another body count. If I didn't, what would happen? Article 15? Court martial? Did the A/C see something about him that I didn't? Did I miss something on the radio?

"Take him out," the A/C reminded me.

Time was running out, yet it felt like it stopped. The other part of me didn't want any part of this plan. I remembered the first guy I killed, still a vivid, daily memory. How was this any different? Closing in on the target. Were we slowing down? Once again, time stood still.

I decided to shoot and miss. Shooting the M-60 from my left armpit, straight ahead from the port-side cargo door, and being right-handed, is not as easy as one might think. The links of ammo fed in from the left side, and the spent brass ejected from the right. At a closing distance of 200 yards I took careful aim and fired a burst of 20-30 rounds.

As planned, the rounds went to the man's left, and some to his right. Puffs of dust kicked up all around. He remained standing, maybe frozen with fear. But, he was physically safe and uninjured. The shooting stopped. Getting closer by the second, we were about twenty-feet above deck and traveling fast. I'll never forget that man's face, vividly pale, as he faced upward to watch us fly overhead. His lips were moving very quickly, almost like he was praying for survival, or cussing us out. I think I detected a brown spot at the seat of his pants, but couldn't be sure. There was no weapon on him or on the ground. Convinced that targeting this man was nothing more than a recreational endeavor, there was nothing more to do but to prepare for the consequences.

I was the butt of a few jokes and ridicule from the A/C and pilot on the way back to base. Some comments were made between them as I monitored the intercom, and a few directed at me.

"How the fuck did you miss him? That gook was an easy target. Why couldn't you hit him? You had all the time in the world to take him out, and missed. What kind of experience did you have during your last tour? What's the matter, are you afraid to kill somebody?"

Letting the verbal assault subside for a few minutes, I asked, "Sir, why was it so important to shoot that guy?"

The A/C answered sarcastically, "'Cuz he wasn't supposed to be there."

All of a sudden, I was ashamed of being in the Sharks. I questioned myself—for the first time, really. Why had I reenlisted for this? Something had changed since my first tour, but I wasn't sure exactly what it was. Almost six months into a six-year enlistment, I felt trapped. Nobody forced me to be here. It was my decision. There was no one else to blame, but me.

Did I think about reporting this attempted murder by gunship of an unarmed man? Yes, but just for an instant. I played out the process and figured I could have been charged with dereliction of duty, disobeying a direct order from the A/C. I knew for sure the pilots, warrant officers, these particular "wobbly ones," were not going to take the fall. They'd put it on me. Nothing more was ever said about this incident, at least to my face.

Chapter 14

Beaucoup Dinky-Dau

The day began as any other. The morning was busy but the activity tapered off as the ships departed on their missions. I made my rounds by driving the jeep to the men's hootch, the ammo dump, operations, and supply room. The Vietnamese men and women had arrived and were already working. Another day, another dollar. I had left my hootch before dawn and returned about mid-day for something.

When I arrived there, Mama-san was upset. Kiém Liên wasn't at work. Angry and tearful, she pointed to a room down the hall. The man who had that room on the other side of the hallway and down two doors was the motor pool sergeant.

"He beaucoup numba ten," as she put it loud and angrily in broken English. "Boom-boom, Kiém Liên, boom-boom numba ten."

"Today?" I asked.

"No, not today." She motioned with her hand in a circular manner in such a way that I understood this taking place the day before.

"Not today. Yesterday?" I asked.

Mama-san nodded her head up and down. She was pissed. "He beaucoup dinky-dau!" she yelled again.[123]

I understood exactly what she was saying. Upset, I searched within myself for a constructive response. This was the first time I ever had to deal with a problem like this and didn't know what to do. Walking the few steps to his room, I pointed at the door to make sure Mama-san had the right man. She nodded in agreement. The motor pool sergeant wasn't there, but I told her I'd take care of it.

This was a problem I was certain I could handle on my own. Going to the motor pool did not seem to be the best option to take, so I tracked down the NCO who supervised the local workers, SFC Zimmerman, and told him what I had learned. He said he'd look into it. It didn't occur to me

---

[123] 'Beaucoup dinky-dau translates roughly as 'very much crazy.'

to report this to Barnett, the first sergeant, the company commander, or the military police. I figured if I was going to be a staff sergeant, I needed to be able to see this thing through, without help from my higher chain of command.

I guess I had a chip on my shoulder for the rest of that afternoon and evening. I felt empathy for Kiém Liên. I couldn't imagine what she had gone through except shame, anger and resentment. She was only fifteen or so, couldn't be much older than that.

Kiém Liên was extremely shy. When she spoke her native language, she did so quietly. I felt protective over her. I had forced myself to think of her more like a younger sister, but was it more? I made sure I didn't let anyone know how much I cared for her. She stood about five-feet tall, couldn't have weighed more than a whisper. Her eyes were dark brown. Black hair hung over her shoulders except for the days she put it in a ponytail. I'd be lying if I said I didn't think a few times about building a romantic relationship with her.

She, and people like her, were the real reason why we were here. It was only by watching her that I shed all the bullshit about being fed up with American politics, draft dodgers, reenlistment bonuses, running away from home again, and any other superficial reason I could come up with at the time to make my decision seem noble. I asked myself what would happen to Kiém Liên, her family, neighbors and village if the communists took over. God, what if we lost the war?

I often wondered, too, if bringing her back to the States might be an option. Would it be difficult for her, trying to learn our language and customs, shopping, or driving a car? How would people treat her? Would she make friends easily? How difficult would it be to take her away from her family and friends to start a new life? She was much too young to have intimate relations. I could imagine a future with her somewhere down the line. Maybe I should stay in Vietnam? Not gonna happen with five years and months remaining on my enlistment.

That evening I went into the enlisted Shark hootch to schedule crews and aircraft for the next day. Two crew chiefs, Bell and Vandiver, were in the hallway standing next to the posting board. They wanted to fly together on the same ship and asked me to schedule them together. We never flew two crew chiefs together unless absolutely necessary, so I said no. As I completed the scheduling on the board, they kept at it, trying to change my mind. They were half-joking, but half-serious too. Bell was from Texas. He was tall, about six feet something, and stocky, as if he worked hard on a ranch his whole life. His buddy, Vandiver, was not as tall. He was heavy, though, and likely weighed the same as Bell. When I wrote the crew names on the board, things got a little more serious. Trying to keep our verbal exchange on the light side wasn't working as well as I hoped.

It became a matter of wills. A few guys in the hootch were standing around watching. Bell and Vandiver's reputation as the informal hootch leaders was on the line, and we all knew it. Many in the hootch looked up to them, while a few just put up with them as there was no way not to. I had to find a way to manage those two to my advantage. Maybe, if I adopted a hard-nose approach, I could meet or exceed their level of self-anointed authority among the men. I had a responsibility to do my job the best I knew how. I knew instinctively that if Bell and Vandiver were to win this time, whatever authority I thought I had would be moot from that day forward. My friend Jim was not around for moral support. I had to guess he was at the NCO Club.

It became clear they couldn't care less if I was the assistant platoon sergeant, or a buck sergeant. We were all the same pay-grade. I was smaller and lighter. I had to get tough. Sometimes humor and friendly talk just didn't work. But as my demeanor changed, theirs did too. Suddenly, Bell grabbed me under one armpit and Vandiver grabbed the other. They lifted me off the floor and carried me backwards, down the hall, in the direction of the back door.

I wanted to tell them to put me down, but I quickly realized how immature that would sound to the others. Resisting as much as I could and making it as difficult as possible, it was for naught. One of them told me I needed to cool off, and they carried me out and sat me down at the foot of a nearby wooden utility pole. Still laughing, they went back inside. I didn't think I was hurt except for my pride.

One or two of the other guys from the hootch followed us out. One stayed with me, helping me get up as I brushed the sand from my uniform. My first concern was to check my .45; still holstered.

"Take it easy," one of the guys said to me. "You ok?"

Looking at my face, he continued, "You can't go into ops now. You cut your face pretty bad. Somebody'll see you looking like this and ask what happened." During the scuffle, I had cut my upper right cheek near the eye socket, and it was bleeding. He continued, "I'll post the crews and ships in ops for you."

"Thanks," I replied.

I realized he was right as I felt the cut and wiped the blood away. If I went, somebody there would definitely be asking questions and I'd have to provide reasonable answers. I figured if I told them I tripped in the dark they wouldn't believe me, anyhow. Most importantly for me, I didn't want Barnett to find out about this scuffle and think he'd made a mistake in selecting me for promotion.

With great reluctance, I retired to my room. The single incandescent light bulb was enough for me to see and clean up the three-inch cut the best I could with what I had available. It was deep, but I didn't think it needed stitches. I also wanted to get out of sight should Barnett come around, or any other senior NCO who would no doubt insist on knowing what happened.

The next morning my upper cheek bone and bruise looked as though I had been in one hellava fight the night before. I hesitantly went to the formation trying to keep that side of my face away from anyone seeing me. I wasn't totally successful, but no one asked me about it. Maybe the attitude I was trying hard to develop had gone too far. Maybe other guys saw that. I certainly didn't. I was a lightweight compared to most of the men—only five-foot-eight, and skinny. To make up for my physical stature, I had to toughen up my mental posture. My efforts to emulate the NCOs I knew failed. I saw them as no nonsense kind of guys; mature, friendly, but don't take any crap from anybody. Barnett had told me that during one of our talks. It wasn't so much who the NCO is, but what he wears on his sleeve or collar. *That* was the authority, not me. So, it goes without question. Even if I'm wrong, I'm right (as long as the lawful order(s) was within Army laws and regulations, and not morally wrong). My error(s) would be addressed later among fellow NCOs. At least, I thought so.

By the time the Vietnamese came in to work, formation was over and our day had begun. I returned to my hootch about 1000 hours, entered and saw both of our hootch-maids. Kiém Liên was back. I tried to read her facial expressions as the two of them, ironing our jungle fatigues, worked close to the floor. She didn't look up as I passed. I didn't want to bother them so I just walked on towards my room. What was I going to say? Should I say anything?

In passing them, Mama-san saw me first and said something in Vietnamese to Kiém Liên. I entered my room and closed the door, but they were right behind me and opened it again. They looked at the cut on my cheekbone and spoke Vietnamese to each other again. Turning to me and inspecting the cut, Mama-san wanted to know how it happened. I told her I tripped, not wanting to get too detailed. This was the same story I told Barnett earlier at formation, but she wasn't buying it. Between the few words of English and gestures, it became obvious that Mama-san knew I had not injured myself as I said.

Kiém Liên's cousin, Kim, worked at the NCO Club as a bartender. For a Vietnamese woman, almost thirty years of age, she spoke English very well, almost fluently. We usually went to the club after dinner for a beer or two, almost daily, so she and I were well acquainted. This day was no different. Kim quietly told me her cousin was attacked by Sergeant Jackson. Everybody knew him. Staff Sergeant Jackson ran his motor pool like a well-oiled machine. At the same time, though, he was easy to get along with, considering. Kim was steadfast; it had been him. Still, it was difficult for me to accept. I believed them, but couldn't believe Jackson would have actually done something like that. He and I were not friends, per se, but we did live in the same hootch and I interacted with him every time I signed the jeep out for the day.

She also told me both Kiém Liên and Mama-san believed I cut myself fighting to protect her honor. Kim smiled and said she believed that, too.

"No," I told her, "I tripped and cut myself. It'll heal." There was no way I was going to admit to her, or anyone else not present at the time, that two of my guys carried me out of their hootch like a bag of potatoes and plopped me down at the foot of a telephone pole.

Try as I did, she didn't believe me, either. I couldn't convince her otherwise. Coincidence or not, the timing of my minor, but very noticeable, injury was their proof. They *knew*, beyond a doubt, that I had fought Jackson to protect Kiém Liên's honor. I was frankly a little embarrassed that I hadn't.

Two days passed. The SFC Zimmerman, the NCOIC of the Vietnamese workers, told me the result of his "investigation", but only after I had to track him down for the answer. Between the ops bunker and my hootch there was a space of about ten feet wide for people to pass from the company area to the tarmac. It was there I caught up to him and we spoke.

"Yeah," he said, "I talked to him. He said she was waiting for him, laying on his bunk, when he returned to his room. They had sex, that's all. He said she was asking for it."

The sandbags of both structures began to close in on me as I stood there in disbelief. Remember, I was still an E-5. He was an E-7 and the motor pool sergeant was an E-6. Who was I to challenge his findings? Was I going to report *him* to the first sergeant for doing what I thought was a crappy job of investigating? No. Was I going to tell Barnett? What chance would that have to resolve his "investigation" to a conclusion that I would accept? Three and a half years of active duty had taught me to keep my mouth shut. Don't challenge authority. Anybody having rank over me *was* authority.

I wanted to dig in deeper. Did he interview the girl? How about Mama-san? Was anybody else in the hootch at that time? The male/female culture at the time was a bit more primitive than it is now, almost fifty years later. I grew up hearing from other guys that all girls say "no" the first time. It's expected, and they want you to keep going. But, when the girl says "no" the second time, you should stop. The first *no* is meant to prove to the guy that she is not a slut, the second is the real one.

How many times did Kiém Liên say no? Did she even know that word in English? I didn't know how to say it in Vietnamese, and I'm somewhat sure he didn't either. Maybe she said, in her native language, "không", pronounced like the last name of King Kong. If she said this word, it meant 'no' to her, but to him it meant nothing. Did she put up a fight? Maybe he liked rough sex. Did she resist? Maybe he also went to the same school of thought. Was she overpowered? These questions weren't part of Zimmerman's investigation, it seemed.

His choice was simple: protect the motor pool sergeant from the accusation of a fifteen-year-old girl.

I didn't know what to think after this. I expected more from him. He was covering for that guy, and I knew it beyond a shadow of doubt. There was no reason for Kiém Liên, and Mama-san, to be angry enough to report this to the only person they trusted, which apparently was me. There was no question that he and Kiém Liên had a sexual encounter. But, for God's sake, Kiém Liên was a young, innocent girl. I refused to believe that she was "asking for it."

After work, I went to the NCO Club for a beer. He was at the bar when he saw me walk inside. His insight surprised me when he suggested we go out back to discuss what happened to the girl. As we walked out, I was making plans about what to do. I wanted to hit him. If I threw the first punch, being an E-5, I could end up with an Article 15, get busted down to a SP/4, kiss my chance at getting promoted down the drain, and maybe pay a fine as well as extra duty. A crappy start to a six-year stint. But if *he* threw the first punch, I would be within my rights to protect myself by whatever means necessary to stop the assault. We stood outside, not three feet from the back door. It was still sunny. I couldn't help but notice the guys across the street playing volleyball next to the mess hall. They were having a good time and couldn't see us, but I was fuming. In fact, I glanced around and saw no one else around. Just him and me. I was ready.

Up to this point, he and I got along fairly well, considering the difference in rank. And, we were neighbors. He told me he understood how angry I was. Confessing to the act, he told me he came back to his room that day to find Kiém Liên laying in his bed. In that he didn't get back to the hootch during the day that often, and with seeing her in his bed, he thought it was an invitation for him to get laid.

"I was horny and made a move," he said." "She didn't fight back much at all, just playing hard to get."

"Didn't she put up a fight? Didn't she say anything?" I asked.

"Not really," he said, "I couldn't understand a word she was saying. Like I told the Zimmerman, she was asking for it." He apologized to me for any misunderstanding. "Look," he said, "I know you have a thing for her"— I was surprised he knew that, maybe it was more obvious than I thought— "but what was I supposed to do? What would you have done?"

I wanted to slug him, hard and fast. My mind calculated the pros and cons very quickly, and I thought I could get away with it. But maybe not.

To describe my behavior after our conversation would be difficult. My right hand closed up. My arm stiffened for the right hook. I looked into his brown eyes as he finished his explanation. I understood why he thought Kiém Liên was coming on to him, laying in his bed. In his own way, I suppose, he apologized to me, but not to Kiém Liên. He deserved the consequence of his actions. My mind's eye envisioned the movement of my right arm, arcing upward, my forearm straight, the fist tight as I aimed at his left jaw bone with every ounce of strength and pushed his brown face into his skull.

As he finished his excuse, I recognized no malice in his words or demeanor. I wanted to be massively angry. I wanted to avenge Kiém Liên's honor. I wanted to punish him, to teach him a lesson. But his story had the ring of plausibility. Then I thought, if I were him and didn't really care for Kiém Liên as a human being but only but as a gook hootch maid, would I have done the same thing? No, but I wasn't him. I did care for her as a human being. I empathized with her shame of being victimized by an American GI who she worked for. I thought his disrespect was not to her, but to people who he looked down to. If I hit him, no lesson would be learned, no honor restored. Shamefully, I stood down.

I followed him back into the club and finished my beer, alone. I had my opportunity and failed to protect her honor. I had my one chance and blew it. Emotionally, it was tearing me apart. I hated this place, the cover ups, the us-against-them mentality. The Americans-can-do-no-wrong mindset. It was all making me beaucoup dinky-dau.

The time finally arrived for our promotion board. Chuck and I each put on our best uniform, all nice and clean, and caught a flight to Chu Lai. We were not competing against each other and knew, if we didn't blow our chances, both of us would get promoted to staff sergeant, E-6. Two open promotions, two men applying. It was early October, sunny, and very warm. We felt good as we arrived and found our way to the battalion headquarters. The sand and dust did a number on my footgear. Very, very carefully, I dusted mine off so as not to ruin the spit shine.

We were directed to a single level, frame building. It was painted a light green. There were no sandbags in sight, none at all. Concrete sidewalks were everywhere in that area. We checked in and sat down in the waiting room, just the two of us. We were early, but not too much. Sitting and eager for our name to be called, we remained silent. My thoughts were consumed with trying to anticipate what would be asked and what my answers would be. I was sure Chuck was doing the same thing. When my name was called, I did a quick check of my gig-line to make sure everything was lined up. I was ready.

I marched inside, making sure I pivoted as I made a turn. Standing next to the chair set before their table, six feet away from dead center, I saluted the officer at the table. At his command, I sat down. Following the preliminary introductions and greetings, each of the three members of the promotion panel asked a few questions about the Code of Conduct, chain of command, leadership, and other general questions about things I should, and did, know. It was over in ten minutes. I left and sat down next to Chuck in one of the waiting room chairs along the wall.

"How'd it go?" he asked.

"Good, no sweat," I told him. We hadn't had much time for further discussion as his name was called. He went in, staying about the same time as I did, and came back out, smiling. Both of us felt confident, but wouldn't know the results for another couple of weeks.

Before heading back to Duc Pho, we checked out the PX. I spent most of my time looking at the electronics: cameras, reel-to-reel tape recorders, cassette tapes, and headphones. I knew that Sony and Aiwa stereo systems were top notch. My eyes feasted on the merchandise, but I bought a cheap tabletop cassette tape player/recorder and three cassettes.

Later that day, back at LZ Bronco, we heard a rumor about a steam bath house to be constructed near the 11th Infantry. It would be open to everyone on base. Its purpose was to be a morale booster for the guys, since the town was still off limits and there was no indication it would be lifted any time soon. Construction was to begin within the next month, and should be done a few weeks later. Oh, boy, a steam bath house. What good was that going to be?

Chapter 15

Stray Bullets

Every now and then, our base took incoming rounds fired from the surrounding landscape. Usually, it was no more than two or three mortars, rockets, or artillery shells; harassment, mostly. The NVA and VC always seemed to pick the late night or early morning hours, between 2300 hours and 0300 hours. To add further excitement, Charlie probed our base perimeter for weakness at least once a week. Claymores[124], M-79 40mm grenade launchers, M-16s and flares from our guards would answer their call. On top of this, insults or greetings were occasionally traded back and forth by our guards with those outside the maze of razor wire coils.

One night, about 2330 hours, the perimeter was quiet. The guards weren't shooting at ghosts in the wire, as some thought happened much too often. No flares, just a quiet night. We had one lieutenant in our company who wanted to make a name for himself. That night he was the officer on duty[125]. He took it upon himself to conduct a surprise inspection of our sector of the perimeter, checking to make sure the sergeant of the guard was supervising properly, guards were rotated correctly, at least one was awake, that all were present in their respective bunker, and (above all) he told a few of his friends he wanted to catch somebody smoking a joint so he could make an example of that man with disciplinary action. He went alone.

The lieutenant went on his rounds at the perimeter. From one of our guard posts, he smelled the scent of marijuana.[126] He investigated the source. No one was actually smoking a joint when he entered the bunker, but the odor was stronger inside. He took their names and told them they would each be on report and to expect further questioning the following morning. He left the bunker. As he walked along Perimeter Road towards the next one, a shot rang out. The lieutenant called out, he was hit. A couple guards quickly responded and provided first aid, while another radioed

---

[124] A 3.5 pound rectangular (8" x 5" x 1.5") remotely detonated anti-personnel explosive device, capable of firing 700 1/8-inch steel balls almost 4,000 feet per second within a 50-meter effective range.

[125] A junior officer acting on behalf of the company commander during the evening. As part of his duties, he inspects the guards and supervises the sergeant of the guard.

[126] Very similar to burnt tree leaves in the fall, but uniquely sweeter.

it in. The wound entered his right shoulder from the back. He was first taken to our field hospital on base. One of our slicks was dispatched to medevac him to Chu Lai. He never returned to Duc Pho.[127]

It was the next morning when I heard the lieutenant was shot, not by the enemy, but by one of the guards. I didn't hear the shot. I was asleep in my hootch. Even if I did, I wouldn't have given it two thoughts. The story circulated just prior to the beginning of morning formation.

The Mafia had a name for it: *Omertà*, the code of silence. Same thing then, nobody knew or saw anything. A few just heard the shot. They saw and treated the wounded lieutenant. Was the shot fired from inside or outside the perimeter? There were about as many opinions as the number of people you asked. The potheads in the company were saying he got what he deserved. The shooter was a guard (nameless, of course) who was pissed because the lieutenant was snooping around trying to catch somebody smoking a joint, no matter what his official purpose for being there was. That man's identity was never revealed.

It was yet another stunning blow for morale. The team-spirit, enthusiasm, and loyalty in our unit, our esprit de corps, was sinking faster than a rock into water. Our purpose of fighting became more of survival than protecting the people of Vietnam from communists. Moral support from home was fading quickly because public opinion began to question the very reason why we were still there and people back home didn't hesitate to let us know.

I think the guys knew we had nothing to do with the outcome of the war. In our area, winning the hearts and minds of the Vietnamese was no longer a priority. The lives of American soldiers were nothing but fodder, as so many were beginning to think. But, the military and political mucky-mucks in Washington, D.C. and Saigon were too far removed (and too high up the chain of command) for these guys to vent their anger and frustration.

The mood of our warfare state of mind, I had noticed, changed. The lower morale in the company was palpable and infectious. There had

---

[127] Our flight surgeon was based at Chu Lai. Normally, he would be stationed with the unit to which he was assigned. But, due to the frequency of incoming rounds, and specifically because of the direct hit on his and our company commander's hooch during March, 1969, he declined to live on our base. We had a dispensary in our unit with one medic, SP/5 Barrett. Next to us was a field hospital, actually more of a triage unit.

been many setbacks since I'd first set foot in Vietnam. The countrywide 1968 Tet Offensive against military bases demoralized our will and swayed American opinion about our involvement in Vietnam. The Battle of Hué[128] resulted in thousands of civilians killed by the VC who had occupied the Imperial City, widespread destruction of most of the city, and door-to-door fighting by the Marines and ARVN soldiers.

The Vietnamese Pacification Program with no-fire zones (even if you were under attack) slowly put a new dynamic to fighting. Fighting became politicized and we were reacting rather than proacting.

President Nixon's campaign promise to end our involvement in Vietnam ("I have a plan. Elect me to find out.") sent the message, "We're out. Save your ass and get back home in one piece." Riots in the streets back home made a lot of us think hard about going home to a new war. Returning Vietnam veterans reported being socially avoided or treated like shit by the general population. The vast number of Americans killed[129] or wounded per week (upwards of 250-plus) in Vietnam made it psychologically dangerous to be here. Ineffectual battle strategies such as Hamburger Hill caused many to question the wisdom of commanding officers. And, atrocities such as My Lai and CYAs[130] were investigated and exposed for all to see.

A lot of the newer and younger guys were naïve, but at the same time very astute. Naïve in the sense of being idealistic and impervious to the dangers of war. After all, aren't all nineteen and twenty-year-olds ready to prove their manhood? They *are* invincible, aren't they? Strategy to them is how to kick ass, take names, and come home to brag about it to anyone who listens. It always makes for a good story over a few beers. (In my experience, many potheads seldom spoke about their combat experiences. They just spaced-out to the rhythm of psychedelic music and got lost in their thoughts.) The younger guys began to wonder what the point of all this was.

---

[128] It was a month-long battle during February, 1968. Following Tet, the VC occupied the city. Around 5,000 civilians died, half of the executed in cold blood. During the battle, it was reported three thousand ARVNs and U.S. Marines died. Approximately eight thousand enemy soldiers were killed. The battle ended at the beginning of March.

[129] Over 58,000+ military personnel died during the Vietnam war. Of those, 47,000+ were killed in action. I would recommend further reading from the "Statistical Information About Fatal Casualties of the Vietnam War", http:www.archives.gov/research/militarywar/casualty-statistics.html.

[130] Cover Your Ass (to avoid blame and/or responsibility when the outcome does not seem favorable).

Still, the newer guys were also very keen. They learned very quickly that more than one war was being fought. One was the extension of the Cold War engaging the communists via proxy wars of Russia and/or China versus the United States and allies. Another was the altruistic motivation to fight in order to save the life of others. Another was the goal to honorably conduct oneself in battle, regardless of temptations to do otherwise. And, lastly, the day-by-day effort to stay alive and go home.

The Black Panther Movement seemed to try very hard to make the argument that the war in Vietnam was a "white man's war" that the black man was being duped to participate in. Rumors about black fatalities being higher than the others had been widely disputed. A few young soldiers believed that propaganda, but not in my platoon (as far as I knew), nor in Chuck's. From my standpoint, keeping the morale up became priority number one, and it was a full-time job.

I began to understand why our gunships broke off a gun run at a thousand feet off the ground. The men began to feel trapped in the traditional baseball pickle. Instead of being tagged out, their life could be snuffed out. At one end, military command pushed for military objectives being met and discipline for the "good of the order." Command expected each man to do his best, to push past physical discomfort and perceived low morale in order to do what was expected of them; to follow orders without question.

At the other end of the pickle was the realization that the enemy had become more powerful. Slowly at first, the methodology of fighting against the small unit tactics of the paramilitary Viet Cong had morphed into a disciplined, organized, and well-equipped fighting force, akin to their North Vietnamese Army counterparts. The battles of Khe Sanh, Huế, Hamburger Hill, and many others were always reminders that our sense of military superiority were subject to circumstances beyond our control. From our enlisted men's point of view, there was absolutely no way of knowing if following the orders of some hot-dog, still wet-behind-the-ears, young officer was going to get them killed that day or the next.

The idea of helping the Vietnamese people fight against the communist forces from within and the north, was fading. The message of war-protesters back in the states had been carried to our unit by some of the new arrivals, letters from home, and being with loved ones while on R &

R in Hawaii. They wanted the war to end, quickly. The discontent and challenge to authority had been field-tested and found to be successful against the *establishment* and *The Man*, meaning us.

Many of the men felt trapped in a situation they could not control. The burden was great; the release was negligible. *I could die tomorrow in this stupid, fucking war and nobody would give two shits about it. For what? For helping the rag-tag ARNVs fight this war?* The ARVNs did not enjoy a popular reputation among the Americans. In battle, they didn't seem to have the will to fight. The frustration the men—not all but a growing number—felt was overwhelming. Day by day, they tried in vain to rationalize their own mortality. Could they trust their leaders? The politicians? They knew, or heard, that we had good men in this company who died. For what? Men, adolescents just yesterday, coping with the question every day: *Is dying here worth it?*

Escape took many forms. A five-day vacation once during the year for rest and relaxation at some exotic location was one way. For some, alcohol drowned out the misery, loneliness, and self-pity. For others, smoking a joint to relieve the tension and anxiety worked better. At the far end of the spectrum, a very small minority chose heroin as their escape vehicle. One of my men at the ammo dump may have taken this last option. How to prove it, get him help or disciplined, was well beyond my level of expertise or understanding.

The construction of the steam bath house, which quickly became known as the "Steam & Cream," was completed about the end of September. About six or seven young Vietnamese women worked there. They weren't too bad looking, either. Each room had a steam box and massage table. The box was large enough for a man to sit inside, with a steam-trapping towel around his neck, allowing the steam to permeate his pores to achieve that deep-down cleansing power—getting rid of the dirt and grim that quick, often times cold, showers could never remove. Then, onto the table for a half-hour massage. From what I was told, the world's oldest profession was not the intended purpose for this business. Using this facility did help morale to some degree, but it didn't really help any of the guys I knew to let off steam (pun intended).

Chuck's and my promotion orders finally came through. As of October 17, we were officially staff sergeants. I wasn't too inclined to celebrate, but Chuck wanted to go to the EM Club and buy the guys from his platoon a beer. That evening we went there together. Most, if not all of the guys, were Spec Four and below. I didn't feel comfortable. I didn't know most of them. But, Chuck did his thing. Everyone had a beer on Chuck. One or two congratulated him on his promotion. A few said thanks for the beer. Most said nothing. And, then we left. All in all, I felt we were like two intruders, being in a place we didn't belong.

One hundred Americans died in Vietnam from October 17-22, 1969[131]. In the 174th, the mourning of the dead seemed to be a private affair. Since I had been there, we lost five crewmen from the slick platoons during August, and we would lose another four crewmen of a slick in November. We did not have a memorial service for any of them. Maybe the pilots memorialized their former companions in the 'O' Club, and maybe the enlisted men did the same in their club. But no chaplains ever showed up, from what I knew. What was with that place, anyway?

We were isolated at LZ Bronco. Our flight surgeon refused to remain stationed there since the company commander and a few other officers were killed, before I arrived. Donut Dollies rarely visited our company area, maybe one time for no more than two hours. The Red Cross didn't visit. Most USO entertainers wouldn't visit us, either. These refusals became well known and grudgingly accepted. But, one group was eventually booked to perform for us. An entertainment troupe from the Philippines was coming to LZ Bronco. Just hearing this news was enough to significantly boost morale. A stage was constructed and a clearing made for the event. There was only a short time to prepare. The anticipation was electrifying.

Guys from all over the base showed up. Infantry, artillery, signal, medical, aviation, transportation, and others were all represented. Nonessential missions were put on hold. One of our fire teams remained on stand-by, just in case. When the troupe arrived, there were about eight to ten entertainers. They had a small band (drums, guitars), singers, and stage dancers. The girls looked hot. They played to the crowd of young, girl-

---

[131] www.vietnamwarcasualty.org/index.php?page=directory&dd=1969.

starved, and horny men. This troupe knew what they were doing. We had fun. We sang along with them. Their girls flirted with the men. They sang many popular and contemporary pop tunes. The girls danced, and the crowd went wild. One of the many songs, our favorite, was "We've Gotta Get Out of This Place," by The Animals. Every man sung along with them. We gotta get outta this place, even if it *is* the last thing we do. Walking or body bag? Some of us didn't care one way or the other anymore.

More than two hundred men sang so loud I'm sure Ho Chi Minh must have heard us in Hanoi. We didn't want the entertainment to end, but an hour and a half later it was over. They were done. We really appreciated the gesture.

About the time when that live entertainment was a fond, but not too distant, memory, the monsoon season began. It rained every day, sometimes a steady downpour, sometimes not. The sun remained hidden from us for days, weeks.

We spent more time inside our hootches than out in the rain. Except for an absolute emergency, flights were limited, as not all pilots had been certified as Instrument Flight Rated (IFR) and able to go from point A to B using only cockpit instruments. We still worked on our ships, either in its revetment or taking it into the maintenance hangar one at a time to complete required inspections and maintenance where it was a little drier. Our daily, quarterly and periodic inspections had to be kept on schedule, rain or not.

Ponchos were used for many reasons. One important use was to cover the mini-guns on the gunships when it was parked in the revetment to keep out rain, blowing sand, dirt, and mud. As rain gear, it pretty much kept the rain off, except for the knees down. That area got soaked, day after day. Most of our ground cover was sand and it got into anything possible. Wet sand is worse. It sticks. Wet sand got everywhere. Boots got soaked. Socks got soaked. Pant legs from the knee down got soaked. Skin on the feet shriveled. During the monsoons, quite a few guys stayed inside their hootch as much as possible rather than wearing a poncho to walk over to the mess hall for chow. They'd stock up on candy, C-Rats, or food bought from the PX in Chu Lai[132] or mailed from home, just to get by.

---

[132] The was no PX at LZ Bronco, no place to purchase any item for personal use. Chu Lai was the

That revealed a lot about us, I guess. Getting wet and sandy during the monsoons was miserable. It got cold (down to 45 degrees Fahrenheit), rainy, and depressingly dark gray from low rain-filled clouds. Staying dry kept us warm. The only place to do that was inside. To this day, I hate getting wet and cold. No matter how miserable it got, I was grateful for what I had, and who I wasn't. The infantry would never see me on their morning report.

No one talked about the guys in the field. We knew we had it good compared to the infantry, artillery, and maybe armor. The infantry had to be the worst career-field job to do in-country. When they're working, they had no hootch to protect them from the elements, only a poncho, if that. Theirs was a difficult job and they have all my respect. But, the choice was theirs from the beginning.

That's why I enlisted the first time. I chose not to work in elephant grass, swampy bogs, stinking rice paddies, being hungry waiting for the re-supply ship to arrive, being eaten alive by bugs, threatened by snakes and carnivorous animals, hunted day and night by an enemy who would rather see you dead; or, putting up with a squad of draftees who carried on with their anti-war and anti-establishment mantra and gave most NCOs trouble, every step of the way.

I want to be clear: I do not want to paint all draftees, and some who enlisted, as troublemakers. A vast majority were good, honest, patriotic men who were simply pursuing other goals in life when they went into military service. But you know what they say about there being a rotten apple in the barrel. It just takes one to spoil the rest.

A few select young men, mostly draftees, had gotten quite vocal in expressing their anger about being in Vietnam. They might have been influenced by the growing anti-war sentiment back in the States. Maybe, one or two of these guys were part of that movement; who knows? From my perspective, the few malcontents were always Privates or Spec Fours, usually with two years or less in the Army.

Aviation occupations were seldom made available to draftees. But, for a while, they got in when crew chiefs and mechanics were running short. Basic training and advanced individual training would use up at

---

closest.

least six months of their two-year stint on active duty. And, as often happened, if a draftee went to Vietnam after training and DEROSed within three or four months of his ETS, he could be discharged upon his return to the States instead of being assigned on a PCS for the last two or three months. The rationale was if the few remaining months would include his customary thirty-day leave and travel delay in getting to his next PCS, it would make no sense for the man to sign into his unit. Hardly a good return on the investment of sending that man to school for avionics, helicopter maintenance, sheet metal, or jet-engine repair.

The draftees we did have in our unit were mostly door-gunners, cooks, motor-pool mechanics, clerks, and drivers. They integrated into our company quite well. Most of them got over their anger early on at having been plucked from civilian life and forced into a military lifestyle. But, some didn't. They seem to have kept vestiges of their former civilian life close and tried to continue behaving as if they were still back home: less-than-favorable attitude, drugs, alcohol, and racial animosity. The degree of discontent varied from one person to another.

Of course, I knew we'd always have people who griped about this or that. That was human nature, especially in military service. I'm certain that years before, my friends and I griped about things. But, mostly we were having fun. Not these guys in 1969. Something had changed. Was it the drug culture, Black Power culture, the hippie sub-culture, or the psychedelic rock music that was becoming so popular? Maybe it was a little of each.

There were a few Black Panther wanna-bes in Duc Pho who, in my opinion, stubbornly pushed the envelope of courtesy, respectfulness, and protocol. They challenged commissioned and non-commissioned officers alike, Army regulations and lawful orders as much as possible. Some outright refused to do what they were told, daring confrontation.

I would guess that less than five percent of all black soldiers subscribed to the ideology of the Black Panthers. The few who did formed into a unique clique, excluding everyone but their own race. Their strength was in numbers. They demanded to do what they wanted, when they wanted, and where they wanted. The phenomena surprised the older lifers more than anyone else. They were not accustomed to anyone challenging their authority, and rightly so. Most would do just what was required to stay out of trouble, and barely at that. Often, they would let their hair grow longer than regulations permitted, and many of them stopped shaving. Do-rags[133] were a new sight, something most of us had never seen before. Some guys asked why could they get away with things like that, and we couldn't. A few white guys began to emulate the look and behavior of their black counter-parts. Challenging authority seemed to work.

And increasingly, more and more soldiers of every color *did* get away with things. As morale continued to plummet, our military chain of command began to crumble. I'm not an expert in military protocols, but I did know how to take orders, how to give lawful orders, what to do, when, and how to get it done right. The guys who were not on flight status and were not crew members usually stayed in the company area, therefore being under the watchful eyes of NCOs who tried their best to get the job done while protecting his own career. Except for the fact of knowing the enemy could launch a rocket and/or mortar barrage into our company area, for these younger guys it was an opportunity for *relaxed military discipline*. You know what they say: give them and inch and they'll take a mile. All too true. I don't know if the senior NCOs just got tired of trying to lead those who didn't want to be led. But, the few dissenters in the company were winning, and gaining in numbers.

Antagonists to authority became widespread. To offer an example of heroic figures to model after, it was no longer John Wayne. A new role model emerged: Paul Newman. His popularity took an uptick in the immensely successful 1967 movie, *Cool Hand Luke*. He played the character of Luke, a loner who would not comply with illogical rules in prison. A much-quoted line from the movie was when a prison captain, who taunted prisoner Luke as often as possible, said in a tenor southern drawl, "What we got he-ear... is a fail-ya... to commune-ee-kate." Luke became the poster-boy of authoritarian resentment.

Slowly at first, I noticed infractions of Army regulations being overlooked, mostly out of my chain-of-command. Maybe it was because I was no longer flying and in the company area more often than before. Fa-

---

[133] A field-expedient 'do-rag' was a woman's cut-off nylon stocking that was placed (as a skull-cap) over close-cropped curly hair in order to control the hairstyle. Personally, I think it became more of a symbol of cultural identity and social rebellion.

tigues weren't being pressed. Mustaches were gaining popularity, and grew longer than regulations permitted.[134] We began seeing mustache curls, Fu Man Chu styles, very bushy and long. Sideburns also got longer, little by little. Regulations required the length of the sideburn to be no longer than the imaginary line between the top of the ear where it's attached to your head and the corner of your eye. Before long, they got as long as the lowest part of the ear, sometimes lower. Being clean-shaven, of course, was required. Some pushed that envelope, too.

In this widespread anti-authority sentiment, I started to feel isolated. I had two people I could ask for help, Barnett and Chuck. Nobody else mattered much. Sergeant First Class Joseph P. Barnett, III, our Shark platoon sergeant, left our company quietly. I knew at the time that I would miss working with him. I liked him a lot. His affection for Cutty Sark Scotch whiskey was legendary in the company. He always drank in the privacy of his room, rarely in the NCO Club, and in the company of a select few friends. He never became overly intoxicated, as far as I knew. He drank like the gentleman he was, with class. I was fortunate to have him as a mentor, of sorts, and for being introduced to his drink of choice. I learned early I did not like double-malt Scotch. It took years for me to first taste, and appreciate, the mellowness of single malt scotch. But now, every glass of Scotch reminds me of Barnett, malt level be damned.

---

[134] A mustache was permitted for Army soldiers during this era IF it was shown on the United States Armed Forces Military ID Card. I myself tried to carefully alter my photo ID by drawing a short horizontal line under my nose. Using a ball-point black pen onto the laminate covering, it wasn't very convincing. Many guys 'lost' their ID card, grew a mustache, and THEN got a new ID. That worked much better. The other acceptable way was to get promoted. That warranted a new ID Card being prepared. The 'official' mustache was not to extend beyond the corners of the upper lip, nor so long that the hairs touched the top of the upper lip.

Chapter 16

Warm and Fuzzy

It got cold in Vietnam. Not cold like in Chicago, but cold like in Miami. During the monsoons, the temperature sometimes dipped pretty low making the rainy weather very miserable. Being acclimated to hot and humid hundred-and-five-plus degree weather during most of the year reduced the ability to adjust to temperatures lower than fifty degrees. I kept no alcohol in my room, so I relied on clean clothes, field jacket, and staying dry as much as possible. I cherished the work done by our hootch maids. No sick days, no weekends, most always showing up for work cheerful and on time.

One morning, our two hootch-maids were inside my room, polishing boots as usual. I didn't mind because I understood they wanted to keep as warm as possible during the monsoon season. Kiém Liên used my room quite often, anyway. The semi-enclosed patio in front of our hootch had no doors, just openings. The windows in each room were also open; no glass, screen, or shutters. There was nothing to keep the elements out.

As Mama-san and I spoke casually, Kiém Liên said something to me. I didn't understand her words, but they sounded sweet and innocent. She must have seen a look of confusion on my face. Shyly, she said it again.

"What'd she say?" I asked Mama-san in a tone of benign inquisitiveness.

She repeated Kiém Liên's words and said, "She loves you very much." I was not ready for that, that's for sure.

Patiently, word by word she helped me repeat those rarely heard Vietnamese words, "Anh Yêu Em Nhiều Lắm" (pronounced quickly and phonetically as On-You-Uhm-You-Lum)[135]. I couldn't believe my ears. Was this simply the result of me treating her with respect? I wasn't sure.

---

[135] The phrase, translated as *I love you very much*, are the words spoken by a girl to her boyfriend. A variation of the words would be used if a boy was saying this to his girlfriend. Such is the Vietnamese language. With practice, it rolls smoothly.

Maybe it was my blonde hair, or my new "almost-mustache." Maybe she was desperate to get out of Vietnam.

Of course, I was immensely flattered. Yet I was confused about my own feelings toward her. She was, after all, a teenager. I could tell her words came directly from her heart, though, and I could not walk away from this. I understood the impact of saying those words out loud, the emotional buildup that was necessary to reveal her emotions toward me, and the potential for heartbreak if she was rebuffed. I did not want to break her heart.

At the same time, it was extremely humbling. Without question, I knew I was returning to the US, and preferred to go back vertically. I was pretty sure this type of situation was not unique, but it was not common. In many ways, I held her future in my hands. It was not impossible, though discouraged, to take this relationship to the next level and eventually bring her back to the States. I didn't care what anybody would think, but I did care about Kiém Liên.

Mama-san was there to translate for me, if I wanted to tell Kiém Liên anything. I could seal the deal right then, so to speak, by telling her I loved her, too. This was the moment. Whatever happened next could alter our lives forever, especially for her. I really didn't know her circumstances, but it wasn't too difficult to imagine. *Just say the words*, I kept thinking for those few seconds. *Do it.* Was it pity I felt in the depth of my soul, or love?

I couldn't say the words. I did not feel warm and fuzzy being with her. I foresaw innumerable challenges, hurtles, and hardship. Happiness was not in the equation. My gut was telling me she was not the one. So very close, and yet so far.

A few GIs routinely treated the Vietnamese with contempt. Our exposure to the local workers in our company area were with the papa-sans who appeared older than sixty but were more likely between forty and fifty, the mama-sans who appeared to be fifty years or older but probably forty, and the few younger women in their mid-to-late teens up to mid-twenties. It was extremely rare, if at all, to have a man between eighteen and thirty years of age working on base. In fact, I rarely saw one unless he was wearing a military uniform of some type.

American troops had no qualms about calling the Vietnamese *dinks*, *slopes*, and *gooks*—though mostly in the field. A few saw no problem addressing them in these generally derogatory terms to their face. I'd also witnessed a very slight minority of GIs who occasionally pushed, kicked, and otherwise belittled the Vietnamese. The vast majority of Americans had little to no interaction with the Vietnamese at all. But if they did, it was usually courteous. I'd like to count myself among the vast majority, though I sometimes used those same derogatory terms when talking with other GIs, most often during combat assaults. It was easier to kill a man when calling him a nasty name.

Keeping busy was the key to making it through one day to the next. My daily routine was becoming predictable and I didn't like that. It was my mission to make sure my men had what they needed, when they needed it, and to support our mission as gunship crews. Monitor aircraft hours, schedule maintenance and supervise the people needed to get that done: my mission. I didn't think much about home or my family, and I had nobody special in my life. I realized my own happiness was an elusive goal. I focused on the here and now.

Prior to his leaving, I convinced Barnett that we needed a fence and bunker at the ammo dump. The ammo dump was located near the northern end of the runway, not a hundred yards from the farthest perimeter wire. It was unbelievable to me that they were so exposed to incoming rounds. A bunker made perfect sense to me, and them.

In all the years the company had been there, the ammo dump remained opened and accessible to anyone, including Charlie, if he managed to make his way in undetected. The new chain-link fencing around the dump helped correct that, but, it needed more. The only protection for the two guys who worked there, as well as any flight crews who were rearming, was a converted aluminum field office removed from an old tech supply truck and used as a make-shift office shed. With a thin layer of aluminum for the walls and roof, it offered no protection from shrapnel or bullets. It provided concealment, not protection.

The first improvement came with the chain link fence. I don't know where Barnett got it from, but a deuce-and-a-half delivered new rolls of the metal fencing one day. We put a detail together and got the posts cemented in and lined up perfectly. Next came stretching the fence and securing it to the posts. With left over material, we got the gate constructed and hung. All that was left to do was the bunker.

With a load of empty sandbags and shovels, off we went. At one point, I helped filling the sandbags. At the bottom of the sandy hole I dug, and no more than eighteen inches down, was a coin. I picked it up and examined it. It was a French Indochina coin. To me, it was buried treasure. I showed it to the guys, but their span of interest was short lived. I kept the coin, hoping it would be worth a fortune. In reality, it wasn't worth more than a dime, as I learned later. But, it was my souvenir from that place and time. I still have it to this day.

Finding that coin was as important to me as finding a real stone arrowhead in the dirt when I was a kid in Illinois. It was a treasure, an historical artifact. Somehow, it told a story of years past, maybe before I was born. How did it end up in that spot? How long ago?

When I showed the coin to Kiém Liên later, I noticed she was getting a little pudgy around the middle. She always wore black silk pants and a black silk-buttoned top, which we usually described as pajamas. It wasn't easy to notice her mid-section getting larger unless she moved about in a certain way. Of course, this was very gradual and almost unnoticeable day to day. I thought she was pregnant, but said nothing. I could have been wrong.

My best friend there, Jim Kildall, DEROSed out, heading back to the states. I would miss that guy. We had many long talks. Jim had about twelve years in the Army and was expecting to PCS to Fort Carson, Colorado for a few years. There was no party for him. He didn't want the attention, being the quiet guy that he was. We saw him off with a few beers at the NCO Club to celebrate his going home in one piece.

Jim missed the big event. Bob Hope came to Chu Lai for a Christmas show. He had been entertaining American GIs in war zones for years, as far back as World War II. He was very funny and an excellent showman. His entourage sometimes included Martha Ray or Ann Margaret. It was a *must-see* event. The sign-up sheet to go had filled up quickly, a specific number from each platoon. I stayed behind.

Christmas arrived. No snow, of course. But, it was cloudy. We had no Christmas decorations to put up, not even individually in the guy's rooms or hootches. I didn't do anything to celebrate, either. It was just another day, another dollar. But, the first sergeant and company commander had cooked up a plan to treat the Vietnamese workers to a holiday meal in the mess hall. It was scheduled between our lunch and dinner. They arrived[136] in the company area like they never did before, all wearing very nice clothing, nothing too fancy though. All the women wore brightly colored clothes, white or yellow long silk dresses over black silk pants (Áo Dài) and wore clean and apparently seldom used wide conical straw sunhats (Nón Lá). Their Sunday best, maybe?

I received a hand delivered Christmas card from Kiém Liên, her cousin Kim, and Mama-san. I was very surprised for a few of reasons. First, except for the Roman Catholic Church in Huế, I didn't know Christianity had found its way locally. It seemed the three of them were Roman Catholics because of the religious Christmas cards they gave. Who would have guessed that? Second, who knew that Christmas cards were even available in the Vietnamese language? Where would they buy them? Certainly, not at a local Hallmark store. Were there such stores in Duc Pho? When the girls arrived to my hootch to deliver the cards, I hid my guilt that overshadowed the pleasure they shared. I had not even considered giving either one a gift or card.

A few minutes later, they left to join the others still milling about. Before they entered the mess hall, I ran in and quickly grabbed a few candy bars, toothpaste, cigarette packs, and gum that was freely available to us (we had no PX at LZ Bronco), and gave them to both of our hootchmaids, and Kim. As I was doing so, I noticed Chuck had done the same thing.

The day after Christmas, I turned twenty-two years old. The day passed just like any other. I received a birthday card from Dad, and a separate one from Mom. I didn't get one from Barb, though I didn't really expect one anymore. It was the first Christmas and birthday in five years that

---

[136] A deuce-and-a-half truck was used to transport the Vietnamese from our main gate to Duc Pho into our company area. They were usually dropped off near the front of my hootch every morning, and picked up there at the end of the day.

she did not send me a card. It had been months since we even wrote to each other. I had long forgotten Nancy by then, I'm sorry to say.

As the weeks passed, Kiém Liên's pregnancy had become unmistakably noticeable. At the NCO Club, I was getting ribbed, not knowing if Kim was having fun or not. She had made the assumption that I was the father of the baby. More than once she asked me if I was going to take Kiém Liên and the baby back to the States. I told her in no uncertain terms that I wasn't the father. It seemed that among a small group of Vietnamese working in our company area, Kiém Liên's crush on me was well known. I'm speculating, but it seemed to me that she did not admit to her community that she had been sexually attacked. It would likely have been devastating to her and her family's honor. Except for Kim, Mama-san, Kiém Liên and me, no one else seemed to be up in arms about her situation.

I wasn't the only one who treated Kiém Liên kindly, but I was the only one she cared for. Kim was becoming quite vocal about this. Not in a loud, boisterous manner of accusation, but as more of a statement of fact that she was very willing to accept. Slowly, I minimized my time at the NCO Club. It had gotten to the point when every time I walked in, Kim was asking about "your baby-san." Maybe this was Kiém Liên's ticket out of Duc Pho and starting a new life in the US. Kim could (or would) not be convinced otherwise. But, I had an ace up my sleeve. The proof of fatherhood would be obvious when the baby was born. The baby would be half-black.

A couple months to go until my DEROS date. Now that made me warm and fuzzy, for sure. My replacement as platoon sergeant had been selected from the maintenance platoon. There was no formality. One day he showed up and introduced himself as Rex Hurst. He was an SFC who always wanted to be a part of the Shark platoon. I found him to be a very nice fellow about thirty-five to forty years of age (an old man by most of our standards). As the days passed, he was there every day. I was surprised by the fact that he came into our platoon to observe, not to take over or countermand anything I did. He didn't challenge anything I did as platoon sergeant. He became a new mentor to me and was simply there, waiting day after day, for his turn to be the platoon sergeant. If I had a question about this or that, I felt very comfortable in asking for his opinion. We soon formed a bond.

Returning from the maintenance area one late afternoon, I saw a gunship parked in front of operations. The blades were at idle RPM. I ran over to speak with the crew chief to learn what they needed. He was nowhere to be found. The gunner was gone. I came around to speak with the peter-pilot, quickly noting the A/C was keying his mic and talking while referencing the tactical map on his lap. It was obvious he was busy. The peter-pilot swung his mic-boom over and told me, in a loud voice to overcome the engine noise and down-drafted wind from the blades, they had just dropped off the crew chief at the med-detachment. He had gotten shot in the stomach. He had his flak-jacket on, but it hadn't been zipped closed. They needed somebody to replace the crew chief, asap. On the way in, they radioed ops to inform them they were dropping off one and needed to pick up another crew chief. They sent the gunner into the company area to look for me.

The pilot had just finished telling me when two crew chiefs arrived at the ship to help out as needed. Rex, who'd been nearby, also approached the ship. He asked me what the pilot said. I yelled the answer in his ear as I was getting the attention of one of the two crew chiefs to climb aboard and take Martinez's place.

Immediately, Rex jumped on board. The speed with which he responded surprised me. He quickly squeezed into the crew chief's flight helmet and flak-jacket. Rex was about six feet tall and weighed probably 250 pounds. The crew chief he replaced was much shorter and lighter. When the gunner returned and saw Rex as the new crew chief, he climbed aboard and donned his gear. They hovered to the north end of the flight line, re-joined the second gunship waiting there, rearmed at the ammo dump, and both left to return to the AO southwest of us. Hindsight is always 20/20. I should have jumped in myself.

It was quiet, again. I walked quickly to the med-detachment to check on his condition. It was just around the corner of our company area, so it didn't take me long to get there. As I approached, Barrett, our medic, was coming out. He told me my man was being prepared for surgery. The wound, in his opinion, might be serious enough to send him home, but he'd survive.

When the ships returned later that overcast day, the guys wanted to know how he was doing. I briefed them. Rex later told me when they returned to the AO, the shooting was over. They stayed in the AO as long as needed before being released by the ground commander. He also told me how exciting it was for him. That was the first time he had ever flown on a mission, let alone in a gunship. He proudly proclaimed it took him only minutes to acquaint himself with the M-60 and belt of ammo, smoke grenades and such, essentially getting ready for battle within minutes of getting airborne. His adrenaline was maxed out. Yeah, he'd do it again, just let him know, anytime. I believe his experience that day was one he would remember for a long time.

We inventoried his gear after I confirmed he would not be returning. It wasn't much, just enough to fill his duffel bag. We tagged the bag and delivered it to the supply room. From there it would be shipped to his home of record back in the States.

Days passed quickly into weeks. It was difficult to remember what day of the week it was, not that it really mattered to anyone not going home or leaving for R & R. It was not as if we had weekends or holidays off. Each day began much like the one before, not knowing what kind of excitement (if any) awaited us.

Some of the guys were still smoking joints, but we'd never been able to catch them during the sweeps. Everyone was quite aware that it took very little evidence to convict someone for a violation, so the guys were *very* careful. To my knowledge, other than the secret hide-a-way CONEX bunker beneath the second platoon's hootch, smoking a joint was never done inside a building or aircraft. During the day, if anyone smoked it, they would go someplace where they could not be seen. It might be near a parked helicopter far away from the company area, down the far end of the flight line, or just about anywhere that was secluded and did not raise suspicion. The ammo dump, for example, would be one such place. I had long stopped participating in the nightly searches by the NCOs. I was in no mood to lift the wrong sandbag to find a live grenade attached. And, I had no interest in getting shot by "accident."

As my time in-country continued, I slowly began to realize we were losing this war. It was becoming more obvious. The will of the guys suffered. We followed the routine that had been in place for years, passed from one guy to the other. New guys learning as the old guys were leaving. We did our jobs because we had to, but there were almost no heroics involved. So very different from my first tour. One day the awards officer, a first lieutenant, addressed the company at our morning formation.

"Men, I'm the one who writes the citations for awards, as many of you know. What you may not know is I've had nothing to write for quite some time. I don't fly with many of you, but I'm certain that your missions out there require some form of bravery above and beyond the call of duty every once in a while. Anyone is free to submit a recommendation for an award for your fellow crewmen. And I mean anyone. Write something down that you believe, or even think, deserves a medal and turn it into me. I'll review it and polish it up, if necessary. Okay? Okay. First sergeant, the men are yours. Thank you."

With that, he walked back to the operations bunker.

"Company," Top hollered, and the platoon sergeants relayed his call to attention back to their men. "Fall out."

In Vietnam, and maybe other places, too, we had a saying about our military/political leadership. It was, "the unwilling led by the unqualified to do the unnecessary." Little did I know then that this was a take-off of a quote by Konstantin Jireček[137] who had said many generations before, "We, the unwilling, led by the unknowing, are doing the impossible for the ungrateful. We have done so much, for so long, with so little, we are now qualified to do anything with nothing." I've since learned this quote was also the motto of the French Foreign Legion who attribute it to an unknown French soldier. At the time, though, I didn't know, nor did I care, who originated the saying. Everything we lived with at the outpost we knew as LZ Bronco—the geographic isolation, terror of incoming, fear of invasion, anger at limitations to fight back, boredom, frustration, homesickness, and countless atrocities—wore on us every day. Except for our own rooms as a physical safe haven, we had no safe place mentally. We had to make our own. We had lost something that would never return.

The smell of Jasmine incense always permeated the hootches in the company area, almost always at night. That sweet, perfumed and unobtrusive odor inside darkened rooms lit only by the dimming of the interior

---

[137] A Bulgarian (1854-1918) author of history.

light by a cloth (usually red) lampshade helped create a pleasant atmosphere, considering the circumstances. Add music by Jimi Hendricks, Janice Joplin, The Who, The Beatles, Jefferson Airplane, or Credence Clearwater Revival and you could create a surreal atmosphere where some of the guys could escape this hellhole and the mental anguish that went along with it, if only for an hour or two. It was rare for anyone to admit loneliness and home sickness. Did that mean they weren't?

If church services existed at LZ Bronco, nobody knew. It wasn't as if we weren't religious. Judaism and Christianity were primarily the default religions in our company. For many, it was the guide to our sense of morality. For others, not so much. Without a synagogue or church, praying and meditation was left to the individual. If he had a religious upbringing, it was easy; if not, many sought artificial means. Music was one way. Norman Greenbaum sang about a friend named Jesus, who, when you died, would set you up with a "spirit in the sky." Life was fragile. These young men tasted death and mayhem, almost daily. Yet, apparently, we had no heroes.

There were all kinds of ways to kill the enemy: napalm and bombs dropped by F-4 Phantom Jets, artillery barrages from Red Legs on land and battleships at sea, hundreds of bombs dropped en masse from 30,000 feet high by flights of B-52 Stratofortress planes, claymore mines, a seemingly never-ending supply of 7.62mm bullets and 2.75 inch HE (high explosive) rockets, and other weapons of war.

Somebody in the supply system placed the requisition for some nasty ordnance. At first, we had a few pallets of these "special" rockets to use at our ammo dump. Rockets with flechettes were used against the NVA, for the most part, due to the sheer number of enemy combatants. This devastating anti-personnel weapon was embedded with a 2.75-inch rocket proximity warhead. At a certain distance off the ground it would detonate, letting loose approximately a hundred three-inch-steel needles to strike the intended target at a high velocity. It could literally shred the body apart if the victim was close enough to the point of detonation. We used them occasionally when the circumstances dictated.

How odd to be thinking of ways to kill and maim the enemy. Odd in the sense that it is not the *civilized* way of thinking. But, it's probably no different than the guy who invented the idea of pouring boiling oil over castle walls onto the wall-climbing invaders, or the guys who invented napalm or the atom bomb. Where is that line where the mathematical, chemical and engineering designs are separated by the cold, uncaring finger that squeezes the trigger?

It's one thing to hear about it or read about it, but totally different when it's you who pulled the trigger. It has a lasting effect on your mind to know your single act let loose a lethal object that was designed to change the course of events forever. Like the genie removed from the lamp, the instrument of death travels the path you selected, and once freed, is impossible to put back. It's too late. That 'you' is me, or it could be you; or, somebody in between. Killing the enemy is sometimes necessary but never easy, though we liked to think it became so. From personal experience, I know that once you've crossed *that* line, you can never go back. Ever.

I understand why many had to find peace, to escape from their reality. They were just trying to survive, one way or another.

In war, the real enemy lies within. It's the devil inside. It's how we behaved, how we reacted and responded to various stimuli, and how we treated others. It was our self-perceived arrogance, sense of moral and materiel superiority, and organizational and personal demeanor that would win or lose the war. As Pogo once said in the cartoon strip[138], "Yep, son, **we have met the enemy and he is us**." We did not win the hearts and minds of the people we tried to protect, and risked our life for, by treating them like shit, scum and inferior people.

Far from us being the knights in shining armor, riding in to save the day, many Vietnamese saw us as just another generation of foreigners invading their country. To some, we were sugar-daddies to be exploited and used for all it was worth. Five or ten dollars a month per man to pay for one hootch maid was an acceptable wage. Our lowest private in the military earned a monthly salary that would take a Vietnamese laborer a year to earn. To others, we were criminals, showing no respect or courtesy. For no reason that made sense to them, we destroyed families, homes,

---

[138] The author was Walt Kelly (1913-1973), a cartoonist, and the award-winning strip was distributed by the Post-Hall Syndicate.

villages, and storages of food and ancestral heirlooms. They would be glad to see us dead or gone.

We could not evaluate the whole of Vietnam by the actions of a few, nor would we expect them to evaluate us by the actions of a few. But, I think many of them did. It was all they knew. Many, unable to read or write, relied on personal encounters to make decisions. Many times, we didn't do so well in that department.

When I was growing up, I often heard that there's more than one way to skin a cat. It did not mean to actually go out, find a *putty-tat*[139] and remove the skin by different techniques. Well, maybe hundreds of years before my time it did. But, to us, it meant there was always more than one way to reach your goal. If one method didn't work, try another. Eventually, one would work. Was it too late to fix the problem of winning their hearts and minds?

Trying to use my time as effectively as possible, I considered my primary job as a motivator. Get the job done, correctly. I could not allow the morale in my platoon to sink. I tried to maintain the standard of high expectations in all the work being done. Lives depended on it. That part was easy because it's what I'd been doing since I arrived. Aircraft maintenance allowed no mistakes. One small error could eventually cause the ship to crash, killing all aboard. The tech inspector drilled that into us every chance he had, just in case we forgot. Details were so important that even a mis-twisted safety wire would not pass inspection.

As I was mentally preparing myself for the final stretch of my tour, I got some unexpected news. Usually, each of us had one R & R per twelve-month tour of duty. Mine had already been used some months back when I went to Sydney. Out of the clear blue, for reasons unknown to me, I was offered a second R & R. A gift from Heaven. Anxious to "get out of Dodge," I gladly accepted. This time I chose to go to Bangkok, Thailand Maybe this was a chance for Rex to get better acquainted with the men of the Shark platoon, and they with him. Though it was never actually confirmed as the reason, it was easy to understand. I was getting short and my DEROS date was fast approaching. Rex would be the next platoon sergeant, and soon.

---

[139] Compliments to Merrie Melodies, 1948, Sylvester the Cat and Tweetie Bird.

My first order of business in Bangkok was getting a room, and then... well, let's just say my time and money would be well spent. I had to get a "date" for the week.

After checking into the Crowne Hotel, I joined two other American GIs in sharing a taxi, and we had one thing on our mind. The drive through the business districts of Bangkok took about twenty minutes. I was surprised at the number of cars, bicycles, and pedestrians going from one place to another. My preconceived image of this city was shattered by reality. It was civilized. The route we took was passed tall buildings, hotels and restaurants, paved sidewalks and streets that were clean and well maintained. I checked the people as we drove past. I could have been in Chicago.

Our taxi driver had reached the destination he recommended. The two-story house, located in the midst of a semi-business neighborhood, had a circular driveway in front. Paying the fare and thanking our driver, we stepped out and approached the front door. There, we were greeted by a middle-aged woman. Our hostess (maybe she was the Madam) was large, but not fat. She escorted us inside and led us through a foyer to a clean and well-lit room. Inside to the right was a three-level semi-circle stage, the type you might expect to be used by a choir. Young women, on pillows or cushions, sat on each level. There must have been no less than forty of them, each well dressed, some in local fashions and others in Western attire. But, what struck me most about them was not their sheer number but the fact that they each wore a numbered placard. Some were pinned to the blouse. Others were hanging from the neck by string or chain. The room was closed off from the hallway, and a large glass-wall separated them from us.

Our hostess stood with us, smiling and obviously very proud of her girls. She invited us each to take our time in selecting our date-for-the-week by the number that girl wore. I stood there in amazement. The girls saw us, we saw them. Panning the room, I spent a split second on each face and realized I was focusing more on their eyes. All brown, all beautiful. The range of ages I'd guess were nineteen to thirty. Some were smiling demurely, a few others were talking to each other, and the rest had no expression that could be detected. Translation: some were interested, others were not. I selected the number on the best-looking girl of the group who appeared to be my age and returned my gaze with a smile.

One morning as I was outside walking around the neighborhood, I returned to the hotel. Seated at an umbrellaed table in a small patio were two guys—one black, one white—drinking coffee. They were wearing civilian clothes, and when they greeted me it sounded as if they were Americans. The white guy tried to start up a conversation. He asked if I was on R & R, if I came to Bangkok from Vietnam, was I in the military, what branch, and finally what unit was I assigned to. To be friendly, I answered most of his questions, but his last one made me stop. I didn't know those guys from a hole in the ground. Why was he pumping me for information? It was more than just casual chit-chat. As I became suspicious of his motive, I clammed up and excused myself. I didn't see them again.

A short time later, it came to me. I had just been talked to by two spies, either ours or theirs. Either way they tried to get as much information from me as possible. If they were American agents, it would reveal a breach in security. If foreign, a bonanza of intel. As I went over the encounter, it wasn't a conversation. He seemed a little too inquisitive. It was more of an interview, a subtle interrogation, a probing for military information. Who knows how far it would have gone?

Relaxed, refreshed, and rejuvenated in every way imaginable, my time in Thailand was over quickly. Upon my return to the company area in Duc Pho, nothing had changed much except that Kiém Liên was no longer working, apparently due to her late stage of pregnancy. She must have been in her eighth month by then. I missed her. Mama-san did the work of two and still kept her cheery disposition. Kim told me Kiém Liên was doing well. Kim and Mama-san were excited about the baby being born soon, but not Kiém Liên. Being Catholic, though, she would be a good and caring mother. She knew the cultural problems she was about to experience when the baby was born. Her secret would be exposed. She and her multi-racial baby would likely be shunned by her community. The Vietnamese, I would later learn, were very persnickety about things like that.[140]

---

[140] Subsequent to 1975 and the war's end, stories abounded about the huge number of Amer-Asian children left

I was relaxed, but careful at the same time. My DEROS date was getting very close. There was a saying among us in country: Be very careful during the first thirty days and last thirty days. You were considered a "cherry" during the first thirty, someone who doesn't know his ass from a hole in the ground. Most guys didn't know what to expect, what to do, and how not to get killed. Training to get here is unlike the real thing when you realize other people are trying very hard to kill you. Then, with that first month under your belt and experience takes hold, you'd learn more as each day passed.

During the last month, you'd be so anxious to get home that thoughts about the future replaced thoughts about surviving. Many guys got careless. They'd lose concentration and begin to daydream about home. They made it so far. What could go wrong? Nothing could stop them from going home at DEROS. Famous last words.

Ninety-nine days or less made the guy a double-digit midget. Other short-timer sayings included, "I'm so short I can stand on a nickel and piss on a dime," or, "I'm so short you'd have to dig a hole to kick me in the ass." My favorites were, "I'm so short I have to jump up to look down," and "I'm so short I have to look up to see down." The countdown was a morale booster in and of itself.

Getting home seemed real, finally, but I had to be careful. If I got careless, I could have gone home in a body bag. It wasn't just Charlie I had to worry about, but guys like the one who shot the lieutenant as well.

My last month there was a lot of fighting activity north of us. Beginning April 1, 1970, Operation Texas Star at the A Shau Valley and the mountains eastward became the scene of a battle between the NVA and the 101st Airborne Division. Problems were also stirring in Cambodia, where a military coup had taken place. Many NVA were headed there in response. These battles did not affect us in Duc Pho too much. We had our own AO to worry about. But news and rumors did make their way to us. Many of the guys were not thinking about winning battles anymore. Their goals narrowed to staying alive and leaving on schedule. Winning the war no longer seemed to be the primary objective. Going home safely, in one piece, was all that mattered.

---

behind by their American fathers and forced into orphanages.

Chapter 17

It Don't Mean Nuthin' Anymore.

By 1970, President Nixon was under a lot of public and political pressure to reduce the number of American troops in Vietnam. At a time when political promises meant something, he publicly promised during April that another 150,000 soldiers would be withdrawn throughout the rest of the year. I became part of that promise and left the 174th about three weeks before my DEROS date.

The day I left, one of the company lieutenants accompanied me on the way to the other side of the tarmac where I would wait for my flight to Da Nang. It was the same shack we used when the cook and I went to Sydney. The lieutenant and I had a pleasant conversation about my "investigation" of drug usage among the men and source of drugs coming into the unit.

What had I learned? I tried to be careful for the past few months, but how did *this* lieutenant know of my inquiries? It was very odd that he would ask. You couldn't trust anybody those days. Was he one of the good guys, or not? Was I going to have an accident on the way out? Who knew? It was my last day at Duc Pho, be careful. *What did I know?* Really? Had I learned the supply chain of drugs coming into the company? Did I know the players? Yes, a few. I hadn't developed much information to answer all of his questions. It was too early. I would have needed more time to find answers—and no, I would not extend my tour by six months to find out. He promised our conversation would be kept confidential, and I'd be obliged to do the same.

When I first arrived to the 174th, a few guys thought I was a CID agent, assigned to investigate their *dirty laundry*. I didn't blame them. I was immediately assigned as a crew chief in the Sharks, ahead of many others-in-waiting. On top of that, getting promoted to staff sergeant five months later? At twenty-one years of age? The frosting on a cake was that unheard of second R & R. Who would not add one and one and get two?

At twenty-two years of age, I left the 174th Assault Helicopter Company. My PCS orders provided a thirty-day delay in travel before reporting to Fort Riley, Kansas. Who did I know there? Absolutely no one.

I finally arrived at Da Nang, duffle bag in hand, wearing my best set of clean and pressed jungle fatigues, ready to go home. My expectations of leaving country early disappeared very quickly as soon as I saw how many men, hundreds, were also part of this troop reduction plan.

Sandy Combs—the one with the CIB who I met when I first arrived about a year before—was there, too. He also had been promoted to staff sergeant. As we talked about our last eleven months, the topic switched to us both leaving at around the same time and other mundane topics. We agreed that Nixon's troop reduction was not about getting us out of the country. It was more about getting us out of the fight. There, in Da Nang, we were non-combatants, not assigned to a unit. We had no weapons. We had no post or assigned area in case we got hit. In fact, I didn't even know where the bunkers were—though, remembering Bien Hoa back in '68, I searched for them each day. Da Nang was safe, almost like a stateside military base: busses, frame buildings, all very spread out. There were too many of us waiting to leave, and not enough planes per day to take us home. So, we waited.

Each morning, we had a casual formation at 0800 hours.

"Bring it in, guys," would say the sergeant. "The names I read will be going home today. The rest of you…" He paused for dramatic effect, looking to his left and right, scanning the crowd. "See you tomorrow, right here, at oh-eight-hundred." Anxiously, a couple hundred guys pressed forward to hear the names being called off.

The names of those scheduled to depart that day were read. My name was not on the list. Okay, not today. We were free to do whatever we wanted, as long as we didn't leave the base and were there the next morning at eight. Worked for me! It didn't take me long to find the Air Force bus stop nearby. Combs and I went to the BX to look around.

During the next ten days or so, it was the same thing: eight o'clock formation, reading of names, released for the day, go to the BX, NCO Club, ocean beach, etc. My funds were limited, but only by choice. I had a few thousand dollars saved up, some from my reenlistment bonus and the rest from my pay each month. As of March 1970, my full monthly pay was:

Basic E-6 pay with three years of active duty: $372.90

Hostile Fire Pay (HFP), a/k/a Combat Pay: 65.00

Proficiency Pay: 50.00

Amount unpaid last account: 95.44 (didn't care where this came from)

SGLI (Insurance):   - 2.00

FICA (tax withheld):   - 17.90

Total Entitlements: $583.44

Total Collections: 19.90

Amount Due: $563.44

Carried forward to next pay period   -.44

Amount Paid: **$563.00**[141]

No longer on flight status, the $70.00 per month flight pay was gone since I was promoted.

While we waited for our freedom bird, Sandy and I were not joined at the hip, so to speak. I spent a lot of time at the beach, alone, sitting on the sand, getting sunburned, ruminating about the past year, and trying to anticipate what I'd do for the next thirty days while on leave. The sand was almost white. The sky, light blue. The water, an opulent blue-green and further out, a darker green. White caps on the waves complimented the scant white clouds on the horizon. There was no war here. It was peaceful, but boring beyond words. Bus to the beach, sit around most of the day, bus back. Day after day. When would I get out of this place?

One or two days before I left, a Spec Four grunt was trying to un-load a painted bronze figurine he had "liberated" from a gravesite in the boonies a few months before. He was afraid it would be taken away from him by customs, therefore didn't want to take it home. So, if nobody wanted it, he was going to throw it away. In the small group, he addressed those around him. No one spoke up. A couple of them turned away and walked off. I patiently waited as I really didn't want the thing to carry around, either. It was heavy. There was no way to mail it home and cer-tainly no way to return it to the gravesite. But finally, I decided to take it

---

[141] Pay scales were public knowledge. What was not were the number of years of active duty the serviceman had that affected his pay scale, except for the three-year service chevrons on the winter Class As.

off his hands. I could see he was glad to get rid of this ten-pound weight he had to lug around. I put it into the bottom of my duffle bag.

If I had a M-60 or an RPG with me, and if it could have fit into my duffel bag, I could have taken that back to the States, too. There was no inspection of duffel bags for weapons or any other contraband. Just load your gear and climb aboard.

On April 16, 1970, my name was called, loud and clear. I left country that afternoon. Sandy Combs, too. We sat next to each other on the plane as we headed to Fort Lewis, Washington.

During the flight home, we talked, laughed, smoked, slept, and ate. One of the topics of conversation was about cars. He was planning to buy an Aston Martin sports car. He just saw a picture of one in the magazine he was reading from the seat-pouch in front of him. I read the same magazine when he was through. In it I saw a picture of a Triumph sports car, among others. I had never seen cars like these before, even when I was in Germany. But that Triumph caught my eye. As far as I was concerned, buying that car was a done deal. My trip back home now had a purpose. Of course, the ads didn't show the price of the car. I'd deal with that, later.

I thought about the rumors of protesters that were supposedly going to screw up our arrival in the States. There had not been much information about it in the *Stars & Stripes*, various magazines, etc. We weren't briefed about them. Most of what we knew was what the guys who went home before us wrote about in their letters. I never got one of those letters. My information was from others, the rumor-mill. But, still, why would the protesters be angry with us?

Having lit yet another Pall Mall cigarette, I shoved the pack and Zippo lighter back into my pocket. I adjusted my butt in the seat and sat back to get comfortable for the long ride home. Thinking about anti-war protesters, I tried to imagine what it would be like to run into them. How angry would they be? I tried to understand their motivation. What did they know about this war? The more I thought about it, the more images of the past year floated through my mind.

The most horrific scene I had witnessed was during a low-level fly-by. The grunts had been inserted into the LZ and spread out. At treetop level, we flew ahead of one squad. I noticed, against a tree trunk, the contorted bloody body of a shirtless, thin and young Vietnamese man, his AK-47 on the ground at his feet. We had been using flechettes that day. This Charlie had obviously been struck with a shitload of steel pins that nearly tore off one arm and pinned him to the tree. I only caught a momentary glimpse due to our speed and the vegetation around the guy. There was no sense alerting the pilots. He was obviously dead. The grunts were headed his way. Did protesters know about things like that?

I remembered the grunt, some time before, who had a string of left ears on his rucksack. Killing people became part of his job. But keeping souvenirs of the kill was weird. Like the saying about Las Vegas, "What happens in Vietnam stays in Vietnam." Did that guy write home about his string of ears? Did he send back a photograph? If he did, how appalling did the recipient think it was? Did protesters know about things like that, too? And, those VC heads on a log, in that picture at the end of my first tour a year before. I could not forget...

I flashed back to the first man I killed back in '67, unarmed in red shorts, running for his life. Other kills, confirmed and not. Getting shot up so bad we couldn't take off to return to the battle. Rolling over at the fuel dump. Cheating the Angel of Death, how many times? Following orders. Flying so much that the company area was a strange and foreign place to be. Each and every mission was a potential death sentence. Be strong, be brave. Somebody cares for those who died, got maimed, or wounded in some other way, don't they?

Bad news always travels faster than good news. And, I would have suspected word-of-mouth descriptions of bad news only got worse along the way. Those American GIs who committed atrocities might have argued that its definition was in the eye of the beholder. But, for the uninitiated, the nitty-gritty of warfare is unimaginable, don't you think?

I wondered how many protesters had been to 'Nam. If any, what did they do? Were they REMFs, or grunts? Many of us on active duty thought the service-age male protestors and draft dodgers were just too chicken-shit to serve. But, on the other hand, maybe they had a point. Maybe the stories they heard about Vietnam, seeming too insane, were true.

I had heard many war stories during my time. Some didn't make sense. Some were completely fabricated, possibly to cover up the guy's lack of *glory-story* due to the mundane, non-combat rear echelon, albeit important support work, he did all year (e.g. clerk, cook, operations and supply, managing an officer's club, etc.). Some other stories were true and could scare the daylights out of you. Other guys simply don't talk about it because either there was no story to tell, or the experience was too painful to remember and talk about. I wondered how many false stories were told to and believed by the protesters and reporters.

But then, suddenly, my mind settled down. I was on the plane taking me back to America, and I realized one essential truth: It don't mean nuthin' anymore. Eventually, I dozed off.

Chapter 18

Stateside

A Porterhouse steak dinner, with all the trimmings, awaited each returning veteran at Fort Lewis, Washington. At their recommendation, we changed into civilian clothes to avoid being targets of the protesters who roamed the airport looking to make a scene. After we ditched our jungle fatigues, filthy by civilian standards but reasonably clean to us, into a large heap of clothing on the floor, only a few of us stayed around for the steak. Most went their separate ways. Sandy was one who didn't want to stick around, so we said our good-byes as he took off on his way to the airport in Tacoma. I stayed.

Having learned about the free steak dinner months ago, I considered it my reward for having returned to the world in one piece. Besides, I was looking forward to some good, free food. In a corner of the dining room, I sat alone. Surprisingly, not many guys were there. Out of a plane-load full of GIs, I would have thought it to be crowded, but there were just seven guys there. A few sat together. My dinner was brought to the table. The steak was superb but smaller than I imagined. The mashed potatoes tasted like the real thing, not powdered like in the mess. The vegetables were fresh.

I wasn't apprehensive during the ride to the airport. Except for my short hair, I looked like a well-tanned civilian. If I had been nearer to a military base my short haircut would have been a dead giveaway as to my status. This was the developing era of long hair for men. I asked the taxi driver about the protesters.

"No," he said, "not so much during the winter. Last summer there was a lot of that going on." The rest of the ride in was quiet for both of us.

At the airport, I don't think anyone even noticed me. Nevertheless, I looked around for any protesters, finding not a single one. I didn't even see a hippie wearing the counter-culture uniform of sandals, jeans, tie-dyed shirt, rose-colored glasses, Comanche-style headband and long hair. Where were the peace signs, the anti-Nixon slogans, and the shouts of "baby-killer"? Not at this airport, it seemed.

It was a good thing I didn't expect any type of welcome home party or celebration when I got back to Chicago, because there wasn't any. My return home, just like the plane ride, was low key. When Dad picked me up, he asked me where my uniform was. I told him it was packed away in my luggage, as suggested, and the reason why. I don't think he was impressed.

A few days had passed. The image of that car in the magazine was not going away. Scott was driving my old Mustang, and I had no desire to take it back. The Triumph seemed like a very good idea, especially after I saw one in person. At a dealership, on St. Charles Road in nearby Glen Ellen, I considered the options of models to select. I chose a red, 1970 Triumph GT-6 two-seater hardtop with five-speed standard transmission. The gearshift was in the center console. Sitting inside was different from American cars in that the legs had to be almost horizontally straight to reach the pedals. After paying slightly over $4,000 in cash as total payment I drove off in my new car as one very happy camper.

I was sure the car would become a babe magnet. I drove it everywhere during the day and evenings, close to home and as far as Old Town in Chicago. Nothing came of it. I drove slower to gain attention. After a week, reality hit. Nobody gave a shit who I was. It was just another flashy car on the street.

Being overseas essentially for the past three years and without the benefit of local mentors, I quickly learned just having the car was not enough. There was something wrong, different maybe, that was pressing on me. I wasn't quite sure what it was. Girls were not flocking to get a ride. Why not? All of the ads on TV and magazines showed good-looking women surrounding the car and driver. Without a doubt, in my mind I had the coolest car in the neighborhood. I'd go to the Dog-n-Suds drive-in for a hamburger, fries and milk shake, food on a tray hanging from my door window. I'd get a few smiles, but that was all.

Most of the people I once knew didn't know I was back in town. For reasons that I still find difficult to understand, I was too embarrassed to track them down. I was not a part of their world, nor where they a part of mine. My last four years were quite unlike theirs, I was sure.

Friendships developed in the Army have always been very unlike those in civilian life. We laughed harder and got drunker and stupider together, sometimes more often than we should. We covered for each other in terms of being accounted for, avoiding both work details and the first sergeant, and protecting each other from harm. We had each other's back. This was our fraternity. We were then, and would always be, brothers in the truest sense of the word. Neither time, nor distance, nor path of life could ever separate us. The bond we shared could never be broken. For some of us, we shared what any sane person would avoid, certain death in the face of the enemy. We thought we knew the risks, and went anyway. When our country needed us, we bravely went. We did not run away to Canada, or get some anti-war-leaning doctor to sign off on a bullshit 4-F rating to keep us out of the military. We answered the call.

Have you ever felt alone in a crowd? Getting back to Villa Park, I did. Friends from high school were gone. Nancy? Well, you know the story on that. Dad and Cathy were like two peas in a pod. Wherever one went, there was the other. Janie was almost five and Scott was a high school junior. I felt like a fifth wheel. Dad and Cathy tried so hard to be accommodating. I ate it up but didn't feel worthy of their gestures. This was my family but at the same time I didn't feel like I belonged. Gone for most of four years, I had become just a visitor, someone to break up their monotonous routine.

While we watched the news on TV at night, complete with vivid images of combat scenes and analytical commentary (usually negative by then) about our involvement in Vietnam, the opportunity to talk took second place to the required politeness developed over years. Don't interrupt the program.

We talked very little about the war, and what we did was restricted to the commercial breaks. How on Earth could I share what I wanted to share (and I really did) during commercials? Isolation is a very lonely feeling, even at home.

What was it that prevented me from truly "coming home"? I was here, physically. That was all. Not emotionally. That part became a casualty of my war. As a very small fish in a very big pond, it became quite difficult to grasp the perception that nobody cared that I went there; or, came back, except for my family.

Was it the same for other returning vets? Nobody seemed to care that battles were fought, guys got hurt or died. It was difficult to express what exactly I had been through and who I was as a result. Me, a twenty-two-year-old single man with a new sports car, a wounded combat veteran of two years in 'Nam with three combat medals (two of them were awarded multiple times), and an active duty staff sergeant in the United States Army. These were adjectives. They were labels that described me, but could not explain me. I was one of many men who were ordered into battle by other men who were following orders from some politician somewhere else. Old, white-haired men, in the comfort of their mahogany-walled offices, were deciding the fate of young men neck deep in muck halfway around the world.

As I sat there in Villa Park, taking it easy, I knew there was a hard firefight going on somewhere in 'Nam. Guys getting shot at, wounded, and maybe killed. Just as I had before, some part of me felt like I should be there, doing my part. A year before, I had quietly left home, alone. I returned home just as quietly, and still alone. Villa Park was the same as when I left. Daily routines, unchanged for most people, I suppose, maintained its constant rhythm and cadence.

There was not one sign, placard, banner, poster, or reference to the veteran returning home from 'Nam. Nothing good to say, nothing bad. Except for grieving families, not one person's lifestyle had changed for the better or worse because of Vietnam. I wasn't expecting a parade. There were no "we support our troops" campaigns then. But I wanted some acknowledgment of my sacrifice, and the sacrifice of my brothers in arms.

Dad was extremely kind and understanding. Because of his own experiences, I believed he understood that sometimes a guy just has to let things play out on their own. So, he let me be. I wanted so much to have a drink with him, to talk about what took place (Kiém Liên, potheads, understanding the war on the ground versus the war shown on TV, the generation gap, the crazy things that no longer made sense). But he was busy with Cathy, and she with him.

Dad didn't drink alcohol. I tried to drop some heavy hints that I was looking forward to having a couple drinks with him. He let me know there was a bottle of whiskey on the top shelf in the pantry that I was welcome to. But that wasn't the point. From early on, I never learned how to communicate very well with him and figured alcohol would help. (Booze, the great liberator of inhibitions.) Down a few drinks and I could talk someone's ear off. Down a few more and I could bare my soul to anyone who'd listen. I wanted so much to talk to somebody, brag a little, tear-up maybe.

On a sunny weekday afternoon, I bought a six-pack from a local convenience store, had my cigarettes and a cassette player with tapes with me, and drove around. I wasn't sure what I was looking for, but I found a secluded empty grassy lot between Villa Park and Lombard, just east of Addison Road and West Division Street. It wasn't exactly a park, per se, but it was rural and a stone's throw from the railroad tracks. Sitting on the grass I opened a beer and started drinking, listening to B.J. Thomas singing "Raindrops Keep Fallin' on My Head," one of Burt Bacharach's pieces. It was from the movie *Butch Cassidy and the Sundance Kid*, released during the fall of 1969, that I had recently seen. The song was easy listening, and I needed easy listening.

I sat there entertained by the squirrels and birds. There was no else one around. Trees and underbrush lined three sides, leaving the open area accessible only by W. Division, a two-lane road on the south side. The temperature was very warm and the beer very cold. I needed peace and quiet, time to think and reminisce. Five years left in the Army, going to Fort Riley, Kansas soon. I had a new car, no girl, no buddies left in town, and Army buddies scattered everywhere. I was beginning to feel sorry for myself.

That place halfway around world was with me, every day. The fighting in Vietnam didn't end just because I left. I didn't need proof to know the 174th was still heavily engaged with NVA and VC in Quáng Ngãi Province. I was pretty certain guys in the bush were still dying, getting maimed, thirsty, hungry, dirty, questioning orders but carrying them out anyway, trying to survive to the next day or week. Always one day closer to DEROS.

The enjoyment of the weather, solitude, music and beer was interrupted when a cop car drove up. I first heard the slow crunch of stones from the tires as it drove onto the shoulder of the road. Quietly, the officer parked next to my car and got out. I had no license plates on my car, only the temporary tag. He wanted to know what I was doing, other than drinking beer and listening to a B.J. Thomas song. I explained, and offered additional information about having recently returned from Vietnam, being on active duty, on leave and such. We talked about my car, recently purchased so no plate, yet. He didn't ask for my driver's license, car registration or military ID. I guess he could tell I was military by my short hair, so seldom seen in those days except for cops and military, and my out-of-season tan.

"Son," he said, "drinking beer on public property is against the law." Illegal? I didn't know, and told him so. What harm was I doing to anyone sitting there, away from everybody, having a beer?

"You have two options here: Pour the rest of that opened beer on the ground and stay. Or pour it out and leave," he said. I poured out the remains of the beer in the bottle, no more than an ounce or two. Without further discussion, I packed up my stuff and drove away.

Before my leave was over, there was a movie that I wanted to see. It was about Army surgeons in Korea during that war. I suggested we, Dad, Cathy and me, go. I never heard of the actors Elliot Gould and Donald Sutherland before, but it had been well advertised. The name of the movie was *MASH*. The storyline is about a mobile Army surgical hospital staff consisting of a clerk who managed every event, another clerk dressed as a woman to qualify for a Section Eight mental discharge, a hot-looking nurse, three main doctors who had their antics, and the fatherly MASH commander who was past his prime. It was a satire and a very good one. I enjoyed the movie. Dad did not.

In his own way, Dad chastised me for selecting that movie. Satire is funny. *Dr. Strangelove* was satirical, mocking the absurdity of nuclear war. Dad took me to that years before and didn't complain. I didn't know what he expected, but *MASH* was certainly not a patriotic, gung-ho flag-waving movie. I think it was a shock to his generally conservative and patriotic sensibilities, and he pouted all the way home. It was the first and only time I suggested a movie for him to see.

Finally, it was time for me to go. I still had some time left on my leave, but I was ready.

Fort Riley, Kansas was about a day's drive away. With duffle and AWOL bags packed, car gassed up, hugs and kisses all around, it was time to go. Leaving Villa Park was a bittersweet occasion, but getting back to the military was better than staying at home. Janie was still as cute as a bug's ear, always happy and smiling. Scott was growing up. He was getting taller by the month and was at least a foot over Dad. I hardly knew him anymore. The last four years had taken its toll. Whatever brotherly bond we had years earlier was gone. I left him and the rest of the family, just as I found them weeks before, in their world, as far as I could tell, of mundane routine and complacency.

The plan was to spend the next two to three years at Fort Riley. I expected being a UH-1 maintenance supervisor was likely going to be my assignment, at least initially. Dad had continued his recommendation that I go to officer candidate school. My GT score had a double-digit increase after re-testing while I was with the 174th, so all that was needed was to get the paperwork going. The downside was this last tour really soured my outlook of the Army in general.

But, with five years to go, maybe serious consideration was due. I'll have to make the best of it, keep my mouth shut and do what I'm told to the best of my ability. Maybe flight school was a better option. There were quite a few enlisted men, many crew chiefs, who later went to flight school and came out as warrant officers. I could do that. Would I be sent back to 'Nam? Didn't know, didn't care.

The drive to Kansas allowed plenty of time to think. Stupidly, I opted out of the radio accessory when I bought the car, thinking I could save a few bucks by buying my own at K-Mart and installing it myself. But I didn't do that. So, except for the wind through the window openings, whine of the engine, and the hum made when the tires roll over the pavement, it was quiet. Once again, I was free. Nobody was around to tell me what to do.

The past couple weeks had been difficult. I didn't understand why, at the time, but I wanted to be left alone. It was really my doing, actually. I needed companionship, but not theirs. I couldn't explain it to myself. I gave a lot of thought about the past year and rehashed my failures: not following orders to shoot that man on the knoll; avoiding the NCO sweeps at night; getting carried out of the Shark hootch like a bag of potatoes; not seeking counsel from my platoon leader and/or first sergeant; not being the knight in shining armor to protect Kiém Liên's honor; literally wasting two R & Rs with wine, women, and song (well, maybe not *wasting*); not doing something to help the guys at the ammo dump with their drug problem; and, not having my head in the game one hundred percent of the time.

But there were some positives about my service. Nobody in my platoon got killed while I was the platoon sergeant. Only one guy got wounded. I had no control over those except for the fact that I insisted on attention to detail and military protocol. I pushed to get the best out of my men, notwithstanding the challenges posed by Bell and Vandiver. I did what I could to identify with each man, to understand the wants and needs of each one.

Sadness was probably what I felt most of all. I was very happy to leave the 174th, but sad that I did. I had lost interest in doing my job, tired of doing my best, trying to support the Army goal of completing our mission honorably while at the same time hating what we were doing. I thought by coming home I'd snap out of my gloom. It didn't work. It just got worse. I missed most of the guys I worked with, and our hootch maids. I would likely never see any of them again. It was time for a beer.

Since I had left Villa Park during the late morning, I expected to stop at a motel en route. So, I did. Being twenty-two, getting a beer wasn't important anymore. It took too many beers to get drunk, and that's what I wanted most of all. I remembered the first can of beer I ever drank at age 16. Dick Johnson and I went to a drive-in movie near Roosevelt and Manheim Roads. We weren't there to watch the movie. We were there to look for girls and to share a six-pack of beer he had hidden under the seat. The beer came from his kitchen refrigerator at home. We both knew it was against the law. It was the most rebellious thing either of us did in high school. We each had three.

Inside the personnel office at Fort Riley, the clerk didn't mince words. They didn't need me at Fort Riley. Not in my MOS, not in another. There's no room for you here, dude.

"But, look," I said, "my orders tell me I'm supposed to be here." That didn't matter. The Spec Five, who incorrectly surmised he was in charge of personnel, told me they had too many Huey-guys already, and being an NCO didn't help. After a wait of an hour or so, he offered me the choice of going to Fort Sam Houston in Texas, or Fort Carson in Colorado.

It was at that point I remembered my buddy from the 174th, Jim Kildall, had gone to Fort Carson. My orders were amended and, after no more than thirty-six hours at Fort Riley, off I went to Colorado in my no-longer-shiny new car without a radio.

Driving west on Interstate 70, I would later learn I entered what they called the eastern plains of Colorado: flat land and wide spaces. It was a beautiful sunny day in May. As I continued driving west, I encountered a few hills and valleys. As I rounded a curve in the road, I saw it. Looming in front of me, as far as I could see to the south and north, were the majestic stretch of the snow-capped Rocky Mountains.

The air was fantastically clean, free of smog and dust. Distances were deceiving. What looked to be close was actually many miles away. It was extremely easy to see things at a distance, so clear you could almost reach out and touch it with your hands.

My first day in Colorado Springs was the day of graduation for the United States Air Force Academy. It was featured on the news when I checked into a motel. I watched part of the ceremony on the small, flickering color TV as I unpacked some of my stuff. The room was small and certainly not five-star accommodations. But, it was clean. This would be my home for a while because my reporting-in date was still a couple days away.

Colorado Springs was not just the home of the Army's Fort Carson and the Air Force Academy. It was also home to at least three college campuses: University of Colorado, Cragmor Campus; Southern Colorado State College; and, El Paso Community College. Additionally, near Fort Carson was Cheyanne Mountain, where NORAD[142] was located in the bowels of this mountain. Of course, there was also Pikes Peak, a tourist attraction at the top. Nearby was the upscale community of Broadmoor, where U.S. Olympians trained at the ice rink. Manitou Springs was somewhat of a hippie community, but I didn't see any sign of protests—only commercialism.

---

[142] North American Aerospace Defense Command, a bi-national organization shared with Canada.

For the new arrivals to this base, especially for those of us returning from Vietnam, the Army provided a required five-day orientation. Of the fifteen guys in our group, two of us were E-6s and excused. That was how I met Duane "Turtle" Gardner. He, too, was a young, single staff sergeant whose MOS was jet engine maintenance (used in UH-1 aircraft). Because we were both staff sergeants, the NCOIC of the orientation excused us from the training. We were free to do whatever we wanted, for a while at least.

Turtle, as he preferred to be called, also just returned from 'Nam. He was from California and before the Army, was a member of the Sports Car Club of America. He once drove a Triumph TR-6, very similar to my GT-6. His was a convertible with a roll bar. He raced in a few circuits, not winning any; he mainly did it for fun. He was really excited to know someone at Fort Carson with a Triumph. He told me he could, and would, teach me some driving techniques. I was interested.

About a week or two later, he signed a lease for an apartment off base at the north end of town. We worked at the same hangar at Butts Army Airfield, a short drive away from our company areas. He was encouraging me to check his apartment, and maybe sign-up for one in the same complex if I liked the area. I told him I'd consider it. But, for the time being, I was living on base until I became better acquainted with the community. He was assigned to one of the companies in the 704th Maintenance Battalion.

Soon after signing into the 283rd Aviation Company, I met up with Staff Sergeant Bob Minton, my former platoon sergeant from Germany, at our company formation. I managed to get near him when the formation was over. Surprised to see me, and I him, we sauntered over to the base snack bar for coffee and catching up. The last time he saw me I was leaving Schweinfurt en route to Fort Dix to be discharged from the Army. More than being surprised of me being here at Fort Carson, he was even more so to learn I had reenlisted for six years, went back to 'Nam, and had been recently promoted.

My NCO colleagues in the 283rd were at least five years older than me, some being in their mid to late thirties. As far as I knew, I was one of two NCOs in the company who was not married. So, at the beginning I was assigned a barracks to live in. This building, one of the same World

War II leftover types, was a wood frame, two-story barracks. On the second floor, I shared the cadre room with the other unmarried E-6, who bore the nickname "Tiny" because of his huge stature. I doubt he liked the nickname, but he took it in stride.

The last I knew, Jim was somewhere on base, unless he, too, was diverted somewhere else like I was at Fort Riley. I went to the base locator's office near the front gate. It was a simple matter of checking the name, Jim Kildall. The Spec Four at the desk confirmed he was at this base, and assigned to the 704th Maintenance Battalion. This was the same one that Turtle was in. I found the battalion area, but not Jim. Turtle wasn't familiar with Jim's name but said he'd check around. I didn't see Jim at the hangar, as I, too, checked around at the different work stations when I had a chance. I was busy there, as well, supervising a small crew of Huey mechanics.

My crew of five, along with other crews, worked on the couple Hueys we had. We'd do the usual inspections, maintenance, rotor blade and flight control adjustments as needed, washing the ship, ordering parts from tech supply. None of my guys were crew chiefs. Actually, I don't recall any enlisted man who was assigned as a regular crew chief for each aircraft. A rumor was circulating about the 283rd being sent[143] to one of the southeast states. Because I had recently arrived, and technically had two PCS assignments during the current fiscal year, I would not be going anywhere except to a new unit on base. Fort Carson would become my home base for the next three years.

It took a while, but I found Jim in the 704th Maintenance Battalion. He was doing well, but not great. Still single, he lived on base in the upper level of the brick building where his company's offices were located. There was something different about him that was difficult for me to pinpoint. He seemed pre-occupied, almost like he missed his Vietnam experience and his job as crew chief. There, at Fort Carson, he was not on flight status. I knew this hurt him because he loved flying, so much that he had passed up a chance at getting promoted almost a year before. But here he was, not flying and still a Spec Five with a lot of time in grade.

---

[143] It was eventually transferred to Ft. Bragg, NC during June 1971.

Jim and I didn't talk about 'Nam as much as I thought we would have. We both knew what the other had experienced. We palled around as much as possible, but protocol did its best to keep the staff sergeants and above at one end of the social spectrum and Spec Fives and below at the other.

To my detriment, we ignored that. When we took a break or lunch at the airfield, many of the other NCOs expected me to sit with them, but I usually chose to sit with Jim. There was no need to broadcast our history to anyone. The building of professional relationships and the mentoring I needed with other more experienced NCOs was not happening. In many ways, the company I kept worked against me. I just didn't know it at the time.

Jim wasn't the same as when we were together in 'Nam. He was still friendly, but seemed distant. One day I asked if he was pissed that he had turned down the promotion, and that I had taken it.

"No, no, nothing like that," he replied.

He didn't seem to be willing to reveal what was on his mind. So, we let it go. We just laughed and got drunk as often as we could. Us 'Nam vets, just doing the best we could to enjoy our stateside duty.

Turtle taught me how to drive my Triumph as a race car driver: downshifting and accelerating to take curves; tail-gating for air-flow drafting purposes; allowing and controlling the sideways movement (drifting) of the car when turning at high speed; and essentially managing the coordination of gas pedal to manual transmission, without relying on the brake. The El Paso (County) Highway Road Commission, the Colorado Department of Transportation, and the U.S. National Park Service all did wonderful jobs maintaining the roads in excellent condition throughout the Colorado Springs area and at the Garden of the Gods National Park.

He had a blue 1970 Ford 'Boss 302', and I had my red 1970 Triumph. We had the world by the tail as we parked our cars in the shade of Tatarian Maples, Mountain Alders, Saskatoon's, or Cherry Dogwoods trees. It seemed Turtle had the same idea I had when it came to getting the girls: impress them with something new, shiny and fast. It seemed perfectly logical to a twenty-two-year old at the time. But it wasn't. Not even close.

Turtle took a short trip to his hometown in California and came back with a small formula racecar on a trailer. It needed a battery and the engine needed work, but otherwise it was ready to drive. He invited me into his place one afternoon to see what had been done. I walked in, finding this massive car engine, with various parts strewn about, a couple cans of beer, and various tools all set up in front of his TV. He was very proud of the set up and his accomplishment. I wasn't around when he and a few others had removed the engine from his race car and carried it into his second-floor apartment, placing it onto a heavy-duty coffee table in the living room.

We ended up as regular (daily) customers at a local Pizza Hut, going there after work and on weekends as much as possible. One of the girls who worked there, Barbara, was single, about twenty, twenty-one years old and extremely cute. I tried for months making my moves to get her to say yes for a date. It was complicated because she lived at home and her father didn't want her dating Army guys.

There was a jukebox inside the restaurant. Every time I arrived, which was usually around six in the evening, I'd tried to impress her by putting a quarter or two into the machine to play the theme song of the movie *2001: A Space Odyssey*. I loved this song, especially the opening. I was also a big fan or Simon and Garfunkel's "Bridge Over Troubled Waters". I don't think Barbara was impressed by that, either. But I was not going to give up. When Turtle wasn't with me, I would stay until closing and help her wash the glassware in the three tubs of soapy, rinse, and clean water. She and I would talk about all sorts of topics, but never the Army or Vietnam.

Turtle suggested I put a Glass-Pac muffler on my car. Removing the one installed at the factory, I liked the sound without the muffler: loud and roaring, backfiring occasionally. I drove over the Pizza Hut to show it off to Barb. She thought I was crazy. A day later I installed the Glas-Pac.

Finally, she agreed to go on a date. Wanting to impress her, I took her to a popular nightclub. I had a few drinks, but she had only one. Afterwards, I took her to the Garden of the Gods park, a natural landmark, to show off my driving skills. In the dark, I hugged every curve. Cresting a small hill, the car went airborne for a few feet. It caused momentary weightlessness. I knew as soon as she bumped her head on the sun visor above her that this was going to be our one and only date.

One Sunday morning, I decided to go for a drive and test out my newfound skills some more. I downshifted and accelerated as I negotiated an upward curve on N. Chestnut going south. Within sight of W. Fillmore Street, some loose stones remained on the asphalt from recent road repair, causing my car to slide sideways off the road at the crest. Downshifting, I accelerated, and slid sideways. The front and back tires on the right side wedged into hardened dirt ruts in the vacant lot. My car rolled over with a three-quarter rotation. When it stopped, I was stunned and realized the driver's door was on the ground. I climbed up and out through the opened passenger door window and jumped to the ground. Except for my car and a bruise on my back, nothing else was damaged.

As the first few minutes passed, getting the car right side up seemed to be the most important thing that needed to be done. Maybe the car still worked. It was no more than a few minutes later when one of Colorado Spring's finest showed up. He assessed the situation and informed me that he was going to have to issue me a citation for careless driving. Without even a hint of being disrespectful, I questioned his decision because, in my mind, my driving wasn't "careless," per se, but a simple accident caused by gravel stones on the road. The only thing I damaged was my car, and it was paid for. At my very respectful request, he explained the difference between careless and reckless driving, the resulting ramifications to my insurance and driving record. I agreed to accept his first offer.

The car was totaled. The roof was caved in. The insurance company made the payout to me, about $2,400, and cancelled further coverage. The next Saturday I went to a Saab dealership looking for a new car.

The Sonnet III was a nice-looking car. The salesman and I went for a test drive. I was being very careful on I-25, driving responsibly, not as Turtle had been teaching. I suppose the salesman thought I was driving like a little old lady, so he asked me to pull over to let him drive and show me what the car could do. I did and we switched places. He immediately exited the highway and took a back road west into a rural area.

The road turned to gravel. I braced as he accelerated into an "S" curve and downshifted. The first turn was to the right. That was easy enough. The back end of the car swung left as he prepared for the next turn. As he steered left, the car drifted to the right, and kept going. We went off the road sideways, sliding about twenty feet into the grass and weeds. The tires on the right side got tangled up in a barbed wire fence, and we stopped abruptly.

When we got towed back to the dealership, the first thing the manager wanted to know was who was driving. No apologies, no concern for my well-being, none of that. The salesman admitted his guilt.

Turtle, who had driven me there and was waiting for me to return, took it all in as a typical sports car story. When we left, I knew I was done with sports cars.

Two serious car wrecks within a week, one my fault, one not. And, twice in one week, I again cheated the Angel of Death. The same dark Angel I cheated in 'Nam, many times over. My car was a wreck, my life was a wreck. By day, going to work and doing what I was told, to the best of my ability, and not complaining was the same old shit I've been doing all along: smiling, getting along, acting fine. But, at night I was alone in my thoughts. I did not smile. I wanted so much to complain, but about what, exactly, and to whom? Jim's malaise was worse than mine. I couldn't complain to him, only sympathize. The only way I could control my ever-present anger was to self-medicate with whatever was available at the time.

I didn't even know exactly what I was angry at; everything, I suppose. I found no one who I could really trust with my innermost feelings and hurt. Jim was the closest guy I could trust, but why burden him with my problems? He seemingly had enough of his own. Together, he and I shared a common bond born of bullets, bombs, dead gooks and that shit-hole we called LZ Bronco. My anger had a hair-trigger and I had to learn how to control that before it controlled me.

Whiskey makes me mean. Almost violent, but not quite. I wanted to get violent, but at the same time knew not to. I learned to keep to myself. Safer that way for everyone. Drinking alone usually produces no problem for me. A good buzz, in the company of songs like "Light My Fire" by the Doors, helps me forget. But, the image of that guy in red shorts running down the tree line, running for his life, was something that haunts me all too often. I can't seem to run fast enough to escape that scene.

God knows I've tried.

I decided to play it safe. Dad drove Oldsmobiles for as long as I could remember, so why not check them out? The next weekend I looked at a "high performance" 1970 Oldsmobile 442 two-door, but with automatic transmission. I bought it at full price, using the insurance money and dipping into my VRB and earnings from 'Nam. When I got home, I parked it alongside Turtle's car, just as I had before with the Triumph.

I woke up the next morning, a Sunday. Walking outside, the air was brisk, the sky clear, and the sun shining. I looked at my new car. I had the day planned out. It felt good sliding into the driver's seat. I wanted to add some gauges to the center console, one for the RPM, vacuum, and electrical. I turned the ignition key… nothing. Not a sound. I popped the hood to find the problem, and I saw it immediately. The battery was missing. Someone had stolen the battery! The first night I brought it home!

I realized in that moment that I wouldn't find the happiness I'd been missing behind the wheel of any car.

Towards the end of summer, I received a letter from Rex[144] who was still in 'Nam. Bell and Vandiver were killed during a mission on July 15, 1970. Though it was an emergency mission, they finally got their way, and it cost them their lives. I can't explain how or why, but knew in my gut they should never have flown together.

Rex informed me about what happened. There had been a huge firefight, and one of our Sharks was damaged. A replacement gunship was needed, immediately. Rex grabbed the first people available, Bell and Vandiver, to crew Pink Panther, my old ship (# 66-00646). They got airborne right away and engaged the NVA at the AO. Within the next hour, the pilot lost power/control while flying too close up a steep ravine. Efforts to regain control failed, causing the ship to fall to the ground, roll

---

[144] He passed away on March 08, 2006. RIP.

over and explode. Three of the four crewmen (WO1 Lenton Mizer, SP/5 Harrison Bell and SP/5 Fred Vandiver) died.

It's difficult to put into words what I felt when I read his letter. I was saddened, and still am to this day. Their laughter was contagious. I can still see their faces and hear their voices. Bell spoke with a thick, boisterous Texan accent. Thinking back, I'm sure Vandiver picked up a little Texan drawl from his buddy. Bell was tall and husky. I almost want to say muscular, but that would be unfair. His face was angular and his dark eyes piercing. He had a dark complexion, almost as if he had a permanent prairie wind burn. Maybe he was, indeed, a rancher in Texas.

Vandiver, on the other hand, had fairer skin tone. He stood not as tall as Bell and looked heavier, though he probably wasn't. His face was rounded, and his physique just as round. I wouldn't want to describe him as fat, but in years he could very well have been without much trouble. Vandiver was not boisterous when compared to Bell, but he was quick witted. They used to spend all their free time together. They lived life to the fullest, considering the circumstances, and were true brothers-in-arms in life, and death. I knew they were well liked by most, and would be missed by friends and family alike.

As I settled into the routine of stateside life, alcoholic beverages became my best friend. They helped me through the rough patches of adjusting to a peacetime Army and later, civilian life. Guys like me were dime-a-dozen, just too many of us to fill available jobs. Military careers were made or broken, not so much because of what we knew but who we knew.

An application for Officer Candidate School (OCS) was submitted and approved. My interview at Ft. Carson went smoothly and my packet was forwarded to 6th Army. There, (they told me) I missed selection by one. The reason: no college degree. Little did I know at the time that the Army was putting into action a Reduction-In-Force (RIF) program. Very qualified pilots (warrant and commissioned officers) in our company, without a degree, were given the option to separate from active duty or revert to an enlisted rank.

The option to go back to Vietnam was always available, though I chose not to return. That summer I busied myself with work, took a night class at the community college, and did my best to put Vietnam behind me. But, the bravado and bragging rights never went away. Many afternoons were spent at the NCO Club, extended lunches, trying to out-do each other by sharing overseas exploits with our close-knit group of Vietnam vets.

I met my first wife, Pam, in Colorado Springs during the fall of 1970. Pam was a pretty, blond-haired, blue-eyed Air Force brat. Her dad retired from the Air Force after a 21-year career and settled in Colorado Springs. He didn't want her to date Army guys, either. But we did and regularly. By December, we decided to get married. Jim Kildall agreed to be my best man, but a family emergency intruded and he went to Michigan. Another Army friend, John Sloan, happily filled in for us.

In 1973, I was transferred to W. Germany with two years and some months remaining on my enlistment. Pam came along and we enjoyed a pleasant tour of duty at Schwaebish Gmuend. I worked at the airfield for a year. There were still too many Huey-guys to assign jobs for everyone. It was clear I needed to change my MOS. Seeking a new career field, I became a director of the local (Dependent) American Youth Activities (AYA) until I learned the MOS wasn't available. My ETS was fast approaching, but I extended for a year due to Pam being pregnant with our first child. During the time of the extension, I successfully completed (95B) OJT during my temporary duty assignment with the military police. But, my pay grade of E-6 prevented that MOS from being awarded. My career in the Army was going nowhere.

At the end of our time in Germany, our full-term son, Jason, was in "good health" while he was in the womb. The obstetrician was confident that the baby would be healthy. Not a hint of trouble. But, Jason did not survive more than five hours after birth and died (cardio-pulmonary dysplasia) in a Huey helicopter atop the U.S. military hospital in Stuttgart, West Germany. His death, as tragic as it was, was one more nail in my coffin of solitude. Pam and my hearts ached beyond belief.

With about six months to go before my ETS, we took a Blue Bird reassignment from Germany to Ft. Sill, Oklahoma (as I was still, officially, assigned to the *once-your-in-you'll-never-get out* 56th Field Artillery Brigade). Eventual assignment to the military police company there did not sway me to remain on active duty. After ten years of active duty, I received an honorable discharge during 1976.

The stigma of being a Vietnam veteran was always present, even in civilian life. The images of our last days in Vietnam on TV and the printed media were painful reminders of our failed outcome of the war. As the NVA brazenly moved towards and into Saigon (and other locations in country), escaping by any means possible translated into retreat. The Vietnamese people who supported the war against the Viet Cong and NVA were marked people. Everyone knew what happened to intellectuals, professionals, and sympathizers of democracy at the hands of the NVA. The horror of Hué during 1967 and 1968, at the hands of the NVA, had not been forgotten. Civilians were killed en masse. The United State Embassy was overwhelmed by Vietnamese ex-soldiers and civilians seeking refuge and trying to board one of the last remaining helicopters leaving. Vietnamese pilots flew and ditched their aircraft off shore on or close to American Navy vessels.

Congress had cut funding for the defense of South Vietnam. The mood of the American public became overwhelmingly against further involvement of trying to support, or save, the government of South Vietnam. As we left, so did our allies. The Republic of Vietnam failed. Likewise, the neighboring country of Cambodia had its trouble.

During the gradual fall of Saigon, the communists gained strength in Cambodia. Thousands of Vietnamese civilian occupants in the country, and newly arrived refugees, were massacred. Hundreds of thousands of civilians in Phnom Penh, maybe millions, who were left with no means to escape, were killed by the communist Khmer Rouge. As the carnage continued, on April 12, 1975 the American Embassy was evacuated. Meanwhile, in Vietnam, the evacuation of Vietnamese people was underway. Finally, the U.S. Ambassador to Vietnam was ordered to leave. The American radio station played, and replayed over and over, the Irving Berlin song, *White Christmas*, sung by Bing Crosby. That was the signal for all Americans to seek evacuation from the country. On April 30th, the Ambassador and his family were evacuated.

The communists won! WTF? It's hard to believe that their win meant we lost.

To recap my mental anguish, I failed over circumstances I had no control: our first-born son's death, the collapse of the Republic of Vietnam, and my dead-end career in the Army. For the first year as a civilian, I enlisted into the U.S. Army Reserves, the 300th Military Police Company in Livonia, MI. After the one-year stint, my colleagues were quite surprised at my decision to not reenlist. I just wanted to try it out. I ended up doing the job of a clerk because the Spec Four whose job I completed, at the orders of the first sergeant, was motivationally challenged. The first sergeant and company commander declined to address his failure to perform his job for fear of repercussions. His being from Detroit, I do not wish to say anything more about that young man.

My marriage to Pam failed after seventeen years and three more sons. I drank too much, too often. I spent too many evenings at the bar with co-workers who pleaded with me to go along with them for the promised *one-drink-only*. That promise was broken every time, and I didn't care. God still protected me, though. No traffic accidents, no driving under the influence tickets, and no understanding whatsoever as to how the hell I ever got home in one piece. It's only when we divorced and I became a single custodial parent that I began to get a grip on things. Fast forward to 2017, our sons have enjoyed very successful careers and have wonderful families of their own.

Tom, Babe and Don are still alive and well. We're in touch with each other fairly often. We all contributed to Babe's book, *Us Guys: The Army, The 60s* (2016, CreateSpace.com). Those stories focused on our friendship during training, the startup of the 187th Aviation Company and the ocean journey to Vietnam.

Epilogue

A Final Thought

For many people in the United States, our active military involvement in Vietnam from 1960 through 1975 was a questionable endeavor. Their reasons were many. It was a civil war and we had no business being there. It was a proxy war between communists and the free world democracies, and we bore the brunt of the fighting among our allies. Our legal obligation, under SEATO, ceased to be well understood. After thirteen years (1960-1973) of military action and an additional two as advisors, the regime of the South Vietnamese government remained criminal in the eyes of many and fragile. Years of escalating manpower and equipment could not halt the constant guerilla tactics of the Viet Cong and the growing presence of the NVA. The United States Congress, a Democrat majority, obliged to public opinion, and the promise of President Richard Nixon to end the war, resulted in further funding being denied for the war effort.

As the North Vietnamese Army advanced on Saigon with tanks, artillery and troops, the last of the Americans in country fled—no, "evacuated"—leaving behind a population of people who would be killed, tortured, or "re-educated" because they supported the Americans and Vietnam's other allies for so many years. The last official date of American presence was April 21, 1975. The official end of the war came on May 7, 1975.

President Jimmy Carter gave amnesty to those young men who avoided the draft and those who fled to Canada, numbering in the hundreds of thousands. This was done during January 1977, one day after his inaugural speech as the newly elected president. To me, then, that was the ultimate slap to veterans who served our nation honorably. But later, I began to understand the nature of forgiveness.

I am proud to be a Vietnam veteran. At eighteen and again at twenty-one, I volunteered to go. At a time when many young men avoided military service by whatever means necessary, my friends and I answered our nation's call to arms. We willingly risked life and limb in support of a little-known country so far, far away. A vast majority of us served honorably, with no malice of forethought. Most of us left our family and friends as innocent and naïve soldiers, sailors, and airmen, not knowing if we'd ever return alive. Many did not.

Our silence should never be misconstrued as an unwillingness to share. Our self-inflicted solitude should never be misunderstood as anti-social behavior. Our gruff demeanor, at times, should not be misinterpreted as being a pain-in-the-ass to others. Our preference to see things in black and white, of not always considering the many shades of gray, should not be misread as having shallow depths of evaluations. We've been taught, and learned through experience, what was necessary to survive: evaluate, decide, act. After months and months of nitty-gritty comradeship, we came home to a hostile nation. We didn't overcome our experience, but we used it and managed to become productive members of society. The war never left us. It's forever a part of who we are and what we've become, whether our nation supported us or not.

We lost approximately 58,500 men and women during the war, an average of one hundred per week. Because of the lasting, latent effects of exposure to Agent Orange[145], an herbicidal-defoliant widely used[146] during the war, Post-Traumatic Stress Disorder, suicide, and serious alcohol and drug abuse, the number of war-dead increases daily. Hundreds of thousands of veterans survived, though they and their families continue to live with the physical, mental, and emotional trauma we endured.

Someone once said that we all die twice. The first time is when our heart stops beating, our lungs stop working, and our brain is no longer in control. Our body turns cold. Our soul, spirit and spark of life leaves the body, never to return again as we once knew it to be. We get buried, or cremated, or both. We cease to exist as living, breathing, thinking creatures on Earth. Some die in peace, some in pain, and some with regret for the things they wished they should have said or done before that fateful day.

But, we leave behind a part of ourselves: a personal history for our family; a philosophy of life that impact others both near and far; and,

---

[145] South Vietnamese President Ngo Dinh Diem sought the application of aerial herbicides from the Americans to be sprayed in South Vietnam. United States President John F. Kennedy authorized its military use. The name, Agent Orange, was derived due to the orange-striped barrels it was stored in for shipment. What made Agent Orange lethal was 2,3,7,8-Tetrachlorodibenzodioxin (TCDD). Applied to the ground, it exceeded safe levels of contamination (as established by the Environmental Protection Agency of the United States much more than a hundred-fold.
[146] Very high concentrations in Tay Ninh Province.

achievements and inventions to, hopefully, better the human experience of those whose paths we cross. In essence, we become a memory. Our second death occurs at the moment that memory, of who and what we were, ends. When our name is spoken, or thought of, for the very last time on Earth.

Wanting to keep the memory of my friends alive, I chose not to change their names to fictitious identities, making this a novel of sorts. It remained my intent to be as honest as my recollection of names and events could make it possible. I trusted these people with my life, and they trusted me with theirs. They are wonderful human beings and each had a profound effect upon my thoughts and dreams. We walked the walk.

Over the years, it is surprising to me how many people who once made every effort to deny themselves the military experience now seem to want to embrace it by talking the talk. As one of many potential examples, I once had an employer who avoided the draft during the late 1960s, meeting every criterion as they came along. He never served in the Armed Forces. But, many years later, with small details gleaned from the experience of me and perhaps others, he would brag that he was a Navy pilot aboard the USS *Enterprise* during the Vietnam War. We can't stop people like this, but it hurts just the same.

The story you have just read covered a period of my life from 1966 to 1970. It was a period of social and cultural change, for me and for our great nation. We were privileged to live during a time of great, and not-so-great, music, thinkers, and leadership. Thank you.

Appendix

A partial list of combat fatalities from the units I served with in the Republic of Vietnam. Listed by the date of death, their names will always be associated with paying the ultimate price for freedom.

For a complete list and (available) narratives, please visit the unit websites as noted in the footnotes.

187th Assault Helicopter Company (1st Aviation Brigade)[147]

4-19-67	**Joe Colotti**
7-07-67	**Thomas DeRosier**
7-07-67	**Charles Sauer**
7-07-67	**Paul Simon**
7-07-67	**Ivra Tatum**
9-20-67	**Billie Presson**
10-11-67	**Ellis Bailey**
11-11-67	**Evert Roberson**
01-05-68	**Kenneth Scruton**
2-17-68	**Dennis Lulofs**
4-12-68	**Harold Tharpe, Jr.**

190th Assault Helicopter Company (1st Aviation Brigade)[148]

11-08-67	**Bill Whitney**

---

[147] www.187thahc.com
[148] www.190thahc.com

12-07-67	Charles Wilcox
1-31-68	Aubrey Goff

174th Assault Helicopter Company (Americal Division)[149]

3-01-69	Ray Davis
3-01-69	Ed Harris
3-01-69	Dave Shultze
3-01-69	Don Zarina
3-11-69	Charles Rogers
3-17-69	Richard Brown, [Company Commander]
5-12-69	Jim Isaac, Jr.
5-12-69	Larry Shepard
5-16-69	Dennis Schmidt
8-02-69	Albert Vaquera
8-14-69	Don Contarino
8-15-69	John Bozinski
8-15-69	Sanchez Del Valle
8-15-69	Johnny Graham
8-15-69	Robert Shields, II
11-15-69	Ron Ducommun
11-15-69	Forest Hodgkin
11-15-69	Ricardo Regaldo
11-15-69	Adam Wilson
12-22-69	Don Selkey, Jr.

---

[149] www.174thahc.org

2-12-70	John Gibbons
5-13-70	Richard Henke
5-13-70	Sidney Jarrell
5-13-70	Ernest Johns
5-13-70	Darek Patrick
5-13-70	Fred Sheffield
7-15-70	Harrison Bell
7-15-70	Lenton Mizer
7-15-70	Fred Vandiver

May their memories be eternal.